Americans and the Unconscious

Robert C. Fuller

New York   Oxford

Oxford University Press

1986

Oxford University Press

Oxford   New York   Toronto
Delhi   Bombay   Calcutta   Madras   Karachi
Petaling Jaya   Singapore   Hong Kong   Tokyo
Nairobi   Dar es Salaam   Cape Town
Melbourne   Auckland

and associated companies in
Beirut   Berlin   Ibadan   Nicosia

Copyright © 1986 by Oxford University Press, Inc.

Published by Oxford University Press, Inc.,
200 Madison Avenue, New York, New York 10016

Oxford is a registered trademark of Oxford University Press

Library of Congress Cataloging-in-Publication Data
Fuller, Robert C., 1952-
m-R Americans and the unconscious.
Includes index.
1. Psychology—United States—History. 2. Subconsciousness.
3. Psychology and religion—United States—History. I. Title.
RC443.F85   1986   150'.973   85-32100
ISBN 0-19-504027-9

9 8 7 6 5 4 3 2 1
Printed in the United States of America

To Chuck and Bette

Acknowledgments

I would like to express my gratitude to a number of individuals and organizations for assistance in the writing of this book. First, I would like to thank Peter Homans of the University of Chicago for sharing with me his expertise in what might be called the "sociology of psychological knowledge." A great deal of the inspiration for this book came from his publications and friendly advice. Don Browning and Jerald Brauer, also of the University of Chicago, have likewise offered wise counsel and spirited collegiality as I labored on this project.

Second, several colleagues at Bradley University were extremely supportive throughout the period during which I worked on this manuscript. Jim Ballowe, Peter Dusenbery, Alan Galsky, Steve Permuth, John Hitt, and Max Kele—all gave generously of themselves and their offices to help make this book possible.

Grant assistance came from the National Endowment for the Humanities, the Midwest Faculty Seminar, and Bradley's Board for Research and Creativity.

Evanne Dorethy and Linda J. Raineri typed numerous drafts of this manuscript; their patience passeth all understanding.

Cynthia Read at Oxford University Press afforded me her

expert editorial skills and guided this manuscript through extensive revisions.

And finally, I wish to thank my family for their love and concern. Matt, Bryan, and Kathy endured my demanding work schedule and have enriched my life immeasurably throughout the course of this project. It is, however, to my parents, Chuck and Bette, that I choose to dedicate this book. It was the spirited discussions around the dinner table that first aroused my interest in the study of religious thought, and I now realize that they have in many ways been my best teachers.

April 1986
Peoria, Illinois   R.C.F.

Contents

Introduction

AMERICANS discovered the unconscious simultaneously with their entry into a modern, secular world. For that matter, the entire discipline of academic psychology is a relatively recent historical phenomenon; not until the mid-1880s did it gain its foothold in American universities. Yet, by the turn of the century, psychology had already established itself as the preeminent authority to which Americans would thereafter turn in their personal quests for identity and wholeness. Replete with scientific-sounding terminology and practical strategies for meeting life's challenges, psychology set itself to the prophetic task of assessing which life-styles and values are most commensurate with a modern world. As Martin Gross has observed, a major consequence of this psychologizing of American thought has been the emergence of

> a civilization in which, as never before, man is preoccupied with Self. We have become fascinated with our madness, motivations and our endless, sometimes wearying search for normality. Modern psychology and psychiatry seek to satisfy that fascination by offering us a full range of systems, from the serious to the whimsical, with which we can understand our confused psyche, then seek to heal it.[1]

Psychology's contribution to modern self-understanding is, as Gross suggests, far from monolithic. So divergent are the major schools of psychological thought and so disputatious are each of their partisan factions that it is almost impossible to assess the cultural import of psychology taken as a whole. Gordon Allport cautions, "Unlike mathematics, physics, or biology, [psychology] is not a cumulative science but rather an assortment of facts, presuppositions, and theories, whose relevance to human welfare depends upon the particular theories, presuppositions, and facts we select for inspection."[2] The purpose of this book is to focus upon one such psychological "fact"—the unconscious mind—and to examine how its relevance to human welfare has been articulated by the American psychological tradition.

This study was inspired in part by Henri Ellenberger's brilliant account of the history of dynamic psychiatry, entitled *The Discovery of the Unconscious.*[3] Ellenberger's study impressively demonstrates that the European "discovery" of the unconscious can be fully understood only within the larger contexts of European social and intellectual history. Various strands of European cultural thought provided the presuppositions upon which individuals such as Mesmer, Freud, and Jung set about interpreting the "facts" of the unconscious.[4] Ellenberger notes that, by 1900, Europeans had come to ascribe four separate functions to the unconscious mind: (1) the conservative function of recording memories and registering perceptions which often escape conscious attention; (2) the dissolutive function, as evidenced by hypnotic behaviors and the multiple or split personalities of schizophrenic patients; (3) the creative function of innovative or inspirational thinking; and (4) the mythopoetic function of fabricating inner romances, fantasies, or dreams which give psychic life a kind of autonomous reality apart from events that transpire in the physical universe. Ellenberger also points out that debates among Continental psychologists concerning which of these functions best defines the unconscious have never been resolvable through normal scientific procedures. Inasmuch as "facts" about the unconscious cannot be ascertained empirically, theories which purport to explain men's and women's hidden depths have almost entirely been shaped by philosophical and cultural factors.

It occurred to me that whatever the difficulty of ascertaining the functions performed by the unconscious, it was evident that the concept of the unconscious has—at least in the United States—performed what might be called a symbolizing function. That is, disputes among American psychologists concerning the existence and activities of the unconscious disclose far more about the basic assumptions and presuppositions which distinguish psychological models from one another than they do about the psyche itself. Disagreements about the unconscious invariably reveal differences in philosophical viewpoint or ideological orientation, not empirical data. For this reason, an examination of the various meanings which the concept of the unconscious has had in American psychology is, in effect, a case study in American cultural and intellectual history.

My objective in surveying the various American psychologies of the unconscious is thus not to assess the scientific basis of psychological concepts so much as their cultural meanings. For although a great many theoretical developments have been achieved in psychology by subjecting hypotheses to rigorous experimentation, this has not been the case in regard to the unconscious. Instead of progressing in the accumulative fashion of positivistic science, theories of the unconscious develop more in accordance with underlying cultural patterns; and, indeed, the following chapters will chronicle the astonishing extent to which modern American psychologies of the unconscious mind represent structural replays of indigenous American religious and cultural traditions. The "American" unconscious has displayed an enduring tendency to symbolize harmony, restoration, and revitalization. In sharp contrast to those European psychologists who saw in the unconscious a symbol of rift, alienation, and inner division, Americans have imbued the unconscious with the function of restoring harmony between the individual and an immanent spiritual power.

Since I will be arguing for the decidedly religious character of most American psychologies of the unconscious, I feel obligated to explain my use of the term *religion*. I am not inferring that the psychologies which I will be treating are merely disguised theologies. Yet, insofar as psychological theories purport to interpret reality and orient individuals within it, they inevitably assume many of the cultural functions traditionally associated with religion. And to the extent that psychological concepts are used to guide individuals toward life's instrinsic values and ultimate mysteries, their religious character becomes prominent. It is helpful in this context to remind ourselves of Paul Tillich's observation that religion "is not a special function of man's spiritual life, but is the dimension of depth in all of its functions."[5] The fact that psychological theory displays this depth (i.e. concern with life's intrinsic values and unconditioned meanings) does not make it any less psychological. It does, however, make it appropriate to speak of the symbolic aspect of psychological thought. A symbol, to quote Tillich once again, is defined by its ability to "open up levels of reality which are otherwise closed for us."[6] To the extent that ideas concerning the unconscious mind have performed this symbolic function, they certainly warrant interpretation from a broadly religious and humanistic perspective.

The first chapter of this book will provide the historical backdrop to Americans' discovery of the unconscious. I will examine the role which the concept of nature has played in the development of a uniquely American mode of spirituality in which the aesthetic—as opposed to the doctrinal or moral—dimension predominates. Aesthetic spirituality consists of those forms of belief and practice based upon the conviction that there are hidden depths to nature in which resides the secret to achieving spiritual composure. Insofar as psychological theories of the unconscious explain how humanity might participate in these non-empirical dimensions of existence, they have had an inherent tendency to become vehicles of this enduring strain of American religious thought.

Chapter 2 chronicles America's first popular psychological system, mesmerism, and its efforts to acquaint Americans with the unconscious depths of the human mind. Shifting the consideration of our higher nature from metaphysical to psychological terminology, the mesmerists made their references to the "influx" of higher spiritual energies into the human mind seem scientifically plausible. The mesmerists' version of humankind's spiritual potentials eventually came to compete with the churches for the loyalty of individuals concerned with innovative approaches to religious living. Insofar as mesmerism arose to fill a cultural niche created by the onset of secularization, it prefigured the many metaphysically charged conceptions of the unconscious which to this day enable Americans to forge a bridge between science and religion.

Chapter 3 will look at the emergence of academic psychology, particularly the functionalist school of thought represented by James Mark Baldwin, G. S. Hall, William James, John Dewey, and J. R. Angell. For all the functionalists' insistence that they had formulated a "new psychology," their writings on the unconscious reveal their indebtedness to a metaphysics rooted in the mystical or aesthetic strain of Puritan piety. This is also, however, the period in which neurophysiological, psychoanalytic, and early behavioristic models began to divide American psychology into diverse methodological orientations. Nowhere is this pluralization of both humanistic and social scientific thinking more apparent than in the ongoing debates concerning the existence or nonexistence of the unconscious.

The fourth chapter focuses upon the writings of America's most influential philosopher/psychologist, William James. At once a creature and creator of modern American thought, James believed the unconscious depths of human personality to be the source of our highest capacities. The unconscious afforded James a single psychological mechanism on the basis of which to argue for the existence of a creative or nondetermined component to mental activity, locate an inexhaustible reservoir of energy which could be activated in the pursuit of the strenuous life, and support his personal "over belief" concerning the individual's inner link with the divine. His genius for psychological description has made him the sole authority called upon by the psychoanalytic, behavioral, and humanistic schools of American psychology alike. James's writings, moreover, provide an important key for interpreting Americans' continuing tendency to endow the unconscious mind with an aura of ultimacy or religious depth.

Chapter 5 explores the major patterns according to which Americans have assimilated the psychoanalytic theory of the unconscious. The Freudian psyche, it seems, is in important respects ideologically incompatible with its essentially Transcendentalism-inspired Yankee counterparts. From James Jackson Putnam to Thomas Harris, American spokesmen for Freud's cause have attracted popular followings primarily by introducing structural changes at the very heart of the psychoanalytic system; and, for that reason, their writings reveal distinctively American assumptions about the nature and utility of the unconscious.

The sixth chapter examines the emergence of behaviorism as a dominant force in American psychology. Over and above behaviorism's obvious usefulness as a methodological or experimental program, it also helped address urban America's need to systematize and gain control over an increasingly unruly world. The vigorous environmentalism which J. B. Watson injected into the lifeblood of American psychology afforded a melioristic approach to life, but did so by grafting psychological thought onto a quite different strand of American religious thought—the moral or ascetic (as opposed to the aesthetic). Behaviorists have enhanced the scientific status of psychology by employing research methods which ignore such terms as *mind* or *consciousness*, for the reason that they are inherently insusceptible to objective measurement. In this view the unconscious becomes a fictitious belief incommensurate with scientific and cultural progress.

Chapter 7 examines recent humanistic psychologists. Abraham Maslow, Carl Rogers, and others have encouraged their readers to cultivate inner awareness and, by so doing, unleash the psyche's creative energies. The unconscious, in their writings, is a reservoir from which flows the power for self-actualization. Humanistic psychology's portrayal of the unconscious invokes a "romantic individualism" similar to that found in Emerson's transcendentalism, the mesmerists' philosophy of our higher nature, and the early functionalists' psychological rendering of Americans' enduring faith in the progressive and evolutionary character of nature. To this extent I think it fair to suggest the existence of a remarkable continuity in the religious and metaphysical assumptions which have guided Americans in their efforts to describe their own unconscious depths. By signifying levels of existence which would otherwise remain closed to the positivistic sciences of our day, the unconscious has emerged as an important symbol which enables many modern Americans to understand themselves as participating in the ultimate nature of things.

This study readily lends itself to a consideration of the often overlooked affinity between professional and popular American cultures. The final chapter will link the theoretical models of the unconscious emanating from academic psychologists with those of spiritualism, theosophy, Christian Science, New Thought, and the American Society for Psychical Research. Popular culture, it would seem, has reacted against the kind of secularizing influences represented by the professionalization of academic psychology by preserving many of the cultural meanings symbolized by the unconscious.

This book does not pretend to be an exhaustive account of the unconscious in the history of American psychology. Authors must select from among their sources only those which best advance the narrative. Since my intention is to demonstrate the various ways in which the unconscious has functioned as a religious symbol, I have selected accordingly and many influential authors and works have therefore been excluded. Often the fact that an author was self-conscious about appropriating—or opposing—a particular conception of the unconscious because of its religious overtones was a more important factor for inclusion than his or her overall contribution to the academic study of this topic. Readers will undoubtedly wonder why one or another psychologist received scant attention. Since errors of omission were both inevitable and necessary, I would ask the reader also to consider them justifiable insofar as the viewpoint in question has been incorporated into the narrative through other means.

One

The Psyche as Symbol: Theological Anticipations

THE unconscious is not so much a thing as it is an idea. Its appearance in the vocabulary of modern psychologists was thus less a sudden discovery than a novel rearrangement of assumptions which were more or less endemic to American culture. As Perry Miller argues in his essay "From Edwards to Emerson," much that emerges in the course of American intellectual history testifies to the fact that "certain basic continuities persist in a culture . . . and underlie the succession of ideas."[1] The continuities that so fascinated Miller concerned a strain of American spirituality which looked to "an indestructible element which was mystical, and a feeling for the universe which was almost pantheistic."[2] This aesthetic spirituality, as William Clebsch aptly labels it, contrasts sharply with the predominant religious outlook of our nation's churches; it involves neither doctrinal creeds nor moral codes. The aesthetic religious posture emphasizes instead the inner experience of beholding God as spiritually present within the natural universe and it equates spirituality with "consciousness of the beauty of living in harmony with divine things."[3]

So pronounced was this aesthetic spirituality in the writings of Jonathan Edwards, Ralph Waldo Emerson, and William

James that it is possible to proclaim them the bearers of a distinct American spirituality.[4] And even though all three drew considerable criticism from their contemporaries for locating the core of spiritual commitment in something so subjective and individualistic as a mode of consciousness, they nonetheless put their respective stamps upon a continuous, if countervailing, tradition in American religious thought. Edwards, for example, felt compelled to chide his contemporaries for what he called the "extraordinary dullness" of their doctrinal and moralistic conceptions of religion. He countered by insisting that "true religion, in great part, consists in holy affections."[5] Holy affections differ qualitatively from other modes of human experience. They are produced not through ordinary sense experience, but can only be known by those who have awakened to "new inward perceptions or sensations of their minds."[6] By rooting religion in the "holy affections," Edwards thought he had made religious experience compatible with the psychology of John Locke, who had insisted that all knowledge derives from sense experience.[7] To Edwards, religious knowledge differs from other kinds only in that it derives from its own, unique range of sensory impressions. Edwards's notion of holy affections thus made the mystical apprehension of God's invisible presence consistent with an empirical psychology. A sermon delivered in 1734 made it clear that true religion proceeds upon "A Divine and Supernatural Light, Immediately Imparted to the Soul by the Spirit of God, Shown to be Both a Scriptural, and Rational Doctrine." Edwards was thus equating religious faith with empiricism of the most radical sort.

God—or more properly, the supernatural light that emanates from God—is thus present to the properly receptive or aesthetic mind.

> The great and last end of God's works . . . is fitly compared to an effulgence or emanation of light from a luminary. . . . It is by this that all nature is quickened and receives life, comfort and joy. . . . In the creature's knowing, esteeming, loving, rejoicing in, and praising God, the glory of God is both

exhibited and acknowledged; His fullness is received and
returned. Here is both emanation and remanation. The
refulgence shines upon and into the creature, and is reflected
back to the luminary.[8]

These references to the "effulgence" or emanation of divine
light reveal the great extent to which Edwards, a Calvinist,
emphasized God's presence within the natural universe. He
wanted to show God's relatedness to the created universe in more
intimate terms than was allowed for in the mechanistic categories
then regnant in the New England theological mind. But to do so
he had to explain how the divine and human realms might come
into contact with one another. Edwards explained that God's
emanative spirit awakens in us a "new sense." He contended that
"this new spiritual sense is not a new faculty of understanding
but it is a new foundation laid in the nature of the soul for a new
kind of exercise of the same faculty of understanding."[9] This new
sense is the source of the holy affections that both promote inner
reconciliation with God and incline us toward "disinterested
benevolence" in our actions toward others.

Edwards's mystical inclinations elevated nature to the status
of a symbol or metaphor for the divine.[10] He wrote that there
exists in nature "an analogy or consent between the beauty of the
skies, trees, fields, flowers, etc., and spiritual excellence."[11] The
"new sense" of which Edwards spoke made it possible for
humans to apprehend "images or shadows of divine things" in
nature. Once God is identified with "being in general," however,
there is little to distinguish between images or shadows and the
immanent deity himself.

The pantheistic tendencies in Edwards's thought, anomalous
though they appear within the Calvinist-inspired American theological tradition, reflect a native metaphysical tradition. According to no less acute an observer of American life and thought than
Alexis de Tocqueville:

If there is a philosophical system which teaches that all things
material and immaterial, visible and invisible, which the

world contains are to be considered as the several parts of an immense Being, who alone remains eternal amid the continual change and ceaseless transformation of all that constitutes him, we may readily infer that such a system . . . will have secret charm for men living in democracies.[12]

As Edwards pointed out, the presence of God's emanative spirit makes divinely infused "life, comfort and joy" available in all of nature. The effulgence of divine light "into the creature" is thus potentially present in every human experience. This notion was open to appealing interpretations. It implied that all people—not just an elect few—were intimately linked with God's providential powers. It also suggested that, because the currents of Being circulate through us, we are all in a sense divine. Of course, neither Edwards nor any of his contemporaries were prepared to follow this idea to such daring conclusions; the Calvinist framework could not stretch that far. But, as Perry Miller wryly comments, "If the inherent mysticism, the ingrained pantheism, of certain Yankees could not be stated in the old terms, it could be couched in the new terms of transcendental idealism, of Platonism, of Swedenborg, of 'Tintern Abbey' and the Bhagavad Gita, in the eclectic and polyglot speech of the Over-Soul, in 'Brahma,' in 'Self-Reliance,' in *Nature*." [13] Which is to say, in the writings of Ralph Waldo Emerson.

Changing Metaphors for Depth

"Nature," Emerson proclaimed, "is the symbol of spirit."[14] His writings extol nature as a kind of meeting point between the divine and human realms. Nature constitutes "the organ through which the universal spirit speaks to the individual, and strives to lead back the individual to it."[15] Edwards's mystical feel for the "emanation and remanation" of spirit endures in the Emersonian vision, but with an important difference.[16] Here there is no transcendent "luminary" or personal God. This is not to say that Emerson failed to recognize the divine as something more than merely the natural order; it shows, however, how fully Emerson represents that tradition in American thought which insists that religious thinking must be grounded in human experience. When he identified nature as the preferred metaphor or symbol of life's spiritual depth, Emerson laid the foundation for a new style of religious thinking; he became, as Sydney Ahlstrom put it, "the theologian of something we may almost term 'the American religion.' "[17]

Once intellectual restraints of the Western monotheistic tradition had been thrown off, claims concerning the in-streaming presence of God became inseparable from descriptions of that state of consciousness in which awareness of such pneumatic transactions is possible. When Emerson went alone into nature, he was moved to testimony reminiscent of a Upanishadic sage: "All mean egotism vanishes. I become a transparent eyeball; I am nothing; I see all; the currents of the Universal Being circulate through me; I am part or parcel of God."[18] In the context of that Protestant tradition which posits an unbridgeable chasm between God and the natural order, this statement is unthinkable. But according to his own lights Emerson was describing the lawful conditions governing intercourse between the divine and human realms.

For Emerson, religion has its foundations in the act of becoming inwardly receptive to the Over-Soul. The self—like the Hindu Atman—was a succession of layers or sheaths. Only by peeling away the outer sheaths can one hope to become a "vehicle of that divine principle that lurks within."[19] Thus, it is not so much nature but a particular state of consciousness that permits "an influx of Divine Mind into our mind."[20] As deeper levels of consciousness are attained, a person becomes "conscious of a universal soul within or behind his individual life, wherein, as a firmament, the natures of Justice, Truth, Love, Freedom, arise and shine."[21] This perception is nothing less than an ecstatic religious event. It is marked by "that shudder of awe and delight with which the individual soul always mingles with the Universal Soul."[22] The self, inwardly connected to nature at a preconceptual level, is instantaneously "filled with the divinity which flows through all things."[23]

Self-reliance is the by-product of such expanded consciousness. The truly self-reliant individual differs from the rest because he has cultivated closer relations with the "supersensible regions":

> The study of many [of these] individuals leads us to an
> elemental region wherein the individual is lost, or wherein all
> touch by their summits. . . . Thought and feeling that break
> out there cannot be impounded by any fence of personality.
> This is the key to the power of great men—their spirit diffuses
> itself.[24]

The true virtuosos of the human species inhabit "a higher sphere of thought." Emerson maintained that the representative man is an "exponent of a vaster mind and will. The opaque self becomes transparent with the light of the First cause."[25] Emerson's point here is that self-reliance is in fact God-reliance. The "self" upon which one must rely is not the self whose identity is derived through the physical senses. It is, rather, the self which has first "become nothing" and thus receptive to the "exertions of a power which exists not in time, or space, but an instantaneous in-streaming causing power."[26] Psychological conditions are thus a necessary but by no means sufficient cause for the act of becoming self-reliant. The ultimate power behind self-reliance derives not from the activities of the rational ego but from "the divinity which flows through all things."

Modern readers are often puzzled by the fact that Emerson never specified the psychological mechanism through which the divine influx enters the human mind. In certain contexts he counseled that the secret to self-reliance lies in our orientation to the outer world; to realize one's full potential one must first know "that beyond the energy of his possessed and conscious intellect he is capable of a new energy (as of an intellect doubled on itself) by *abandonment to the nature of things*." [27] Yet, elsewhere Emerson used intrapsychic terms: "As fast as you conform your life to the pure idea in your mind, that will unfold its great proportions. A correspondent revolution in things will attend the influx of the spirit."[28] Probably Emerson was himself unsure about the exact relationship between states of our own minds and the divinity immanent in nature. His comment that "the power to produce this delight does not reside in nature, but in man, or in a harmony of both" seems to reflect the thinking of a period still more comfortable with metaphysical than with psychological categories.[29]

Emerson's contemporary and fellow Transcendentalist George Ripley stated the agenda that those committed to aesthetic spirituality would follow for the remainder of the nineteenth century:

> The time has come when a revision of theology is demanded.
> Let the study of theology commence with the study of human consciousness.[30]

The aesthetic strain in American religious thought was, in Emerson, freed from dependence upon scriptural language. Religious truths, he claimed, "arise to us out of the recesses of consciousness."[31] As Ripley so presciently observed, the very credibility of theological discourse would henceforth be determined by its ability to educe a psychologically nuanced description of "the recesses of consciousness." In the 1840s and 1850s the mesmerists would attempt to do precisely this, while heralding their discovery of the unconscious. And, from William James in the 1890s to the humanistic psychologists of the 1970s, American psychologists have continued in this aesthetic strain of American religious thought, using the psyche as a powerful symbol of our unconscious connection with higher spiritual realms.

Harmonial Piety and the Cultural Roots of American Psychology

The metaphysical assumptions behind this "From Edwards to Emerson" tradition of American religious thought promoted a distinctive form of piety in which "harmony" rather than contrition or repentance is the sine qua non of the regenerated life. As Sydney Ahlstrom describes it, harmonial religion "encompasses those forms of piety and belief in which spiritual composure, physical health, and even economic well-being are understood to flow from a person's rapport with the cosmos."[32] The deity—here conceived as an indwelling cosmic force—is approached not via petitionary prayer or acts of worship, but through a series of inner adjustments. As the mental barriers separating the finite personality from the "divinity which flows through all things" are gradually penetrated, abundance spontaneously manifests itself in every dimension of personal life.

Harmonial piety is essentially faithful to the Puritan-Protestant world view. Notwithstanding the somewhat heterodox denial of any "gulf" between God and humanity, the harmonial outlook retains the Protestant emphasis upon the individual as alone before God and the conviction that faith (inner transformation) precedes good works. The aesthetic or harmonial tradition also retains intact what intellectual historians such as Perry Miller, Ralph Gabriel, and William McLoughlin have identified as the core conceptions that shape American culture:

> the chosen nation; the covenant with God; . . . the higher
> (biblical or natural) law, against which private and social
> behavior is to be judged; . . . the laws of science presumed to
> be from the creator, and evolutionary or progressive in their
> purpose; the free and morally responsible individual, whose
> political liberty and liberty of conscience are inalienable; the
> work ethic (or "Protestant ethic"), which holds that equal
> opportunity and hard work will bring economic success and
> public respect to all who assert and discipline themselves; and
> the benevolence of nature under the exploiting or controlling
> hand of man (i.e., nature was made for man).[33]

These interrelated assumptions have given direction to the personal as well as the collective sense of identity throughout American history. Over time, however, they have been reformulated and given new applications. For some, the need to make these conceptions more compatible with changing socio-cultural realities has been acute. It was, for example, Emerson's genius to bring the aesthetic or harmonial understanding of the relationship between man and God to bear upon the interpretation of these widely held beliefs and in so doing make them more appealing to those who shared his doubts about orthodox theology. This also seems to have been true for many intellectuals in the 1880s and 1890s as well as for seekers of many varieties in the 1960s.

The harmonial understanding of the individual's relationship to nature is perhaps best illustrated by the notion of a covenant between God and His creation. Since Old Testament times, the concept of the covenant enabled individuals to know the actions and attitudes upon which their hope for salvation depends. By locating God's dealings with humans within the confines of a lawful system, the covenant encourages belief that the natural world is essentially melioristic. Covenantal theology has in the same way served as a bulwark against determinisms of every kind—historical, political, social, psychological, even theological. The final outcome of all things depends upon the freedom of both parties—humans and God—to act in accordance with the stipulated conditions. In the American context, covenantal theology thus helped to offset Calvinism's emphasis upon God's seemingly fickle selection of which souls shall and which shall not be granted salvation.

American theologies have largely reflected the conviction that "in some fashion the transcendent God had to be chained, made less inscrutable, less mysterious, less unpredictable—He had to be made, again, understandable in human terms."[34] By the time of the Second Great Awakening (1800–1830), a belief in humanity's active role in initiating the salvatory process held sway in the popular religious climate. Whereas the conversion or rebirth experience had once been thought to be wholly dependent upon the initiative of the Almighty, by the 1830s it was generally considered to be amenable to human engineering. Popular—and eminently successful—revivalists had forged a consensus of theological opinion to the effect that humans can manipulate their and others' inner lives to bring about a profound encounter with the Holy Spirit.

Charles Grandison Finney epitomized antebellum America's changing attitudes toward both the covenant and the process of spiritual rebirth. Finney, articulating the progressivist temper of the Jacksonian era, wrote that "new measures are necessary from time to time to awaken attention and to bring the gospel to bear upon the public mind."[35] The "new measures" Finney had in mind were the empirically tested techniques he had used so effectively to elicit conversion experiences. His *Lectures on Revivals*, published in 1835, was essentially a technical manual for those who shared his assumption that the revivalist ministry could be reduced to a science. To Finney's way of thinking, a conversion "is not a miracle or dependent upon a miracle in any sense . . . it consists entirely in the right exercise of the powers of nature."[36] The theological corollary of this assertion was that "God had connected means with ends through all departments of his government—in nature and in grace."[37]

Finney was not one to miss the utilitarian applications of his theology. In order to reap a bumper crop of converts, he urged, "he who deals with souls should study well the laws of the mind."[38] To be sure, Finney's religious temperament was far removed from that of his harmonially minded contemporaries such as George Ripley and the Transcendentalists, but they shared an experimental attitude toward religion, which tested "truth" by its empirical or experiential consequences. And it was the Finneyite attitude, rather than that of the Boston Brahmins, which set thousands of nineteenth-century Americans off on the search for novel modes of religion—modes that were expected, as Whitney Cross puts it, to get "the automatically operant Holy Spirit to descend and symbolize the start of the New Life."[39] The growth of mesmerist psychology in the 1840s and 1850s and the mind-cure movement in the 1880s and 1890s can be directly linked to these popular expectations of "the laws of the mind."

Harmonial or aesthetic piety thus predisposed individuals to view psychology in an essentially religious light; namely,that studying the laws of the mind and questing for the covenantal terms whereby we can be restored to harmony with God are, in this religious union, virtually synonomous. Furthermore, during the nineteenth century the harmonial understanding of the relation between the divine and human realms was often fused with the Swedenborgian/Emersonian concept of "correspondence." Correspondence was not simply a method for studying nature (i.e., "the fine secret that little explains large, and large, little. . . . Nature iterates her means perpetually on successive planes"). More important, it involved a belief in interpenetrating spheres of causality. When inner harmony, or resonance between realms, is established, guiding wisdom and energy automatically flow from the "higher" to the "lower" plane. On this view, the idea that there are laws governing human participation in God's redemptive scheme entails not only obligation but opportunity as well. According to the harmonial understanding, the covenant, rather than restraining humanity's natural tendencies, promises their almost unlimited fulfillment. All of us carry within ourselves the key to happiness, success, and spiritual advancement. We need but to attune ourselves to the inflow of what Emerson described as that "force always at work to make the best better and the worst good."[40] This notion of the inner resources of the individual powerfully strengthens belief in the principles of democratic thought, commitment to the work ethic, and confidence in God's providential activity. Psychology, when approached from the standpoint of aesthetic spirituality, had the potential to reinforce both Americans' religious and cultural faiths.

From Nature to Psychological Nature in American Theology

Underlying the ability of late nineteenth-century Americans to embrace scientific psychology as a source of spiritual edification was a long tradition of seeing nature as fraught with theological significance. Throughout the first half of the nineteenth century, American Protestants were increasingly fascinated by scientific method. Speculation came to be seen as an inadequate basis for theology, and many set themselves to the task of producing an empirical or natural theology. Natural theology was based on the assumption that God has revealed Himself to humankind through two mediums: Scripture (special revelation) and nature (general revelation). This view could accommodate the Baconian insistence that nothing could be accepted as true unless founded on hard empirical evidence. If knowledge of God and knowledge of the world were of the same order, it was possible to derive theological conclusions from observations of natural phenomena. Herbert Hovenkamp notes that in the mid-nineteenth century

> Orthodox Protestants believed that the Baconian method was
> useful for both science and theology. For them, doing theology
> was a scientific activity. It employed the inductive method
> and drew its data from the world of nature. As orthodox
> Baconians conceived it, natural theology was also like the
> sciences in one other respect: its conclusions could be
> demonstrated empirically. The men who engaged in natural
> theology believed it could prove, beyond any reasonable
> doubt, God's existence and sovereignty.[41]

Nature was thought to display a divinely ordered, rational design. Although this design was statically and mechanistically conceived, natural theology infected antebellum Americans with a kind of cosmic optimism. Amherst President Edward Hitchcock voiced the progressivist message of natural theology in his book *The Religion of Geology and Its Connected Sciences* (1851). Progress, he affirmed, occurs whenever "we conform to the laws which God has established."[42]

Hovenkamp believes that the 1850s were a watershed for American natural theology:

> Up to the middle of the century the work in natural theology
> gradually became more sophisticated, more responsive to the

natural sciences. It was generally acclaimed by Christians of
all persuasions as an effective way of demonstrating the
existence and attributes of God. After *On the Origins of
Species*, however, the emphases in theology changed
dramatically.[43]

The Darwinian theories of random variation and natural
selection were diametrically opposed to the Christian concept of
design. Darwin's discovery undercut both confidence in biblical
authority and the concept of divine providence. Science was
proving to be something of an embarrassment to orthodox Protestant theology. Understandably, interest in natural theology
waned. Conservative theologians could no longer proceed on the
assumption that science would be a faithful ally to them in their
theological efforts.

This is not to imply that nature ceased to serve as a primary
symbol of American religious thought; it is only to note its final
divorce from the methods and scope of conservative Protestant
theology. Intellectuals of more liberal or progressivist persuasions would continue to make nature the cornerstone of their
religious reflections, without, however, feeling obliged to square
their reasoning with Scripture as had their antebellum predecessors. And it was they who, according to historian William
McLoughlin, responded most creatively to the challenges posed
to faith by a modern, scientifically oriented society. As
McLoughlin notes, events of the final two decades of the nineteenth century eroded older concepts of the covenant and providence. And, not surprisingly, it was largely nonecclesiastical
thinkers—philosophers, humanists, sociologists, and psychologists—who were inventive enough "to undertake an enormous
rescue operation to sustain the culture. They had to redefine and
relocate God, provide means of access to Him, and sacralize a
new world view."[44]

It was the Romantic or aesthetic spirit, prefigured in Edwards
and amplified by Emerson, that animated this "rescue operation," and by the 1880s there were many new voices in the

aesthetic chorus: Schelling, Kant, Hegel, and Schleiermacher. Schleiermacher, because of his overt identification with the Protestant tradition, did most to legitimate the return to natural theology of a particular, radically empirical sort. Schleiermacher went the "cultured despisers" of religion one better. He totally concurred with the modern mind and its honest doubts concerning the validity of church doctrines; but Schleiermacher shifted the ground of the debate from theology to psychology. Religion, he contended, possesses its own unique data, its own unique mode of experience and feeling. It is known inwardly, immediately, and intuitively by a prereflective, preconscious dimension of the personality. Like Emerson, Schleiermacher failed to specify the psychological mechanism through which we derive this preconscious knowledge of God. Yet his writings enabled countless American intellectuals to believe that the investigation of the mind's hidden depths, even when pursued with "secular" methodologies, would ultimately lend empirical support to religious faith.

The natural theology of the late nineteenth century differed from its predecessors in two important ways: (1) It turned away from anthropomorphic conceptions of God in favor of abstract notions like "Cosmic Force" or "Infinite and Eternal Energy" and (2), increasingly, it neglected the Bible as a source of religious knowledge and—following Schleiermacher—looked to some prerational mode of thinking and feeling for evidence of God's presence in nature. In such paradigmatic works as John Fiske's *Through Nature to God* (1899), Lyman Abbott's *The Theology of an Evolutionist* (1897), and John Bascom's *Evolution and Religion* (1897), evolution came to figure as a substitute for Christian cosmology. Fiske declared that "the lesson of evolution is that . . . [the soul] has been rising to the recognition of its essential kinship with the ever-living God."[45] Despite his avowed intention to preserve a personal deity, Fiske is found referring to this "ever-living God" as "Absolute Power" or "the Power which is disclosed in every throb of the mighty rhythmic life of the universe."

Unlike Fiske, Abbott jettisoned theistic language unapologetically. Evolution represented for him "the doctrine of growth applied to life . . . of continuous progressive growth, from a lower to a higher, from a simpler to a more complex organization, under the influence of resident forces and in accordance with law."[46] Abbott defined God as the necessary postulate of this progressive series: "the Infinite and Eternal Energy from which all things proceed." God was not to be thought of as a discrete entity residing in a celestial kingdom, but as a dimension of "all the multifarious forces of nature." Abbott spoke for many scientifically inclined Americans in the late nineteenth century when he reasoned that the "foundation of spiritual faith is neither in the church nor in the Bible, but in the spiritual consciousness of man."[47]

Abbott's contention that religious belief was still possible in an age of science depended a great deal on the existence of this "spiritual consciousness." Similarly, John Bascom's effort to reconcile evolutionary science with religion depended in part upon his argument that in addition to our five physical senses,

> there is also a spiritual sense, a power to feel spiritual
> connections and to discover their implications. It is an
> inductive tendency exercised in a higher region. It has the
> constructive force of an artistic temper. . . . God is a being to
> be thought of less and less sensuously, to be rejoiced in more
> and more super-sensuously.[48]

Later nineteenth-century Americans were still trying to find the functional equivalent of Emerson's "transparent eyeballs." The sense of urgency about finding new scientific evidence in support of the Christian faith is particularly evident in liberal Protestant churchmen such as Horace Bushnell and Henry Ward Beecher. Bushnell's so-called sentimental theology was born of the Romantic spirit set loose in New England intellectual circles through the writings of Schelling, Schleiermacher, Coleridge, and Emerson. He applied their ideas to his own theory concerning the progressive development of personality. The cause of such development was, he reasoned, "a flowing-in of God's righteousness upon the believing soul."[49] But Bushnell recognized that neither the science nor the orthodox theology of his day possessed adequate tools for conceptualizing God's availability to the individual self. He appealed instead to the more aesthetic, symbolic, and intuitive functions of consciousness. "Religion," he wrote, "has a natural and profound alliance with poetry. . . . The poetic forms of utterance are closer to the fires of religion within us, more adequate revelations of consciousness."[50]

Henry Ward Beecher also struggled to make the interaction between the divine and human minds intelligible. Describing God's radiant influence by means of an analogy to electricity, Beecher said that we are in some way specially constituted to receive the spirit "which fills the universe with the energy that men call force or natural law."[51] Beecher was uncertain about the exact nature of this receptive faculty, and he conjectured that to explore the fathomless, dark sea of the mind would be—like Columbus—to set out on a journey destined to lead to marvelous new terrain:

> The human mind is the kernel; the material world is but the shell or rind. As yet science has chiefly concerned itself with the shell. The unexplored soul is yet to be found out.[52]

Even as Beecher and Bushnell were writing, many of their contemporaries were busily investigating these uncharted mental territories. Nature—or, more precisely, psychological nature—was thought to contain the mechanism for the harmonization of individual selves with the World Spirit. At the level of popular culture, groups like New Thought, Theosophy, spiritualism, and the American Society for Psychical Research were all promulgating doctrines concerning humanity's inner connection with the higher cosmic spheres. Among the ranks of academic psychologists, James Mark Baldwin was writing about the superlogical state of consciousness while William James was preparing a study of the varieties of religious experience considered solely in terms of the psychological doctrine of the subliminal self. The human psyche was, in short, being seized upon as a passageway to higher metaphysical realms.

Americans had discovered the unconscious.

Two

The Unconscious Discovered: The Mesmerists' Legacy

APATHY, scorn, and derision met Charles Poyen at the beginning of his American lecture tour in 1836. His audiences knew virtually nothing about his subject and, what is more, seemed to prefer it that way. Poyen consoled himself with the knowledge that all great truths—even when espoused by the likes of Galileo, Columbus, or Christ—are initially dismissed by the general populace. His confidence and evangelical zeal emanated from the conviction that he was speaking on the basis of "well-authenticated facts concerning an order of phenomena so important to science and so glorious to human nature."[1] And, though Americans were as yet not interested in "yielding to its reality," he persisted in his prophetic mission to acquaint them with Franz Anton Mesmer's science of animal magnetism.

Mesmer (1734-1815) had attracted a good deal of attention when he presented himself in European intellectual circles as the bearer of an epoch-making discovery. The Viennese physician claimed to have detected the existence of a superfine substance or fluid which had until then managed to elude scientific notice. Mesmer referred to this invisible fluid as animal magnetism and postulated that it permeated the physical universe. He further explained that animal magnetism constituted the etheric medium through which sensations of every kind—light, heat, magnetism, electricity—passed as they traveled from one physical object to another. Every event transpiring throughout nature depended upon the fact that animal magnetism linked physical objects together and made possible the transmission of influences from one to another. Mesmer believed that his discovery had removed the basic impediment to scientific progress and that every area of human knowledge would soon undergo rapid transformation and advancement.

Mesmer was most concerned with the application of his discovery to the treatment of sickness and disease. Animal magnetism was said to be evenly distributed throughout the healthy human body. If for any reason an individual's supply of animal magnetism was thrown out of equilibrium, one or more bodily organs would consequently be deprived of sufficient amounts of this vital force and would eventually begin to falter. "There is," Mesmer reasoned, "only one illness and one healing."[2] In other words, since any and all illnesses can ultimately be traced back to a disturbance in the body's supply of animal magnetism, medical science could be reduced to a simple set of procedures aimed at supercharging a patient's nervous system with this mysterious life-giving energy.

Before Mesmer's theory reached American shores, his pupils had introduced significant changes which would drastically alter the science of animal magnetism. The Marquis de Puysegur exerted the greatest influence upon subsequent interpretations of his teacher's remarkable healing talents. Puysegur had faithfully imitated Mesmer's techniques only to have his patients fall into unusual, sleeplike states of consciousness. They had, so to speak, become "mesmerized." What made this phenomenon so important was that these entranced individuals exhibited the most extraordinary behaviors. Puysegur's subjects responded to his questions with more intelligent and nuanced replies than could possibly be expected given their educational and socioeconomic background. Many subjects suddenly remembered long-forgotten experiences with astonishing accuracy and attention to detail. A select few appeared to drift into a much deeper state of consciousness, which Puysegur described as one of "extraordinary lucidity." These subjects spontaneously performed feats of telepathy, clairvoyance, and precognition. Puysegur had stumbled upon the fact that just below the threshold of ordinary consciousness exists a stratum of mental life quite superior to anything of which anyone had been aware. In discovering the means of inducing persons into this unconscious mental realm, Puysegur had initiated a revolution in the study of human nature.

Journey Across the Atlantic

Charles Poyen had studied directly under Puysegur and thus confidently stood before his American audiences as a self-appointed Professor of Animal Magnetism. Like his mentor, Poyen believed that mesmerism's single most important discovery was the somnambulic, or mesmeric, state of consciousness. His public lectures centered on an actual demonstration of the mesmeric state of consciousness and all of its attendant phenomena, among which, as he described it, were:

> Suspension, more or less complete, of the external sensibility;
> intimate connexion with the magnetizer and with no other
> one; influence of the will; communication of thought;
> clairvoyance, or the faculty of seeing through various parts of
> the body, the eyes remaining closed; unusual development of
> sympathy, of memory, and of the power of imagination;
> faculty for sensing the symptoms of diseases and prescribing
> proper remedies for them; entire forgetting, after awakening,
> of what had transpired during the state of somnambulism.[3]

In addition to employing the services of a professional somnambule, Poyen also made a practice of enlisting a few volunteers from the audience. He explained to his subjects that his manual gestures heightened the activity of their system's animal magnetism to the point where their "external sensibilities" temporarily receded from consciousness, inducing a sleeplike condition. Whatever the explanation, he succeeded in putting about half of his volunteers into a trance which rendered them peculiarly unresponsive to their surroundings. Loud hand clapping and jars of ammonia passed under their noses failed to evoke even the slightest response. To all appearances, their minds had withdrawn from the physical world.

Staged exhibitions of mesmerism proved to be great theater. Crowds thronged to see their friends and relatives transformed before their very eyes. The entertainment value of these demonstrations obviously outstripped their application to contemporary medical science. The frivolity which inevitably developed during the demonstrations predictably disenfranchised mesmerism from the established scientific community. But for all their unintended disservice to the science of animal magnetism, Poyen's lecture-demonstrations effectively stimulated the public's imagination with novel "facts" about human nature—facts which, if not as "important to science" as Poyen had hoped, were soon thought to be more "glorious to human nature" than even he had ever dreamed.

Many of Poyen's volunteers came in hope of obtaining a medical cure. He obliged by making repeated "passes" with his hands in an effort to direct the flow of animal magnetism to the appropriate part of the body. A large proportion of those receiving this treatment awoke from their mesmeric sleep and, remembering nothing of what had transpired, claimed cure. Poyen's own account, in many cases supported with newspaper reports and letters to the editor, lists successful treatment of such disorders as rheumatism, nervousness, back troubles, and liver ailments.

Roughly 10 percent of subjects mesmerized by Poyen attained the "highest degree" of the magnetic condition. Their behavior went beyond the peculiar, to the extraordinary. The onset of this stage in the mesmerizing process was marked by the formation of an especially intense rapport between the subject and the operator. The crucial ingredient of this rapport was the establishment of some nonverbal means of communication through which the subject telepathically received unspoken thoughts from the operator. Most subjects obligingly attributed this ability to their heightened receptivity to animal magnetism. Some actually reported feeling animal magnetism impinge upon their nervous systems; they felt prickly sensations running up and down their bodies. Others claimed to "see" dazzling bright lights. Nor was it uncommon for subjects to perform feats of clairvoyance and extrasensory perception. They might locate lost objects, describe events transpiring in distant locales, or telepathically read the minds of persons in the audience. Yet, upon returning to the waking state, they remembered little of their trance-bound experiences. It was as if they had temporarily existed in an altogether different realm. They knew only that they were now more refreshed, energetic, and healed of their former ailments.

Word of Poyen's fantastic healing methods spread throughout New England. His 1837 treatise on the progress of animal magnetism in New England declares that "nineteen months have elapsed since that period and already Animal Magnetism has sprung from a complete state of obscurity and neglect into general notice, and become the object of a lively interest throughout the country."[4] Newspapers began to take notice. The *Providence Journal* reported that more than one hundred cases of "Magnetic Somnambulism" had been reported in Rhode Island alone. Poyen's system was, according to one observer, fast becoming a "steady theme of interest in New England papers" and making "a deep impression upon some of the soundest and best balanced minds."[5] Poyen cited articles from Rhode Island, Maine, and Connecticut supporting his contention that the science of animal magnetism had become a topic of conversation in all classes of society, especially—as he was quick to point out—among the learned and well-to-do.

Poyen returned to his native France in 1839. The same year, an Englishman by the name of Robert Collyer began a lecture tour in America which helped spread mesmerism's sensational discoveries all along the Atlantic seaboard. In Boston, Collyer managed to attract "large and intelligent audiences" to his nightly lectures for three straight months. The city council finally deemed it necessary to appoint a committee "consisting of twenty-four gentlemen selected from the learned professions" to investigate Collyer's practices.[6] The committee refused to give mesmerism its full endorsement but did assure the citizenry that there was no reason to suspect Collyer of engaging in deceptive practices. They even went on record as corroborating the major issue at stake in the public controversy: the reality of a distinct mesmeric state. The report concludes that "while this committee refrains from expressing any opinion as to the science or principle of animal magnetism, they freely confess that in the experiments of Dr. Collyer, certain appearances have been presented which cannot be explained upon the supposition of collusion, or by reference to any physiological principle known to them."[7]

Poyen's and Collyer's efforts attracted a host of newcomers eager to become spokesmen for the science of animal magnetism. According to one estimate, by 1843 more than two hundred "magnetizers" were selling their services in the city of Boston alone.[8] Growing public interest stimulated demand for books and pamphlets, and the American mesmerists willingly complied.[9] Most of the dozens of works to appear over the next twenty years followed a common format: an introductory exhortation of open-mindedness; a short history of Mesmer's discovery; a cataloging of typical cures; documented reports of clairvoyance and telepathy; and last, but not least, a set of do-it-yourself instructions. For example, one widely circulated pamphlet bore the appropriate title *The History and Philosophy of Animal Magnetism with Practical Instruction for the Exercise of this Power.* Another included in its title the promise to explain "the system of manipulating adopted to produce ecstasy and somnambulism."[10]

A consensus as to the scientific principles established by mesmeric phenomena soon emerged in the literature. Relying heavily on the writings of a British mesmerist named Chauncy Townshend, American investigators came to view the mesmerizing process as a technique for shifting mental activity along a continuum.[11] Each stage or point along the continuum was said to correspond to a successively deeper level of consciousness. The mesmerizing process dismantled the normal waking state of consciousness and induced individuals to shift their attention inward, away from events occurring in the physical world. As the sensations supplied by the five physical senses gradually receded from consciousness, subjects start to enter the beginning stage or level of the mesmeric trance. This relatively light trance state was one in which subjects would appear totally insensible to any external sensation other than the voice of the mesmerist. The behaviors exhibited by subjects in this entranced condition fell well within the standard repertoire of modern stage hypnotists.

The most distinctive claim being made by the mesmerists, however, was their insistence that the mind could be moved even farther along this continuum until, at last freed from bondage to the five physical senses, it opens up to wholly new ranges of experience. Or, as Townshend had put it, mesmerism brings about "the inaction of the external operations of the sense, coexistent with the life and activity of some *inner source of feeling*." [12] The mesmeric state had made possible a giant breakthrough in the scientific study of the brain. The mesmerists' experiments were hailed as having empirically proven that there exists "a sense in man which perceives the presences and qualities of things without the use of . . . the external organs of sense."[13] At this deeper level, the mind detects orders of sensation never monitored by the physical senses. Some mesmerized subjects became

clairvoyant, or capable of seeing objects at any distance,
without even the assistance of sympathy [with their operator];
they are prevoyant, or capable of foreseeing future events; and
they have also intuitive knowledge as to the thought and
characters of persons to whom they direct their attention. . . .
In truth, there is no definite limit to the range of their
intuitive knowledge [whether] in medicine, mental
philosophy, theology, chemistry, geology, etc.[14]

These deeper realms of the mesmeric state had a decidedly mystical element to them. Subjects felt that they had transcended the affairs of mundane existence and entered into an intimate rapport with the cosmos. In the mesmeric state persons temporarily felt endowed with omnipresent and omniscient mental powers. As one investigator reported, mesmerized subjects "speak as if, to their own consciousness, they had undergone an inward translation by which they had passed out of a material into a spiritual body. . . . The state into which a subject is brought by the mesmerizing process is a state in which the spirit predominates for the time being over the body."[15]

It was inevitable that the mesmerists' psychological continuum would be thought also to define a metaphysical hierarchy. That is, the "deeper" levels of consciousness opened the individual to qualitatively "higher" planes of mental existence. The mesmerists confidently proclaimed that the key to achieving personal harmony with these deeper levels of ultimate reality lies quite literally within ourselves.

From Fluidic Theory to Psychology

Poyen had heralded mesmerism as the "science of the psychological constitution of man."[16] Unfortunately, he was not exactly sure what this might entail. While a great deal of attention had been given to validating their observations, mesmerists had as yet offered very little in the way of a scientific rationale. For his own part, Poyen hypothesized that "every human being carries within himself a nervous, magnetic, or vital atmosphere."[17] But beyond that he had little to say.

The mesmerists' effort to expand their observations into a comprehensive theory of human nature was complicated by the fact that Mesmer had bequeathed them a theory modeled after the physical sciences. It was only gradually—and with considerable awkwardness—that they were able to educe a more fully psychological perspective from the phenomena observed of mesmerized subjects. The first problem they faced was to decide whether the mesmeric state was produced by animal magnetism or by the mind itself. Unable to accept the consequences of either hypothesis, they took a safer route and chose both. An article that appeared in *Buchanan's Journal of Man* in 1849 registers the confusion:

> The established fact, that imagination may effect the most wonderful cures . . . seems to have been overlooked by the early magnetizers; they could see nothing in all their experiments but the potency of the wonderful and mysterious "fluid." On the other hand, the antimesmeric party, knowing the powers of the imagination, were blind to the existence of any other agent. . . . It is probable that, in this matter, both the mesmerizers and their opponents were wrong in the ultra and exclusive doctrine which each party maintained—but with the lapse of time, we now see that each party had progressed nearer the truth. The opponents of animal magnetism have yielded by thousands to the conviction that there are forces of some kind emitted by the human constitution which had not been recognized in their philosophy; and, on the other hand, many mesmerizers (in the United States at least) have learned that many of their most interesting results are really the product of imagination.[18]

The American mesmerists were awakening to the fact that their experiments attested to an autonomous psychological realm. Well aware of the role that "suggestion" (i.e., the mesmerized subject's tendency to comply with the wishes of the operator) and prior expectations played in determining the behavior of a person in the magnetic state, mesmerists became the first Americans directly to study the psychodynamic nature of interpersonal relationships. Not that their insights were particularly impressive. Poyen picked up the scent when it dawned on him that he had not once encountered a subject who could clairvoyantly describe scenes of a city which he had not previously visited. Puzzled as to just what this might mean, he concluded that "such a thing is inexplicable and cannot be referred to any philosophical principle."[19]

La Roy Sunderland ventured a bit further when he proposed that the mental influence which the mesmeric operator wields over the subject is not transmitted through some external agency (animal magnetism), but rather is on a continuum with the influence one mind always has over another.[20] J. Stanley Grimes pushed this interpretation furthest, arguing that the behaviors of entranced subjects were largely the products of unintentional self-deception.[21] Most, if not all, of these strange phenomena could be interpreted as a consequence of the subject's subdued will and abnormally active phrenological propensities for imitation, credulity, trust, and—above all—conformity. Interestingly, Grimes did not suppose that this reductionistic interpretation in any way vitiated the evidence which he had garnered in support of telepathy and clairvoyance.

Most American mesmerists, however, were by no means convinced that the "imagination" or "suggestibility" could account for their data. They feared that without the premise of animal magnetism, however interpreted, their theory quite literally lacked substance. A purely subjective psychological reality was beyond their conceptual horizons. And, for that matter, it was not supported by the data. Mesmerized subjects detected a discrete and palpable force impinging upon their nervous systems from without. The American mesmerists therefore did not feel justified in pursuing the theory of suggestion as relentlessly as did their later European counterparts. While Charcot, Breuer, Janet, and, finally, Freud followed the notion of suggestion to a more or less mechanistic view of intrapsychic mental processes, the mesmerists remained committed to their belief that an individual's "inner source of feeling" somehow opens the finite mind to a nonphysical, transpersonal realm.

Convinced that their observations could be accounted for within a suitably enlarged science, the mesmerists offered as detailed neurophysiological explanations as contemporary medical research permitted. The mesmerists' journals, incidentally, contributed significantly to the study of the physiological structure of the brain. The articles and neurophysiological charts that they circulated throughout the 1840s and 1850s constituted the period's most significant attempt to correlate physiological and psychological perspectives on the nature of consciousness. However, it must be pointed out that the mesmerists were as reluctant to follow a neurophysiological viewpoint to its logical conclusion as a psychodynamic one. The phenomena of direct thought transference, clairvoyance, and prevision defied explanation by reference to neural forces within the brain. As one early researcher insisted, the "doctrine of animal magnetism is the connecting link between physiology and psychology . . . it demonstrates the intimate interconnection between the natural and the spiritual."[22] The mesmerists believed that although it is possible to offer physiological descriptions of any and all mental processes, these descriptions could never constitute final explanations of mesmeric phenomena. Mental processes, at least those occurring spontaneously to individuals in the mesmeric state, demand an explanation at once psychological and metaphysical—that is, they testify to the existence of animal magnetism.

The mesmerists thus found themselves committed to a psychological perspective that limited the usefulness of physiological and interpersonal data and theories to the explanation of the material or efficient causes of human behavior. The ultimate cause of conscious experience (i.e., animal magnetism) belonged by definition to the realm of philosophy and metaphysics. It was, in fact, precisely this eclecticism (and ambiguity) that attracted researchers to the field. By investigating this "science of the soul considered physiologically and philosophically," they could think of themselves as furthering both the scientific and spiritual aims of man.[23] In the words of one midwestern professor of physiology, the doctrine of animal magnetism taught that "positive material existence and positive Spiritual existence—however far apart they stand and however striking the contrast between their properties—are connected by these fine gradations . . . both are subject to the same great system of laws which each obeys in its own sphere."[24] Mesmerism's discovery of the mind's receptivity to these refined spiritual energies made it possible to speak of ecstatic self-transcendence and mystical illumination as lawful possibilities of human nature. It was at last possible to affirm that "the power of disembodied mind and intellectual manifestations . . . fall within the scope of the fundamental principles of the constitution of man, and spiritual mysteries, too, are beautifully elucidated by the complete correspondence, and mathematical harmony, between the spiritual and material laws of our being."[25]

Whereas Mesmer had intended his theory to show that medical and nonmedical healings were but variations of the selfsame principle, mesmerism's Yankee offspring were thought to explain the commonalities shared by normal and transcendent states of consciousness. Which is to say, the American mesmerists had transformed the science of animal magnetism into a theory whose chief value was that it sanctioned, and could even help engineer, mystical union with a transcendent spiritual order.

Engineering Cosmic Consciousness

The mesmerists' difficulty in defining the exact nature of their psychological science was compounded by the fact that their work preceded by fifty years the establishment of the first department of psychology at an American university. Their theories consequently lacked the kind of focus that collegiality, corroborative research, and professional associations impart to a theoretical discipline. The audience to which the mesmerists addressed their theories was the general public. It would be unreasonable, then, to expect mesmerist psychology to have developed in accordance with the kinds of criteria appropriate to disinterested scientific observers. A psychological theory attracts a popular following not by virtue of its formal scientific standing, but rather because it promises practical solutions to problems of everyday life. The path followed by a "popular psychology" is, for this reason, determined by the very needs and interests that it endeavors to satisfy. The fact that the American mesmerists were able to win a constituency testifies less to the scientific merit of their theory than to its resonance with the needs and motivations of nineteenth-century American culture.

Though Poyen, a Frenchman, was all but oblivious to the close connection between mesmerist psychology and the popular religious climate, as early as February 1837 a letter addressed to the editor of the *Boston Recorder* would testify:

> George was converted from materialism to Christianity by the
> facts in Animal Magnetism developed under his [Poyen's]
> practice . . . it proves the power of mind over matter . . .
> informs our faith in the spirituality and immortality of our
> nature, and encourages us to renewed efforts to live up to its
> transcendent powers.[26]

A high school teacher wrote to the *Providence Journal* that "God and eternity are the only answer to these mysterious phenomena—these apparitions of the Infinity and the Unknown."[27]

Americans were apparently far more disposed to emphasize the religious import of mesmerism than Europeans had been. An early tract was quick to point out that it casts "light on how we are constituted, how nearly we are related to, and how far we resemble our original . . . God who is a pure spiritual essence."[28] This same author went on to boast that mesmerism "shows that man has within him a spiritual nature, which can live without the body . . . in the eternal NOW of a future existence."[29]

Entrance into the mesmeric state was thought to be a decidedly numinous experience. Direct contact with the instreaming animal magnetic forces momentarily transforms and elevates a person's very being. A typical account of this encounter relates that

> the whole moral and intellectual character becomes changed
> from the degraded condition of earth to the exalted
> intelligence of a spiritual state. The external senses are all
> suspended and the internal sense of spirit acts with its natural
> power as it will when entirely freed from the body after death.
> No person, we think, can listen to the revelations of a subject

in a magnetic state, respecting the mysteries of our nature,
and continue to doubt the existence of a never dying soul and
the existence of a future or heavenly life.[30]

It is evident that Americans saw mesmerism as treating the
whole person and not just isolated complaints. They believed
that the mesmerizing process helped them to reestablish inner
harmony with the very source of physical and emotional well-
being. In the mesmeric state, they learned that disease and even
moral confusion were but the unfortunate consequences of having fallen out of rapport with the invisible spiritual workings of
the universe. Conversely, health and personal virtue were the
automatic rewards of living in accordance with the cosmic order.
When patients returned from their ecstatic mental journey, they
knew themselves to have been raised to a higher level of participation in the life-power that "activates the whole frame of nature
and produces all the phenomena that transpire throughout the
realms of unbounded space."[31]

Although mesmerism had no overt connections with insti-
tutional religion, it was nonetheless interpreted as a progressive
variation of the religious revivals which had long since become
the most effective institution in American religious life. Appearing in the mid-1830s, mesmerism was simply swept along in the
wake of the religious enthusiasm unleashed by the outburst of
revivalist activity which historians call the Second Great Awakening. Numerous revivalist preachers had disposed the popular
religious climate toward an "alleviated Calvinism" in which sin,
rather than originating in humankind's inherent depravity, was
understood as a function of ignorance or lack of self-discipline,
or as the result of faulty social institutions. Man's "lower nature"
was, therefore, considered to be potentially correctable through
humanly initiated reforms. Renewed emphasis upon the perfectibility of the human condition made it possible to redefine the
covenantal conditions believed indispensable to the fulfillment
of human destiny. As a consequence, American religious thought

during this period implicitly sanctioned experimental doctrines aiming toward the immediate and total renovation of humanity. Mesmerism, with its doctrine of the unconscious, recapitulated the themes of the nation's revivalist heritage almost perfectly. Like the revivalists, the mesmerists were preaching that individuals would continue to be plagued by confusion, self-doubt, and emotional unrest so long as they refused to open themselves up to a higher spiritual power. Mesmerism provided inwardly troubled persons with an intense experience thought to be restoring them to harmony with unseen spiritual forces. The mesmeric state, no less than the emotion-laden conversion experience, gave powerful and convincing experiential grounds for the belief that humanity's lower nature can be utterly transformed and elevated when brought under the guiding influence of spirit.

Yet the mesmerists differed from revivalists in at least one important respect. Far from reproaching individuals for challenging orthodox religious thinking, they encouraged them to do so. Mesmerism, like so many of the "isms" to appear in the nineteenth century, was at the far forefront of the liberating tendencies spawned by American Protestant culture. Its doctrines tended to appeal to those whose religious sensibilities could not be constrained by scriptural piety and who yearned instead for a progressive, co-scientific religious outlook. Mesmerism, since it "not only disposes the mind to adopt religious principles, but also tends to free us from the errors of superstition by reducing to natural causes many phenomena," enabled many who had become intellectually disenfranchised from the churches to find a new focus for their religious convictions.[32]

Among the first to recognize mesmerist psychology's contributions to innovative religious thinking was a Universalist minister by the name of John Dods. Having struggled throughout his career to make a convincing case for God's universal and redemptive presence in nature, Dods was quick to appreciate mesmerism's religious and metaphysical implications. The science of animal magnetism confirmed Dods's aesthetic and harmonial conviction "that God is electrically and magnetically connected to His universe, that this is how He stamps upon the world its BEAUTY, ORDER, and HARMONY."[33] And, what is more, mesmerist psychology afforded empirical proof that each and every human being is inwardly connected with "the grand agent employed by the Creator to move and govern the universe."[34] The mesmerizing process could be likened to a sacrament. When properly employed, it had the power to "enlarge and elevate the mind . . . to impress upon it more exalted ideas of the infinite wisdom and goodness of the Deity."[35]

Mesmerist psychology afforded Dods a scientific basis for his theological understanding of the *imago dei*. He argued that just as the human mind has both a cerebrum (associated with voluntary actions) and a cerebellum (the executor of unconscious, involuntary movements), so can divine mind be said to exhibit both voluntary and involuntary powers. God's voluntary powers are evident in those rare instances in which He miraculously intervenes in the lawful operations of nature. His involuntary powers are executed through the laws and processes of nature as established at the time of creation. Among the foremost of these is the continuously instreaming presence of animal magnetism through which His design is made manifest in the physical universe. Mesmerism, by demonstrating that the preconscious levels of mind provide a conduit for these divine emanations, furnished Dods "positive proof that man has instinct and intuition in the back of his brain . . . it is through these that God inspires man."[36]

The mesmerists' discovery of the unconscious was part and parcel of nineteenth-century optimism and faith in human progress. Mesmerism, like all other sciences, was seen as harnessing formerly hidden forces for human use. As Dods boasted, mesmerism had climbed aboard that "glorious chariot of science with its ever increasing power, magnificence and glory . . . ever obeying the command of God: ONWARD."[37] Yet mesmerism went all other sciences of the period one better. It showed that human experience potentially extends well beyond the boundaries of the physical senses. Mesmerized subjects proved that the normal waking state of consciousness was not the only, nor even the highest, mental condition. A spokesman for the Swedenborgian cause asserted that the investigations of the mesmeric state pointed to "an entirely new class of facts in psychology."[38] Here at last was empirical confirmation of "the grand principle that man is a spirit as to his interiors and that his spiritual nature in the body often manifests itself according to the laws which govern it out of the body."[39] Convinced that mesmerism had uncovered the point of connection between our two natures, he concluded that it had opened "a new chapter in the philosophy of mind and in man's relations to a higher sphere."[40]

The vast body of literature written by American mesmerists reveals that they had discovered in it much more than a key to physical health. The findings of the mesmerists were being lauded on the grounds that "they present a new view of the interior genius of the inspired Word, and of the whole body of Christian doctrine."[41] To those seeking confirmation of the living realities of faith, the unconscious appeared to be a promising pathway through which one might hope to experience a sense of participation in the higher reaches of the cosmos.

From Edwards to Emerson to Quimby

In 1838, on his proselytizing tour through New England, Charles Poyen stopped in Belfast, Maine. Attending his lecture-demonstration was a young clockmaker who was destined to become the most successful mesmerist in the United States. Phineas Parkhurst Quimby (1802-1866) was inspired by Poyen's astonishing exhibition to begin investigating the science of animal magnetism on his own. With the help of a particularly adept trance subject by the name of Lucius Burkmar, Quimby was soon established in a highly successful healing practice. Quimby would put Lucius into the mesmeric state and direct him to use his clairvoyant powers first to diagnose a person's illness and then to prescribe a medicinal remedy to rejuvenate the vital fluids. On some occasions Quimby dispensed with Lucius's assistance and would instead make the classic mesmeric "passes" over his patients' heads in an effort to recharge their systems directly with animal magnetism. Whichever method was used, Quimby believed that the resultant healings were "the result of animal magnetism, and that electricity had more or less to do with it."[42]

With the passage of time Quimby became increasingly skeptical that animal magnetism alone could be responsible for all of his therapeutic successes. It dawned on him that Lucius might not be diagnosing the patients' ailments at all. Quimby thought it more likely that Lucius was "merely" using his telepathic powers to learn what the patients already believed to be the cause of their troubles. His "accurate" diagnoses so utterly astonished patients that they put their full confidence in his curative powers. Thus, the herbal remedies Lucius prescribed worked more upon the patients' beliefs about their problems than upon the actual physical disorder. Most of the remedies were innocuous substances that proved equally effective on any number of ailments. On one occasion Quimby actually substituted a less expensive substance for the costly one Lucius had suggested—and the patient recovered just the same!

Many mesmerists had deduced that the patients' beliefs and expectations were at least partially responsible for their rapid recoveries. But Quimby arrived at the more radical conclusion that the illnesses were caused by their ideas or beliefs in the first place. He said that our minds are the sum total of our beliefs, and that if a person is "deceived into a belief that he has, or is liable to have a disease, the belief is catching and the effects follow from it."[43] Quimby moved mesmerism one step closer to modern psychiatry by specifically identifying faulty ideas—not magnetic fluids—as the root cause of both physical and emotional disorders. In Quimby's words, "all sickness is in the mind or belief . . . to cure the disease is to correct the error, destroy the cause, and the effect will cease."[44]

It is important to note that Quimby's theory of human illness was not the mentalistic explanation for which many of his interpreters have mistaken it. He saw the patients' beliefs only as intervening variables. He held that the real source of human health was the magnetic fluid, or vital force, flowing into the human nervous system from some deeper level of the mind. Beliefs function like control valves or floodgates: They serve to connect or disconnect the conscious mind and its unconscious depths. "Disease," Quimby insisted, "is the effect of a wrong direction given to the mind."[45] When persons identify themselves solely in terms of outer conditions, they place their minds at the mercy of noxious external stimuli. As long as the mind is reacting to sensations received through the physical senses, it is unreceptive to the inflow of magnetic forces; and, depleted of its proactive energies, the body eventually lapses into disease.

According to Quimby, health could be achieved only by permanently banishing self-defeating attitudes. It followed that "the theory of correcting diseases is the introduction to life."[46] If he could just show his patients "that a man's happiness is in his belief, and his misery is the effect of his belief, then I have done what never has been done before. Establish this and man rises to a higher state of wisdom, not of this world, but of that World of Science . . . the Wisdom of Science is Life eternal."[47]

Quimby's gospel of mind cure had a beautiful simplicity. Right beliefs channel health, happiness, and wisdom out of the cosmic ethers and into the individual's mental atmosphere. If we can control our beliefs, we will control the shunting valve that connects us to psychological abundance. The essential thing, Quimby counseled, was to identify ourselves in terms of internal rather than external reference points. If persons believe that the external environment is their only source of measures of self-worth, they lose contact with their inner, spiritual selves. The human nervous system cannot rely solely upon the capricious messages supplied by the physical senses without eventually becoming embroiled in fear, worry, and finally disease. Human misery, then, is the necessary consequence of allowing other persons and outer events to supply us with our sense of self-worth.

In Quimby's own words, "disease is something made by belief or forced upon us by our parents or public opinion . . . . Now if you can face the error and argue it down you can cure the sick."[48]

"There are," Quimby declared, "two sciences, one of this world, and the other of a spiritual world, or two effects produced upon the mind by two directions."[49] Mesmerist psychology seemed empirically to verify the characteristic American belief that humans possess both a lower, animal nature and a higher, spiritual nature. The difference between the two natures could now be expressed in psychological rather than scriptural or theological terms. By turning the mind inward, toward its own psychic depths, men and women are, for the first time, able to apprehend the true purpose or design behind their seemingly amorphous lives. The Scientific Man is a medium of higher, spiritual forces. His mind is attuned to the First Cause behind every event in nature.

Quimby had managed to translate the rather vague metaphysical language of an Edwards or Emerson into the semblance of an empirically based science. In effect, his mind-cure philosophy provided a middle-class clientele with a reified version of Transcendentalism. Edwards's notion of emanations of divine light and Emerson's references to the influx of spirit from the Over-Soul had their counterparts in Quimby's descriptions of right thinking and the need for occasional moments of silence during which dynamic mental energies could flow into and rejuvenate the conscious personality. In this way the aesthetic conviction that we each possess the ability to achieve harmony with an immanent divine force could receive practical application in what amounts to a set of "how to" exercises. Practitioners of Quimby's mind-cure system could, by making appropriate adjustments in the microcosm of the psyche, establish rapport with the very powers that activate the macrocosm.

Quimby also psychologized the Protestant ethic. His philosophy of mind-cure continued to affirm the intimate connection between religious conviction and material prosperity, but shifted inward the realm in which one is to be held accountable. The mind-cure approach to religious and material well-being supported the democratic vision according to which everyone exercises dominion over his or her own psychological realm. Quimby seemed to be saying that even if every other area of life seems to be beyond personal control, we can at least adjust ourselves. And, in the mind-cure scheme, this is more than sufficient. Right thinking, accompanied by occasional moments of silence for the purpose of enhancing the inflow of dynamic personal energies, was thought to ensure prosperity of every sort. This psychologized version of the Protestant ethic had one more advantage over its theological predecessors: Those who desired to move beyond the confines of conventional religious thought had equal, if not greater, access to both spiritual and material abundance.

Quimby's patients tended to become students and eventually disciples of his mind-cure philosophy. For them, what had once been a quasi-medical theory of physical healing was now a full-blown philosophy of life. Quimby's ideas spread rapidly throughout New England. Antedating the establishment of academic departments of psychology by twenty years, Quimby played a major role in predisposing Americans to view psychology as a systematic technique for commanding subconscious energies in the service of the whole personality. For some, Quimby's science of mind cure proved that the physical universe contains a mystical dimension. For others, it bespoke self-help techniques for better adjusting oneself to the demands of everyday living. For still others, it promised a kind of high-powered telepathy by which to employ magical forces in the quest for financial success. But for all, mesmerist psychology had come to imply that the key to personal well-being lies within oneself.

The American public had discovered the unconscious and had found there a wondrous psychological territory.

Three

Science Appropriates
the Unconscious: The Birth
of Academic Psychology

QUIMBY and his followers had given birth to a movement that spread rapidly among the members of New England's large middle class. As William James observed, large numbers of Americans had come to the conclusion that "things are wrong with them."[1] And most had at least a dim sense that the source of their difficulties was none other than "their little private convulsive selves."[2] Quimby's science of mental healing offered them relief from a range of psychosomatic illnesses for which their ministers and doctors had shown nothing but contempt. Instead of lecturing them about their lack of inner resolve, mind-curists showed them how to turn inward and discover there the secret of health, happiness, and prosperous living. Reports of remarkable healings abounded, and people who claimed to have literally found new life through the movement's teachings were everywhere proselytizing on behalf of the power of mind over matter.

In challenging the materialistic assumptions both of nineteenth-century medicine and of mainline Protestant theology, mind-cure was a harbinger of the intellectual struggles through which Americans would pass en route to the twentieth century. Physicians were understandably upset to find themselves losing patients to individuals who claimed to heal on the basis of the most ethereal of all substances—mind. Ministers were naturally incensed by the theological implications of a philosophy which taught dependence on powers immanent in nature rather than obedience to a transcendent Being. And citizens from every walk of life were more than a little perplexed by their neighbors' constant urgings on behalf of this new mental science.

"Mind cure," wrote Henry H. Goddard, "suggests psychology, and the psychologist is appealed to for the laws of mind which may explain the phenomenon and give the rationale in question."[3] Goddard, who was just completing his Ph.D. in psychology at Clark University, believed Quimby's discoveries to be "worthy of praise, help, and encouragement." For, while Quimby

> was undoubtedly hampered by some superstitions, for which
> the age was more responsible than he, and which his
> successors have in part perpetuated and increased and in part
> outgrown; yet to him, undoubtedly, belongs the credit not of
> discovering that mind influences matter, nor yet of originating
> the philosophy that all matter is the creation of mind, but
> rather of practically applying the principles to the prevention
> and cure of disease.[4]

Goddard considered himself a representative of what he called the "New Psychology" and was well aware of the peculiar relationship between his fledgling discipline and Quimby's practices. On the one hand, the New Psychology claimed to be at last in a position to liberate Quimby's theories from superstition and refine them into scientific principles. On the other hand, it owed Quimby and his followers a tremendous debt. It was they who had successfully disproven the materialistic assumptions upon which the period's medical profession operated; and it was they who had convinced large segments of the population that mental and physical health are greatly influenced by a "psychical region that is not in full view of the ordinary consciousness, the so-called subliminal consciousness."[5]

Goddard acknowledged, however, that although all psychologists now recognized "that consciousness holds only a small part of man's mental stock," none had as yet advanced a definitive explanation of the nature or activities of the subliminal reaches of the mind.[6] Goddard believed that the closest thing to a real improvement over Quimby's system was the theory of the subliminal self put forward by famed psychical researcher F. W. Myers. He credited Myers with having demonstrated that mental functions acquired early in the evolutionary history of humankind continue to operate at a profound psychical depth and in certain instances irrupt into consciousness. Knowing full well that Myers believed his theory to lend credibility to telepathy, clairvoyance, and mediumistic seances, Goddard was quick to reaffirm his own rigorously scientific intentions and observed that "in the hypothesis of Myers there seems to be a flavor of mysticism which is not entirely satisfactory and not easy to comprehend."[7]

It was apparently both the promise and the burden of the New Psychology to eliminate the "not entirely satisfactory" flavor of mysticism from discussions of the unconscious mind. The promise was full scientific recognition for the new discipline. The burden was the difficulty of disassociating the New Psychology's interpretation of the unconscious from popular theories without stripping psychology of its most important discoveries.

The New Psychology

Goddard's reference to something called the New Psychology reflects the prophetic aspirations of a doctoral candidate more than it does historical reality. For by 1899, when he penned these words, the infant discipline of psychology had already divided itself into various methodological orientations that differed radically one from another. There was no one "new psychology," but rather several new schools of psychological thought each competing for jurisdiction over the discipline. True, the functionalist school in which Goddard had himself been trained held sway temporarily, but its hegemony would soon yield to the pressures brought to bear by the physiological, psychoanalytic, and early behavioral points of view.

These differences notwithstanding, the term *New Psychology* does focus attention on an important fact; namely, the academic world had recognized psychology as an autonomous discipline. Historian A. A. Roback finds no one spectacular event that marks the emergence of academic psychology. He does, however, assert that "we can say with certainty that somewhere between 1885 and 1890, American psychology had definitely turned a corner."[8] A quick chronological review supports Roback's selection of dates: In 1883 G. S. Hall's psychological laboratory at Johns Hopkins University was in full operation; in 1886 James Jastrow became the first individual to receive a Ph.D. in psychology from an American university; in 1887 Ladd published his *Elements of Physiological Psychology* and Hall inaugurated *The American Journal of Psychology;* in 1890 William James's monumental *The Principles of Psychology* appeared; and in 1892 the American Psychological Association was formed and would see its membership quadruple over the next decade. It was becoming clear that psychology was not simply a handmaiden to philosophy but an academic discipline with both subject matter and research methods all its own.

Whatever the differences among the various factions concerning the exact procedures to be followed by a scientific psychology, all implicitly consented to certain minimal requirements of their discipline: the conscious effort to limit their theories to the explanation of empirical data; the necessity of recognizing the physiological components of psychological phenomena; the quest for causal explanations; and adherence to a scientific method which—like those of biology and chemistry—would test and revise hypotheses through laboratory experimentation. The intense commitment to derive a "psychology without a soul" that characterized early researchers had several long-lasting consequences. For one thing, it signaled the growing preference for research and theoretical construction at the molecular rather than molar level of analysis. It also meant that those things that could be measured and in some way quantified would command more scientific attention than those which could not. And, as in most groups struggling to earn professional status, slavish imitation of accepted procedures was to be admired far more than innovation.

None of this boded well for the academic study of the unconscious.

The Functionalist School

The distinction of being the first indigenous school of American psychology is generally accorded to the functionalist movement, which emerged and enjoyed its heyday between 1890 and 1920.[9] Much like the New Psychology, however, the functionalist school is an elusive historical entity. Rather than a discrete system of thought, functionalism was a general outlook, loosely structured around several universities and individuals.[10] William James, James Mark Baldwin, G. Stanley Hall, J. R. Angell, John Dewey, Robert Woodworth, and Harvey Carr can all be said to have been a part of the movement; none ever attempted to define the formal propositions of a functionalist theory. Yet, however amorphous the functionalist point of view may have been, according to Edwin Boring "it was nevertheless in a broad way an expression—the only formal communal expression—of the epistemological attitude in American psychology in general."[11]

The clearest claim attributable to this "epistemological attitude" was the conceptual inadequacy of its major rival, structuralist psychology. The structuralist position, which was being promoted in the United States by Titchener and others, defined psychology as the study of consciousness.[12] Following the philosophical reasoning laid down by Locke and Hume, structuralism viewed the mind as a succession of discrete states of consciousness formed in large part by sensory impressions. Structuralism relied heavily upon introspection and concerned itself both with observing and with classifying these elementary units, or structures, of consciousness. One corollary of the structuralist position was that anything which is not conscious is not a mental state and consequently does not belong to the field of psychology.

The functionalists repudiated the static conception of the mind associated with the structuralist position. Psychology, they countered, ought to be concerned not with what consciousness is, but rather with what it does. In his inaugural address as president of the American Psychological Association, James Rowland Angell argued that the only proper data for psychological investigation are the "typical operations of consciousness under actual life conditions."[13] The address was entitled "The Province of Functional Psychology" and maintained that the proper role of psychology is to interpret mental activities solely in terms of their function in adapting the individual organism to the larger environment.

What Angell referred to as "the broad biological ideal of functional psychology" is the assumption that the mind is a product of evolution and its biological function is to coordinate adaptive processes. In the vast majority of cases, the adaptive activity directed by the brain is not conscious. Instinct and habit automatically adapt the individual to the environment without any need for deliberate mental effort. But when confronted with novel or complex situations in which neither instinct nor habit is an adequate guide to action, an individual inevitably becomes conscious of the necessity of selecting among several possible actions. Consciousness can therefore be defined as "the selective variation of response to stimulation." It temporarily suspends the relatively fixed and automatic unconscious operations of habit and instinct in order to further the organism's innate biological purposes. Functionalism thus seemed to suggest that what distinguishes humans from lower species is their greater capacity for consciousness; what is unconscious, therefore, was by implication subhuman.

It is important to note that implicit in Angell's writings, as in those of nearly all the early functionalists, was the unquestioned assumption that successive adjustments to the outer environment ipso facto represent ontogenetic growth or advancement. The functionalists' belief that life's evolutionary movement has a forward directional tendency, even if unknown to the acting individual, gave early American psychology a decidedly vitalistic and teleological orientation.[14] In this respect, the evolutionary framework within which functionalism cast its descriptions of the mind—including the unconscious mind—showed a greater affinity with Hegel or Bergson than with Darwin.

Functionalism's insistence that the mind influences the organism's adaptation to the environment obliged it to address the perennially thorny mind-body problem. Angell cautioned that there was a wide variety of opinion on this subject and that almost no one claimed the issue to have been resolved. But he added that the movement as a whole displayed a tendency to define the problem out of existence by insisting that there were no such things as purely physical or purely psychical substances. Reality was said instead to be psychophysical throughout. Angell here rearticulated the position taken ten years earlier by John Dewey in his celebrated essay decrying the dehumanizing consequences of molecularism in psychological thinking.[15] He was, furthermore, identifying philosophical and metaphysical undercurrents in the functionalists' writings which, with the exceptions of James's "radical empiricism" and Baldwin's "pancalism," were rarely made explicit.

The functionalists' belief in a psychophysical universe permitted them to escape the consequences of subscribing to a strictly physiological, behavioral, or subjectivist perspective; it also abetted fuzzy thinking. On the one hand, functionalism insisted that the mind is a biological agent ceaselessly engaged in transactions with the surrounding environment. This emphasis upon the mind's adaptive functions promised to reduce complex mental events to observable cause-and-effect relationships and lay the foundations for an empirical, research-oriented science. At the same time, however, its premise that all biological organisms possess an innate directional tendency lessened the significance of empirically derived explanations of human behavior. With nature defined as psychophysical, it was possible to interpret an individual's creative accomplishments as caused by a cosmic push from within as opposed to a merely mechanical reaction to environmental stimuli. There was, then, an ambivalence at the very heart of functionalism's master image of human nature. While it fully surrendered the mind to the realm of nature, it also asserted that nature itself contained immanent adaptive forces. It followed that successful adaptation to the environment requires psychological attunement to the forward thrust inherent in all life processes.

Functionalism and the Unconscious

The concept of the unconscious mind was simultaneously an essential postulate and anathema to the majority of these early functionalists. Because the functionalists had repudiated mental structures in favor of adaptive activities, it was difficult for them to speak of an unconscious mind as a distinct entity. Yet their theory required them to recognize those innate directional tendencies that push life forward at a preconscious or organismic level.

The precarious position of the unconscious in functionalist-oriented American psychologies is evident in Angell's highly successful college text, *Psychology* (1904). It is interesting to note that Angell did not get around to the unconscious until the final two pages of his lengthy book. Yet his discussion of nearly every topic in psychology was predicated upon his contention that

> consciousness does not terminate with sharp edges which
> mark it off definitely and finally from the non-conscious. On
> the contrary, . . . there is a gradual fading out from a focal
> centre of clearest consciousness toward a dimmer region of
> partial consciousness, which we may designate the zone of the
> subconscious. The subconscious area again gives way to a
> region of entire non-consciousness.[16]

Interestingly, Angell reports that "there are many alleged facts in the realm of telepathy, clairvoyance and mediumistic trance which have led psychologists of repute to hold that our conscious minds are subconsciously in touch with psychic influences belonging to a far wider order than common sense ever suspects."[17] He also said that recent experimental work in this area seemed to be making progress toward substantiation of these claims, but, he hastily added, "this is hardly the 'scientifically' accepted view" and most rank-and-file experimental psychologists considered such evidence "as presumptively insusceptible of scientific treatment and therefore as irrelevant to the science of psychology."[18] Angell wished to avoid what he called the "philosophical difficulty" of a wide-sweeping interpretation of the unconscious and instead commended to his students' attention the more defensible position that the unconscious is "practically synonymous with the physiological." In this way Angell sidestepped the issue of the existence and attributes of a qualitatively unique state of consciousness such as the mesmerists and mind curists had described, while yet retaining a functional role for unconscious forces in directing human behavior.

A very similar treatment of the unconscious appeared in Robert S. Woodworth's *Psychology: A Study of Mental Life* (1923). Woodworth had little more to say about the unconscious than had Angell.[19] Aware that most readers believed the unconscious mind to be "the core of the whole subject of psychology," and that there is "a sort of fascination about the notion of a subconscious mind," he devoted the last eight pages (roughly 1 percent of his introductory text) to the subject.[20] Woodworth prefaced his remarks on the subconscious with a warning that "psychologists, as a rule, are inclined to be wary and critical in dealing with it."[21] Woodworth wished to be known as no exception to that rule.

The term *unconscious mind,* said Woodworth, is itself misleading. It unnecessarily postulates a separate or distinct psychical entity. Psychological phenomena such as instincts and the retention of memories—though executed without conscious effort—require no such explanatory construct. It was simply common sense that all mental activity contains elements which are unanalyzed or unattended to. This does not, however, mean that these elements must be qualitatively different, nor does it necessitate the postulation of a separate compartment of the mind.

This is not to imply that Woodworth's functional psychology had no constructive role for the notion of an unconscious. It is just that the functions which enable the organism "unconsciously" to adapt to its environment were grounded in the philosophical or metaphysical presuppositions of his system and therefore did not require the postulation of a distinct psychological entity:

> Schopenhauer wrote much of the "will to live," which was, in his view, as unconscious as it was fundamental, and only secondarily gave rise to the conscious life of sensations and ideas. Bergson's "élan vital" has much the same meaning. . . . The will to live is in a sense unconscious, since it is seldom present simply in that bald, abstract form. But since life is activity, any will to act is the will to live in a special form.[22]

As Angell and Woodworth demonstrate, the functionalists' efforts to situate the mind in an evolutionary-adaptive context effectively fixed the parameters for their interpretation of the nature and functions of the unconscious. Any adaptive function not performed by conscious mental processes was attributed to the progressive tendencies of nature. The unconscious performs a preservative or restorative role in mental life. It links the individual organism with an "élan vital" and, in so doing, gives to individual existence its fundamentally progressive character. Woodworth was thus methodologically predisposed to find Freud's theory of the unconscious "much too narrow":

> There is not half enough room in his scheme of things for life as it is willed and lived. There is not room in it even for all the instincts, nor for the "native likes and dislikes"; and there is still less room for the will to live, in the sense of the zest for

all forms of activity, each for its own sake as a form of vital activity.[23]

The "epistemological attitude in American psychology in general," then, seems to have been characterized more by commitment to common philosophical and metaphysical assumptions than commitment to any rigorously articulated psychological doctrines. Functionalism, while not altogether certain what the unconscious mind was, certainly knew what it was supposed to do.

The Cultural Context

Henri Ellenberger has argued persuasively that the various functions which European psychiatrists attributed to the unconscious can scarcely be understood independent of their social contexts. Partisan involvement in social or intellectual disputes furnished researchers such as Mesmer, Freud, and Jung with presuppositions and agendas which guided their interpretations of the unconscious. The alleged "facts" of the unconscious, since they were the least empirically verifiable data in their systems, invariably attest to cultural rather than scientific standards of truth.

The American functionalists' identification of the preservative or harmonizing function of the unconscious was similarly influenced by larger social and cultural processes. The thirty-year period between 1890 and 1920, during which functionalism thrived as a school of psychological thought, was an era of dramatic change in the development of American civilization.[24] The nation no longer consisted of a network of small communities, each organized around uncoerced commitment to one or another version of the Protestant faith. It had suddenly been transformed into an urban, industrial, and intellectually pluralistic society. The impact upon both personal identity and the national character was as unsettling as it was profound. It called for new terms and strategies with which to take one's bearings on life. Unfortunately, none were easily garnered from the theological tradition that had formerly given both substance and direction to the American identity.

Urbanization, industrialization, and seemingly endless new waves of immigration combined to erode the nation's religious heritage. White Anglo-Saxons and their Puritan faith were losing their hegemenous cultural influence. Society had become pluralized to the point where no one theological creed—much less one demanding assent to the infallibility of an ancient, prescientific text—sufficed to impose order on the bits and pieces of modern life. In the words of historian Robert Wiebe, Americans were forced to engage in a "search for order":

> As the network of relations affecting men's lives each year
> became more entangled and more distended, Americans in a
> basic sense no longer knew who or where they were. The
> setting had altered beyond their power to understand it, and
> within an alien context they had lost themselves.[25]

The functionalists were part of an entire generation of scholars who set themselves to the task of revitalizing Americans' sense of meaning and identity, and as such they made a significant contribution to what historian William McLoughlin calls the "Third Great Awakening" in American culture, which occurred between 1880 and 1920. The inquiries of the functionalists helped to inject added vigor into what McLoughlin describes as "an enormous rescue operation to sustain the culture . . . [an effort] to redefine and relocate God, provide means of access to him, and sacralize a new world view."[26] The most salient contribution of the functionalist perspective was the accommodation of Darwinian biology to deeply ingrained American philosophical and metaphysical assumptions. Approaching Darwin's developmental-evolutionary theory armed with the romantic philosophies of Hegel, Schelling, and eventually Bergson, the functionalists robbed Darwinian biology of its reductionistic sting. Henceforth all discussions of nature—even when couched in scientific terms—could be interpreted as descriptions of the concrete processes whereby an immanent divine force progressively unfolds its creative potential. By implication, psychology is essentially a special instance of a distinct metaphysical interpretation of reality. Psychological descriptions of human nature, though framed in the language of secular science, could yet be understood as defining the structures that allow us to participate in nature's upward surge.

Just as earlier generations of Americans had sought to supplement scriptural revelation about God by discovering traces of His presence in nature, the functionalists turned to our psychological nature in the hope of discovering our rightful place in the greater scheme of things. Psychology was, in a manner of speaking, the lowest common denominator to which modern Americans could reduce metaphysical considerations of their moral and religious responsibilities. The functionalists' writings furnished intellectual warrant for continuing faith in conceptions as fundamental to the American experience as the work ethic, democratic belief in each individual's equal access to the means of self-improvement, and the essentially progressive character of natural law. True, psychology saw the human mind as little more than a biological response mechanism; but, as Angell pointed out in his address to the American Psychological Association:

> if one assumes the vitalistic point of view for one's more final
> interpretations, if one regards the furtherance of life in
> breadth and depth and permanence *as an end in itself,* and if
> one derives his scale of values from a contemplation of the
> several considerations toward this end represented by the
> great types of mental phenomena, with their apex in the
> moral, scientific, and aesthetic realms, one must find [the
> functionalist point of view] more fundamental than others.[27]

In other words, given their pantheisitic views of evolutionary progress, the functionalists could affirm the laws of psychological development as descriptions of God's ongoing creative activity in the world.

In the broader context of American intellectual dispositions, the functionalists' insistence upon a psychophysical universe is much less puzzling. Their rejection of dualistic thinking in favor of a view of mind and matter as interpenetrating realities resembles the pantheistic leanings of Edwards and Emerson before them. The message in both cases is clear: Life cannot be reduced to material forces. The functionalists' idea of nature also protected the American belief in the moral and religious value of self-determination against theories of environmental determinism. Even if the mind was eventually proved to be merely "matter," as suggested by the functionalists' constant use of biological metaphors, this need not mean that the complex achievements of the individual mind were mechanistically determined by environmental forces. The functionalists' aversion to stimulus-response constructions was thus ideological. This is, for example, clearly evident in Baldwin's assertion that he rejected a purely mechanistic psychology because it presupposed an ontology "with no teleology in its movements, no ulterior organic ends."[28] A broader metaphysical understanding of psychological processes "renders the organism much less dependent upon such regularity and constancy in the environment. Creatures which have, in their own methods of reaction, a way of retaining contact with the source of supply . . . find or make for themselves the regularities which the environment may not guarantee."[29] Angell, too, was concerned that many saw psychology as a way to define human nature without engaging either ethical or metaphysical principles; he reminded his fellow psychologists that "anything approaching a complete and permanent divorce of psychology from philosophy is surely improbable as long as we cultivate the functionalist faith."[30]

To the modern conscience no longer able confidently to confess a universal ethical "truth," it was extremely reassuring to learn that "functional psychology reveals conclusively that the deeper springs of life are in motivated conduct and not in thoughts about the good life."[31] The functionalists succeeded in preserving the nation's Puritan heritage in a new secular, pluralistic setting. By focusing upon the psychological rather than the properly theological dimensions of the good life, they helped to reduce the arena of individual responsibility to more manageable proportions. If modern Americans could no longer systematically demonstrate order in every department of their outer lives, they could at least still discipline the way they thought about themselves. In this way, psychological theories—particularly those describing our preconscious connection with adaptive forces—kept the Protestant work ethic intact despite modern uncertainty concerning the ends to which it should be directed.

The Unconscious and Individual Fulfillment

The functionalists' efforts to produce a psychology without a soul placed them at the forefront of a major shift in American cultural thought. The nation's Protestant heritage had lost much of its socializing powers. No longer could Protestantism effectively induce in individuals the conversion experience that would mark their passage from adolescent self-preoccupation to responsible adulthood. Nor could the absolutes of scriptural religion provide infallible guides to action in the new pluralistic intellectual climate.

The functionalist model, by picturing mental life as an endless series of adjustments to changing environmental conditions, helped legitimate and give new direction to the philosophical stirrings of the age. It remained for the New Psychology to translate the "all or nothing" model of human development, epitomized by the conversion experience, into a new, inductively reasoned guide to individual fulfillment. It was at this point that the functionalists found the unconscious most clearly suited to their larger theoretical goals.

The confrontation between psychological and theological models of human development came to a head in the context of the psychology-of-religion movement, which lasted from about 1880 to 1930.[32] Prominent psychologists like James, Dewey, Hall, Baldwin, and Leuba would all publish psychological analyses of religion during this period. The need was real. As most saw in their own lives, conversion—and the belief system that supported it—was a declining cultural force.[33] The conversion experience no longer successfully guided individuals into responsible participation within a unified community of believers. It was up to early psychologists to redefine the "real" essence of religious experience in new, more culturally viable terms.[34]

Perhaps the clearest example of the functionalists' intention to subsume theological explanations of personal growth under a new cultural paradigm was Edwin Starbuck's *The Psychology of Religion* (1899). A student of both James and Hall, Starbuck maintained that conversion was nothing more than a particularly dramatic variation upon the lawful stages of psychological development. The most critical phase of this developmental process ordinarily occurs in adolescence and entails what Starbuck termed "unselfing." It is in this stage that our altruistic impulses become sufficiently strong for us to transcend adolescent self-absorption and become socially responsible adults. Starbuck observed that evangelical religion has long made use of this psychological process and brought it to a climactic resolution in the conversion experience. This sudden transformation was in reality a psychological—not theological—process. The new, or "born-again," self had been germinating all along in the individual's unconscious mind. "Spontaneous awakenings are, in short, the fructification of that which has been ripening within the subliminal consciousness."[35]

> The picture seems to be that of a *flow of unconscious life* rising now and then into conscious will, which, in turn, sets going new forces that readjust the sum of old thoughts and feelings and actions.[36]

The unconscious, Starbuck explained, contains innate "tendencies of growth" which propel the mind to ever higher levels of development. By allowing the full range of these unconscious growth tendencies to flow into awareness, "the individual learns to transform himself from a centre of self-activity into an organ of revelation of universal being."[37] Starbuck knew that his theories constituted an attack on conventional theistic belief, but he also recognized that his description of the creative powers operative through the unconscious articulated a religious vision all its own. He described his outlook as "a sort of pantheism—or panpsychism or pankalonism—a sense of Interfusing Presence."[38] Starbuck believed that by explicating our relationship to this Interfusing Presence with psychological rather than theological categories he had helped make "thinkable and usable the elusive reals of religion."[39]

A very similar veneration of the mind's unconscious depths was evident in the functionalists' writings on child and developmental psychology. G. Stanley Hall's pioneering contributions to this field vividly illustrate the way in which the unconscious helped the first generation of American psychologists to mediate between the new demands of science and those of their cultural heritage. Originally slated for the Protestant ministry, Hall's early confrontation with arguments against a scripturally-based theology started him instead upon a lifelong quest for some new intellectual synthesis. Like so many of his contemporaries, Hall found inspiration in the buoyant vision of such Romantic luminaries as Emerson, Tennyson, Schleiermacher, and Schelling. According to his biographer, Dorothy Ross, Hall found in their aesthetic intuitions "as much a statement of faith in the ultimate rationality and moral beneficence of nature as of God, less a confession of theism than of pantheism."[40] It was Hegel, however, who enabled Hall to give scientific expression to his newly found faith in nature's depths. Hall read Hegel as philosophically sanctioning the view that evolution is the means by which a pantheistic deity has gradually come to consciousness in humanity. Hegel, with Schelling, inspired Hall to envision "all organic and even inorganic nature as steps in the unfoldment of a mighty process."[41] If psychology was approached as the scientific analog of Hegel's developmental philosophy, it could dispense with the hypothesis of a separate soul. The higher, providential powers were within nature, not outside of it. For this reason, when Hall set about describing the laws governing our psychological nature, he saw himself as a prophet of a new era in humanity's religious development.

> The new psychology, which brings simply a new method and a new standpoint to philosophy, is I believe Christian to its roots and centre; and its final mission in the world is not merely to trace petty harmonies and small adjustments between science and religion, but to flood and transfuse the new and vaster conceptions of the universe and man's place in it . . . with the old Scriptural sense of unity, rationality, and love beneath and above all, with all its wide consequences.[42]

Hall accounted for the "unity, rationality, and love" that lie beneath us by postulating a direct connection between the course of individual development and the phylogenetic history of the human species. The *élan vital* which has progressively given rise to ever greater levels of consciousness during the span of natural evolution is also a guiding power in our individual lives:

> Consciousness is of the individual; the substratum on which it is developed is of the race. By brooding and incubation the conscious person communes with the species, and perhaps even with the genus to which he belongs; receives messages from and perchance occasionally gives them to it; appeals to mighty soul powers not his own, but which are so wise, benignant, and energetic . . . and come from the larger self . . . with which we are continuous. It is beneath, and not above us, immanent and not transcendent.[43]

Our conscious lives, according to Hall, are intimately connected with the deeper "will to live" underlying nature's evolutionary tendencies. Hall was thus able to romanticize our instinctual tendencies and credit them with furnishing consciousness with "what is a priori and innate in man."[44] Hall found in the unconscious strata of mental life a guiding wisdom which could not so easily be attributed to the more precarious realm of conscious thought. It is, he wrote, this immanent force that "makes the human soul really great and good."[45] Our unconscious promptings furnish mental life with a "wisdom beneath us we cannot escape if we would, and on which, when conscious purpose and endeavor droop, we can rest back, with trust, as on 'everlasting arms.' "[46]

Hall's studies of mental development offered a reassuringly optimistic vision of humankind's innate tendencies. Since the course of individual development was subconsciously linked to the evolutionary endowment of the entire species, personal growth could be trusted to proceed in line with a predetermined harmony among all human beings. Moral conscience is a built-in component of each and every individual's unconscious, instinctual nature. Needless to say, Hall's belief that we all inwardly participate in a superindividual reality caused him to view the unconscious roots of motivation in a very different light from Freud:

> As Freudians find sex, so our analysis finds religion at the root
> of all. Religion is a passion of the soul comparable in
> universality and intensity with sex. . . . As the root impulse of
> sex is to propagate another generation, so the root impulse of
> religion is to prolong the life of the individual by getting his
> soul born into another world. Both are forms of
> Schopenhauer's will to life, which is the Grund-Trieb of all
> life.[47]

Implicit in Hall's remark is the assumption that a psychological description of personality development discloses the true essence of religious living in a way that philosophy or theology never could. Empirical knowledge concerning the successive stages of individual development simultaneously discloses values and tendencies innate to Being. Psychology thus offered Hall and other early American psychologists a satisfactory compromise between their head and their heart, between their desire for progressive knowledge and their irrepressible religious intuitions.

While Hall initiated the child study movement in American psychology, James Mark Baldwin (1861-1934) stands out as the architect of modern developmental psychology. Baldwin's writings had a profound influence on Piaget's conception of the invariant stages of cognitive development and can be considered a precursor of recent theories concerning both moral and religious development such as those advanced by Lawrence Kohlberg and James Fowler.[48] After abandoning his early inclination to enter the ministry, Baldwin traveled to Germany, where he studied experimental methods at Wundt's famed laboratory and to France, where he became acquainted with the hypnosis research of Charcot, Janet, and Bernheim.[49] Equipped with polished philosophical skills acquired at Princeton Theological Seminary (where he had found theology "rigid and intolerant"), Baldwin was well suited to the task of weaving empirical data into larger theoretical systems.[50] Baldwin's many books, articles, and his active role in editing *The Psychological Review* and the *Psychological Bulletin* made him a dominant force in early American psychology.

Baldwin grounded his developmental theory upon the functionalist credo that cognitive abilities emerge as part of the organism's effort to adapt to the environment. In a formidable array of publications, he argued that mental growth occurs through three distinct and invariant developmental stages: the prelogical stage of infancy and early childhood, the logical stage that emerges in late childhood and continues to develop into adulthood, and the hyperlogical stage of aesthetic contemplation.[51] His descriptions of the last of these stages reflect the continuing tendency among American psychologists to interpret the cognitive functions associated with the unconscious as the very pinnacle of mental development.[52]

Baldwin was concerned lest the study of human development become too rigidly empirical. Empirical method tends to be associated with an extremely nominalistic theory of reality. According to Baldwin, pragmatic or functional tests of psychological functions rule out of court those mental processes which yield access to the general, the universal, or the normative in human experience.[53] Indeed, functionalist psychology gives the impression that the end state of mental development is the attainment of technical, cost-benefit reasoning capacities. The fully developed adult mind would be characterized by the dualistic categories of logical analysis (e.g., being versus becoming, mind versus matter). Although Baldwin agreed with the empiricists' mandate that all forms of mental life should be interpreted (1) genetically and (2) in terms of what they add to the organism's internal satisfaction, he believed that equal attention should be given to those psychological activities which transcend the dualistic categories of ordinary logical analysis. He further argued that in the aesthetic experience such transcendence "does take place as a real experience."[54]

Whatever use logical thinking serves in furthering our adaptive responses to the environment, for Baldwin it was neither the sole—nor even the most developed—cognitive form. The culmination of mental development in Baldwin's opinion is the aesthetic or hyperlogical mode of consciousness, which transcends the dualistic constraints of logical analysis. The aesthetic consciousness is self-existent and underived. The values it detects in experience are intrinsic rather than instrumental. Of all states of consciousness, it alone "seeks the intrinsic meaning of the object, not a meaning foreign to or beyond the object."[55] For this reason it is the most appropriate for the interpretation of reality. The aesthetic or hyperlogical state is one in which "reality discloses to rational intuition its own intrinsic nature."[56] The experience, Baldwin notes, is "so protoplasmic that the distinction between consciousness and non-consciousness itself seems to disappear."[57] In other words, it transcends the subject-object relationship and permits a rapport with reality undistorted by instrumental reason. Baldwin was careful to point out that while the aesthetic fusion with the wider universe has "the calmness and disinterestedness found in simple mystical contemplation," it does not represent a regression to primitive religious forms of thought such as are found in the earliest, pre-logical stages of mental development.[58] It is, rather, an advanced developmental achievement in which the immediate or intuitive character of prelogical thinking and the abstract, rational character of logical thinking are finally united in a higher synthesis. Baldwin insisted that the aesthetic state was the culmination, not the dissolution, of the entire course of ontogenetic development. Baldwin's exposure to the work of Charcot and Breuer apparently had little impact upon his conceptualization of the farther reaches of consciousness.[59] Like the mesmerists before him, Baldwin preferred to identify what is "deepest" in human consciousness as "higher" in the context of humankind's relationship to the structures and forces of Being.

Genetic psychology provided Baldwin with what he called a "pancalist theory of reality." His study of individual development from prelogical to hyperlogical cognitive levels supported the radical claim that "the individual consciousness is the organ of reality."[60] Each and every stage in our ontogenetic development is part and parcel of the movement of Being: "The progress of reality is real progress, the constant achievement of new modes and phases . . . the whole representing an ever widening and enriched contemplation."[61]

Baldwin thought that his pancalist philosophy offered a more precise and psychologically nuanced interpretation of Hegel's description of nature as "objectified mind" and Schopenhauer's notion of "unconscious will." Everywhere nature pushes toward more comprehensive states of consciousness. Humans, by following the developmental laws of their psychological nature, automatically take their place in this progressive movement of Being toward some higher cosmic synthesis.

Splintering of Consensus

By the early 1900s, academic psychology had largely succeeded in establishing itself as the preeminent interpreter of humanity's mental and emotional constitution. But the same pluralizing tendencies which had allowed the New Psychology to distance itself from the nation's theological heritage soon splintered the fledgling science into diverse methodological orientations. Functionalism, having failed to generate a distinctive program of research, faded from the forefront of psychological science (although it exerted continuing influence as a highly generalized set of attitudes loosely embodied in newly developing theoretical positions). As researchers forged theoretical perspectives more susceptible to empirical verification, a variety of American schools of psychological thought emerged, each organized around a particular methodological program. The psychoanalytic, behavioral, and humanistic schools of American psychology in large measure developed by defining themselves vis-à-vis the research strategies advocated by their counterparts. Debates among the three are rarely reducible to issues of fact; they are, rather, largely metaphysical or ideological disputes about the nature, scope, and meaning of psychological discourse.

The unconscious, as a subject inherently resistant to empirical observation, conjured up a host of meanings to America's early psychologists—none of which could command recognition across the emerging schisms. Each of the four properties that Ellenberger distinguished in European descriptions of the unconscious could be found in the newly founded journals of American psychology, but their advocacy reflected partisan metaphysical commitments more than detached inductive reasoning. The "conservative" function of the unconscious (i.e., retention of forgotten perceptions and regulation of habitual behaviors) was an inference, not an empirically ascertained fact. Hall was but one of many who had pressed the conserving functions of the mind into service in support of the theory that the unconscious serves as a repository of the species' phylogenetic history.[62] But this demanded the further postulation of either a subterranean labyrinth of genetically encoded memories or the equally speculative assumption of a nonphysical atmosphere containing a planetary consciousness for which the unconscious was a psychic conduit. Experimental psychologists dismissed the former hypothesis as an unacceptable variant of instinct psychology and the latter as fantastical nonsense. At any rate, the attribution of conserving properties to an unconscious mental agent was easily criticized as either unpsychological or unscientific, or both.

What Ellenberger termed the dissolutive function of the unconscious (i.e., the pathological disintegration of the personality as evidenced in schizophrenia or hypnosis) was also well known to the American reading public. James J. Putnam and William A. White were early champions of the psychoanalytic system in the United States and worked diligently to bring its clinical insights to bear upon the diagnosis and treatments of psychopathological disorders. Yet, however grounded in clinical evidence the psychoanalytic system may have been, it had to fight an uphill battle to win even a modest following among American psychologists. As we shall see in Chapter 5, indigenous intellectual dispositions ultimately forced American psychoanalysts to modify their account of unconscious mental forces to accommodate to the prevailing cultural climate.

The unconscious was endowed by some with creative and mythopoetic properties. In his *The Subconscious Self and Its Relation to Education and Health,* an M.D. by the name of Louis Waldstein explained that "the creations of genius, for instance, can only be explained by assuming that they result from the spontaneous action of that part of man's mind freed from the chains which the intellect, the purposively 'educated' part of the mind, has wound around it."[63] Yet the majority of those Americans who were enamored of the creative properties of the unconscious shared the functionalists' faith in its intimate connection with a transindividual spiritual force. The marvelous functions performed by the unconscious were ultimately attributable to its role in preserving harmony between the acting individual and the ontological ground of life's creative surge. As one early essay on the unconscious explained, the purposive character of consciousness "can never be understood or interpreted except in the light of the greater psychic life of which it is a part."[64] This greater psychic life was, moreover, said to contain a "storehouse of dynamic power" potentially at the service of the conscious mind.

In this mesmerist-sounding view, the unconscious acted as the connecting link between the finite personality and unlimited creative potentials. On this, too, there was little agreement in the eyes of the New Psychology.

The continued professionalization of academic psychology further intensified the conflict over the status of unconscious mental processes. Each year between 1912 and 1920 *The Psychological Bulletin* included an essay entitled "Consciousness and the Unconscious," which reviewed recent literature bearing upon the scientific status of these subjectivistic terms.[65] In each successive year the authors became increasingly disinclined to acknowledge the scientific relevance of anything outside the parameters of experimental research. Approvingly citing John B. Watson's behavioral dismissal of all things nonempirical, the journal reported that the concept of consciousness, like the word soul, was rapidly falling into disuse among academic psychologists.[66] By 1917, the journal announced that "there can be no question that consciousness is rapidly losing its standing as a respectable member of the psychologist's vocabulary."[67]

If consciousness was suspect, the unconscious was anathema. Noting that Watson's behavioral program reduced the so-called subconscious to the ostensibly more scientific category of a "habit twist," the 1917 issue went on to state:

> It seems a pity that a part of the immense labor which Jung
> must have undergone in writing his *Psychology of the
> Unconscious* could not have been expended in learning
> something of modern psychology, of which he shows an
> amazing ignorance.[68]

William James, too, raised the question "Does Consciousness Exist?" and likewise answered no. But he, a radical empiricist, did so en route to declaring the universe psychophysical throughout; "matter" and "mind" represent but different organizations of a panpsychic universe.[69] His fellow empiricists were not nearly so radically inclined. Unlike James, for whom the unconscious formed the point of interconnection between the conscious personality and a psychic "more," they showed an increasing desire to dismiss the unconscious as belonging "to the realm of poetry or mythology; not to science."[70] By 1919, the "Consciousness and the Unconscious" department of *The Psychological Bulletin* had about written itself out of existence: "The opinions of the professional psychologists on the topic of consciousness and mind seem to have shaken down to a degree that does not call out lengthy discussion."[71]

Needless to say, the unconscious had likewise become a moot issue to experimental psychologists. It could not be quantified and was consequently dropped from the vocabulary of those psychologists who adhered to the behavioral and experimental point of view.

The vicissitudes of the unconscious implicate American psychology in a wider cultural drama. The paradigm shifts occurring in the New Psychology show at least partial complicity in the creation of what Robert Wiebe has termed the "new scheme" which had finally emerged by 1920. Wiebe writes that "the new scheme was derived from the regulative, hierarchical needs of urban-industrial life . . . it sought control and prediction in a world of endless change."[72] Experimental psychology confidently addressed itself to the regulative needs of the era: Applied psychology furnished industry, schools, and even the churches with new regimens for the efficient use of human resources; developmental psychology churned out schedules and timetables with which to assess individual productivity; and differential psychology supplied new, technical-sounding measures for classifying individuals according to skill and inner merit.[73] The dominant thrust of American psychology had, in short, aligned itself with the goals of secularization: efficiency, control, and the banishment of the intangible.

The experimental and behavioral psychology of twentieth-century America furnished a new world view that located the mechanisms of both individual and social control. In the process, however, it robbed the psyche of its unconscious depths and extirpated the aesthetic side of the American mind. Severed from an *élan vital,* the self was now at the mercy of myriad environmental determinisms which it could hope to manage—but never transcend.

The New Psychology's efforts to gain scientific jurisdiction over the interpretation of human depth can be read as a chronicle of the fate of Americans' religious and cultural heritage as it collided with modernity. For even as some would repudiate the unconscious in favor of a strictly scientific interpretation of human nature, others would find in it a necessary bulwark against the dehumanizing and desacralizing tendencies in modern thought. The unconscious, by making it possible to identify the psychological mechanism through which men and women participate in nature's proactive forces, promised to sustain the aesthetic strain of American cultural thought against the onslaught of scientific reductionism. In fact, just such an interpretation of the unconscious received eloquent expression in the writings of America's most celebrated psychologist, William James.

Four

Psychology, Religion, and the Unconscious: The Jamesian Synthesis

EVERY now and then an idea is reformulated in a striking new way that enables individuals suddenly to see important patterns in their lives which they had previously neglected or dismissed as inconsequential. This awakening of perception can inaugurate a new cultural epoch or give rise to an enduring philosophical tradition bearing the name of its author. Such "discoverers" become eponyms, their names synonymous with their insights. Darwin(ism) and Marx(ism) are ready examples. Thus, the views of Edwards and Emerson concerning God's availability to the properly attuned mind are, even today, being promulgated by self-proclaimed Edwardsians and Emersonians.

One individual symbolizes the modern attitude that equates religious inwardness with the pursuit of self-enrichment. When William James interpreted the unconscious as humankind's link with a spiritual "more," he gave shape to a peculiarly modern spirituality.[1] James's vision of the unconscious depths of human personality as at once psychological and spiritual made it possible for modern Americans to view self-exploration as spiritually significant and religious experience as psychologically profound.

William James (1842-1910) is at once a creature and creator of modern American culture. His contributions to psychology, philosophy, and religious studies—which reflect the distinctive spirit of his native New England—are still the working capital that is the basis of the continuing prosperity of these disciplines. James is, perhaps, best known as the foremost spokesman for the philosophical position known as pragmatism. As a single measure of his career, this does James a great injustice. It tends to associate him with a crass utilitarianism that is very far from his intentions. James's pragmatism was an agenda for bringing new order to the society in which he lived. He wanted to help his contemporaries discover "what works best in the way of leading us, what fits every part of life best and combines with the collectivity of experience's demands, nothing being omitted."[2] Not the least of these demands was spiritual satisfaction. Pragmatism, James explained, searches for new, empirical warrants for religious belief; it "widens the field of search for God."[3] It was his special genius to bring the pragmatic method to the understanding of the depths of the human psyche. In so doing he succeeded in recasting his philosophical and theological heritage in new, culturally relevant terminology.[4]

Personal Crisis

The new life to which James beckoned his contemporaries was one that he had struggled desperately to win for himself.[5] Growing up under the close scrutiny of a domineering father, William managed to achieve a sense of self-worth in large measure by dutifully appropriating his father's outlook—but restated in his own terms. This was no mean task.

Henry James, Sr., cast an aura about himself and his ideas which far exceeded their substance. His character, like his writings, was a labyrinth of inconsistencies. An inheritor of the Calvinist tradition, Henry James, Sr., insisted upon the "death of the natural man and of a supernatural redemption."[6] His insistence upon the insufficiency of unredeemed humanity was peculiar, however, in that it was predicated upon monistic spirituality and cosmic optimism. Conversion was not accomplished by professing Jesus's divine nature, but rather by the individual's discovery that God's spirit was "a life within him, and no longer without him."[7] Men and women contain God's very being within them; the establishment of the Kingdom of God on earth only awaits humanity's recognition and embodiment of this indwelling spiritual consciousness.

Henry James, Sr., devoted his entire life to exploring cosmic mysteries. Inspired by Swedenborg's mystical writings, he sought an understanding of the inner, metaphysical message of the Christian faith that was beyond the ken of the ordinary individual. Eschewing churches as mundane perversions of spiritual truths, Henry was a member of that band of saints and mystics "whose quests keep religion 'forever alive.' "[8] Into his home he invited metaphysicians of every stripe to assist him in piecing together the fragments of the cosmic puzzle. Perpetual seeking and self-scrutinizing inquiry seemed the sine qua non for finding one's place in the universal scheme of things.

Aware of the impracticality of his own rather ethereal vocation, Henry James, Sr., urged his eldest son to devote himself to a discipline more respected by the age—science.[9] The advice, however, conflicted with Henry's own conviction that metaphysics was the highest realm of human thought. William, sensitized to the potentially cosmic repercussions of any and all decisions, began to crumble under the pressure of deciding his life course. He found little comfort or support in his father's speculative philosophies; they constantly reminded him of the larger, spiritual consequences of failure to bring his life into harmony with the greater cosmic scheme. He developed nervous disorders, which were to plague him the rest of his life. Chronic insomnia, eye trouble, digestive problems, and back pains were cruel reminders that his upbringing had done little to help him come to grips with the world. His inability to impose direction on his life finally gave rise to an all-encompassing sense of despair, futility, and worthlessness. He described his condition as that of acedia, the feeling "that everything is hollow, unreal, dead ... [when] nothing is believed in ... all sense of reality is fled from life."[10]

James was in many ways a prototype of the modern individual who yearns for a grand spiritual dimension to his life, yet feels alienated from conventional religious forms. By discovering a path leading through the stages from initial despair to final union with a higher power, James—as Erik Erikson has said of Luther—was able "to lift his individual patienthood to the level of a universal one and try to solve for all what he could not solve for himself alone."[11] The first step on this pilgrimage was his humble recognition that "if we have to give up all hope of seeing into the purposes of God, or to give up theoretically the idea of final cause, and of God anyhow as vain and leading to nothing for us, then the only thing left to us is will."[12]

His father's faith in higher powers had failed him when he needed its guidance most. William now concentrated his energies on improving his capacity for self-determination. He wrote to his brother, "It seems to me that all a man has to depend on in this world is, in the last resort, mere brute power of resistance."[13] His belief in willpower gave William growing confidence that, on a purely humanistic basis, he could transcend his incapacitation and take control of his life. As his medical studies came to an end, however, his penchant for grander things seemed to surface once more. President Eliot of Harvard offered him a teaching position in physiology but he at first declined, declaring that he would rather "fight it out" in the disciplines of philosophy and psychology. After further consideration, James finally accepted the position. Philosophical endeavors were to be shunned, he wrote, because:

> To make the form of all possible thought the prevailing
> matter of one's thought breeds hypochondria. Of course my
> deepest interest will be with the most general problems. *But
> my strongest moral and intellectual craving is for some stable
> reality to lean upon.* [14]

With this resolve, James embarked upon a career in physiological research that soon took him into the area of neurophysiology. With this "stable reality to lean upon," he proceeded to make great professional progress in the burgeoning field of scientific psychology. Here was an intellectual enterprise that gave him free rein to study the role of free will in helping the individuals surmount life's challenges.

Metaphysics and Psychology

The psychological science on which James leaned as a stable reality proved more pliable than he had reckoned. So new was the discipline that an early pioneer could explore, discover, and describe freely at his own choosing. For this reason James's psychological writings, like those of his contemporaries, often read more like personal documents than scientific treatises. James began with the task of modeling psychology after the natural sciences. His training in both medical physiology and evolutionary biology gave a thoroughly functionalist character to his psychology.[15] After twelve years of painstaking research, James finally issued his monumental *Principles of Psychology,* comprising some fourteen hundred pages of rigorous exposition. It remains the single greatest work in the history of American psychology.[16]

In his preface James stated his intention to keep "close to the point of view of natural science throughout the book."[17] He was not unaware of the epistemological difficulties inherent in the attempt to educe a "science of mental life, both of its phenomena and of their conditions."[18] He realized that a periodic overhaul of theoretical assumptions was indispensable to scientific progress. What he called metaphysics—the disciplined scrutiny of the relationship among facts, theories, and presuppositions—would lead the way to any theoretical breakthrough in scientific psychology. But, he warned, "metaphysics fragmentary, irresponsible, and half-awake, and unconscious that she is metaphysical, spoils two good things when she injects herself into a natural science."[19] In the desire to keep his young discipline free from such disruptive influences, James declared a moratorium on these metaphysical incursions, at least for the time being. He was apparently unaware of the patently metaphysical character of his own stance, readily seen in his assertion that "the pursuance of future ends and the choice of means for their attainment are . . . the mark and criterion of the presence of mentality in a phenomenon."[20] It was, after all, James's belief in the power of free will that had rescued him from acedia and enabled him to pursue a scientific career in the first place; his resulting bias against a rigid determinism in psychology was destined eventually to set him at odds with the accepted canons of natural science.

Just two years later, James added an epilogue entitled "Psychology and Philosophy" to the abridged edition of his text. Despite his best intentions, his discussion of free will had entangled him in metaphysical questions. The total determinism postulated by natural science makes discussions of free will awkward, and proof impossible. James had informed his readers that the assumption of determinism was only a methodological convenience for academic psychologists and in no way settled the issue. Debates concerning psychological issues such as free will are not resolvable on purely scientific grounds and must finally be adjudicated by appeal to the higher court of metaphysics. He was not about to press the case for free will in his introductory textbook to psychology, but he cautioned:

> When, then, we talk of "psychology as a natural science," we must not assume that that means a sort of psychology that stands at last on solid ground. It means just the reverse; it means a psychology particularly fragile, and into which the waters of metaphysical criticism leak at every joint.[21]

James stressed that the data and assumptions of psychology "must be reconsidered in wider connections and translated into other terms."[22] It followed that if and when significant advances are ever to be made in psychology, "the necessities of the case will make them metaphysical. Meanwhile the best way in which we can facilitate their advent is to understand how great is the darkness in which we grope and never forget that the natural-science assumptions with which we started are provisional and revisable things."[23]

James had by this point realized that he had been revising and improvising all along. After a number of long, unexciting chapters on the physiology of brain processes came what is probably the most famous chapter in his, or any other, psychology text, "The Stream of Thought." In this chapter James unwittingly abandoned his natural science viewpoint and signalled the emergence of what is now recognized as the phenomenological dimension in his psychology.[24] Here he ceased forcing psychology to conform to a predetermined scientific language and instead focused on the individual's actual experience of the surrounding world. And although James did not maintain this phenomenological viewpoint consistently throughout *The Principles,* it was when pursuing this particular mode of empirical investigation that he most successfully depicted humanity's innate capacity to transcend environmental determinisms in a free and morally responsible way.

James eventually came to describe his phenomenological method as radical empiricism. Radical empiricism differs from ordinary empiricism in that it concedes no a priori or preconceived limits to what constitutes a "fact." The task of a radical empiricism is purely and simply to uncover the full psychological fact: "A conscious field plus its object as felt or thought of plus an attitude towards the object plus the sense of a self to whom the attitude belongs—such a concrete bit of personal experience may be a small bit, but . . . it is of the kind to which all realities whatsoever must belong."[25]

From the time he penned "The Stream of Thought," James would argue that the basic datum of psychological science was neither the neural event nor the isolated sensory impression, but rather the entire field of consciousness including its margins or fringes. James lambasted "ordinary psychology" for arbitrarily assuming that "what is absolutely extramarginal is absolutely non-existent, and cannot be a fact of consciousness at all."[26] On the contrary, he argued,

> the most important step forward that has occurred in psychology since I have been a student of that science is the discovery, first made in 1886, that, in certain subjects at least, there is not only the consciousness of the ordinary field, with its usual centre and margin, but an addition thereto in the shape of a set of memories, thoughts, and feelings which are extra-marginal and outside of the primary consciousness altogether. . . .[27]

James gave the credit for this discovery of an extra-marginal consciousness to F. W. Myers. Myers's scientific interest in the paranormal did not prevent James (unlike Goddard) from acknowledging that his work on the fringes of consciousness threw "a wholly new light upon our natural constitution."[28] James was persuaded by Myers's argument that each of us possesses a "subliminal self":

> Each of us is in reality an abiding psychical entity far more extensive than he knows—an individuality which can never express itself completely through any corporeal manifestation. The self manifests itself through the organism; but there is always some part of the self unmanifested, and always, as it seems, some power of organic expression in abeyance or reserve.[29]

James agreed with Myers that human consciousness can be likened to the light spectrum. Because of the limitations of our physical senses, we ordinarily perceive only a small fraction of the total spectrum of consciousness; there are types of consciousness outside our awareness at both the lower and upper ends. The lower end, James wrote, is "the depository of our forgotten memories" as well as physiological activities.[30] On other occasions he added "silly jingles, inhibitive timidities," and the "numerous facts of divided or split personality."[31] Also among the functions of the lower reaches of the unconscious are the various psychopathological disorders. James had never undertaken a sustained investigation of pathological mental processes and thus deferred to others in his description of the debilitating effect of certain unconscious phenomena:

> In the wonderful explorations by Binet, Janet, Breuer, Freud, Mason, Prince and others, of the subliminal consciousness of patients with hysteria, we have revealed to us whole systems of underground life, in the shape of memories of a painful sort which lead a parasitic existence buried outside of the primary fields of consciousness, and making irruptions thereinto with hallucinations, pains, convulsions, paralyses of feeling and of motion, and the whole procession of hysteric disease of body and of mind.[32]

James insisted, however, that these psychopathological manifestations of the unconscious reflected "too limited a number of cases to cover the whole ground."[33] A properly empirical psychology must also include the upper or higher reaches of the unconscious. These farther reaches of consciousness can be studied in such phenomena as telepathy, clairvoyance, religious experience, and the mediumistic trance state.

Once James had recognized the subliminal self as a "well-accredited psychological entity," he was forced to return to metaphysics proper. The research of Drs. Janet, Freud, and Prince—as well as Mr. Myers and the Society for Psychical Research—showed conclusively that now and then the threshold of awareness lowers or a barrier is lifted and the self opens up to entirely new ranges of experience. These investigations had established the existence of "wider connections" in terms of which all psychological data had to be reconsidered. Henceforth, James was to redefine "ordinary psychology" in terms of those metaphysical horizons that had been opened up by the discovery of "the continuity of our consciousness with a wider spiritual environment from which the ordinary prudential man (who is the only man that scientific psychology, so called, takes cognizance of) is shut off."[34]

Inhabiting a Wider Universe

James had earlier proclaimed that advancements in psychology would be derived from metaphysics. Slowly he realized that this could also work in reverse. "We can invent no new form of conception," he wrote, "applicable to the whole exclusively, and not suggested originally by the parts."[35] Influenced by the philosophical ideas of Fechner, James believed it possible to arrive at an empirically based metaphysics by means of "a vast analogical series in which the basis of the analogy consists of facts directly observable in ourselves."[36] The observed facts, in this case, supported the belief that

> the world of our present consciousness is only one out of
> many worlds of consciousness that exist, and that these other
> worlds must contain experiences which have a meaning for
> our life also; and that although in the main their experiences
> and those of this world keep discrete, yet the two become
> continuous at certain points, and higher energies filter in.[37]

By extending his functional point of view to include the subliminal realms of experience, James was able to define the "wider environment" as a "world wider than either physics or philistine ethics can imagine."[38] His functional psychology had, ironically, brought him back to his father's Swedenborgian-inspired belief in "correspondence" and "influx." A properly empirical science confirms the religious conviction that humanity—no matter how successfully individuals or groups may accomplish their goals—cannot complete itself solely in terms of material achievements. Wholeness, salvation if you will, depends upon our successful adaptation to a much wider environment:

> The further limits of our being plunge, it seems to me, into an
> altogether other dimension of existence from the sensible and
> merely "understandable" world. Name it the mystical region,
> or the supernatural region, whichever you choose. . . . we
> belong to it in a more intimate sense than that in which we

belong to the visible world, for we belong in the most intimate sense wherever our ideals belong.[39]

James's psychological investigations eventually led him to the same conclusion that the mesmerists and mind-curists had been proclaiming all along: "We inhabit an invisible spiritual environment *from which* help comes."[40] Adapting ourselves to this wider, spiritual environment requires the cultivation of our subliminal minds. By dismantling the structures of our narrowly focused minds we can finally discover that "there are resources in us that naturalism with its literal and legal virtues never recks of, possibilities that take our breath away, of another kind of happiness and power based upon giving up our own will and letting something higher work for us."[41] In this psychological adjustment "our deepest destiny is fulfilled . . . work is actually done upon our finite personality. For we are turned into new men, and consequences in the way of conduct follow in the natural world upon our regenerative changes.[42]

The James whose earlier writings had so strongly supported reliance on strenuous, willful activity had gradually evolved a new sanative philosophy. Drawing upon Starbuck's work on self-surrender, he wrote, "There is thus a conscious and voluntary way and an involuntary and unconscious way in which mental results may get accomplished."[43] While the former is associated with an ascetic, ethical approach to life, the latter invokes receptivity.

James believed that modern life made demands upon our voluntary mental faculties that tended to produce what he called the "over-contracted" personality. The "over-tense and excited habit of mind" characteristic of modern individuals tragically makes us our own worst enemies. "Under these circumstances the way to success . . . is by surrender."[44] Self-surrender, according to James, allows the entire personality to avail itself of higher mental energies. "The transition from tenseness, self-responsibility, and worry, to equanimity, receptivity, and peace, is the most wonderful of all those shiftings of inner equilibrium, those changes of the personal centre of energy."[45] This shifting of consciousness toward the deeper reaches of our personality "actually exerts an influence, raises our centre of personal energy, and produces regenerative effects unattainable in other ways."[46]

James's radical empiricism thus postulated new facts about our psychological commerce with reality. He firmly believed that the discovery of the subliminal reaches of experience softens "nature's outlines and open[s] out the strangest possibilities and perspectives."[47] The world, once interpreted in light of the farther reaches of the human unconscious,

> is not the materialistic world over again, with an altered
> expression; it must have, over and above the altered
> expression, a natural constitution different at some point from
> that which a materialistic world would have. It must be such
> that different events can be expected in it, different conduct
> must be required.[48]

Because the unconscious is our inner point of contact with the non-material constitution of the universe, James made it the focus of his description of the "different conduct" required by his radical empiricism. James insisted that "not to demand intimate relations with the universe, and not to wish them satisfactory, should be counted as signs of something wrong."[49] He even suggested some practical strategies for becoming receptive to the higher energies that filter into mental life through our unconscious. In his popular addresses "The Gospel on Relaxation" and "Energies of Men," James commended to our attention a variety of practices ranging from Yoga to the meditational practices then being advocated by the mind-curists. He was even exhortatory on this subject. He alone among the intellectuals of his day recognized the social and religious importance of popular metaphysical movements such as mind-cure. Their ideas about humanity's higher nature were effecting "a copious unlocking of energies." James attributed the popularity of the movement to the fact that "mind-cure has made what in our protestant coun-

tries is an unprecedentedly great use of the subconscious life . . .
[and thereby] gives to some of us serenity, moral poise, and happiness, and prevents certain forms of disease as well as science
does, or even better in a certain class of persons."[50].

The Unconscious and Religion

The "fact" that transmundane energies filter through the unconscious and enhance the quality of personal life invites metaphysical and theological speculation. James thought it possible to
arrive at an inductively reasoned religious philosophy solely on
the basis of data supplied by psychological science. He reasoned
that "whatever it may be on its farther side, the 'more' with
which in religious experience we feel ourselves connected is on
its hither side the subconscious continuation of our conscious
life."[51] The scientific investigation of the "higher" regions of the
unconscious provides empirical grounds for religious reflection:
"Starting thus with a recognized psychological fact as our basis,
we seem to preserve a contact with 'science' which the ordinary
theologian lacks."[52]

The unconscious provided James with the mediating term
necessary to reconcile the conflicting methods of science and religion. The scientific psychologist and the theologian could agree
upon "the fact that the conscious person is continuous with a
wider self through which saving experiences come."[53] A science
of religion could build this datum of experience into a developed
philosophical system while avoiding the reductionism of either
dogmatic theology or scientific materialism. James saw *The Varieties of Religious Experience* as a "crumb-like contribution" to
this project. In this book, one of the few classic texts ever written
by an American author, James deftly combined the most dramatic examples of religious life in his own psychological crucible.
Reinterpreting the seemingly contradictory beliefs of Protestants,
Catholics, Buddhists, Transcendentalists, Vedantists, drug-tak-
ers, and Muslims in light of his theory of the subliminal self,

James thought that he had distilled from them a common essence:

> The warring gods and formulas of the various religions do indeed cancel each other, but there is a certain uniform deliverance in which religions all appear to meet.
>
> It consists of two parts:—
>
> 1. An uneasiness . . . a sense that there is something wrong about us as we naturally stand; and
>
> 2. Its solution . . . a sense that we are saved from the wrongness by making proper connection with the higher powers.[54]

Psychological analysis can strip the world's great religious traditions of their cultural accretions and disclose a common transformational process: a divided self, a struggle to achieve wholeness solely in terms of material satisfactions, and a final surrender to some higher power that brings about a change in the center of personal energy. The last stage in this process is effected by the psychological mechanism of the unconscious. Spiritual renewal thus hinges upon an unusually active subliminal consciousness such that an individual can identify "his real being with the germinal higher part of himself. . . . He becomes conscious that this higher part is conterminous and continuous with a MORE of the same quality, which is operative in the universe outside of him, and which he can keep in working touch with, and in a fashion get on board of and save himself when all his lower being has gone to pieces in the wreck."[55]

Over and above laying the foundations for a purely descriptive science of religion, the psychology of the unconscious also supplies broad hints as to the nature of this psychic "MORE." James cautioned that any interpretation of this farther side of the unconscious takes us beyond science proper and into the realm of over-beliefs. James did not, however, hesitate to confess that he himself believed that the farther reaches of our unconscious minds lead directly to the Over-Soul, or God.[56] James thought that the regenerative properties of the unconscious were a type of proof of the existence of God. "God is real since he produces real effects."[57] But, James cautioned, this cannot be taken as a blanket vindication of traditional Christian theology:

> That the God with whom, starting from the hither side of our own extra-marginal self, we come at its remoter margin into commerce should be the absolute world-ruler, is of course a very considerable over-belief. . . . All that the facts require is that the power should be both other and larger than our conscious selves.[58]

Radical empiricism warranted belief in the existence of some power greater than ourselves; it could not, however, prove this power to be infinite. James cautioned that empiricism cannot offer the emotional comforts of conventional theism. It reveals a pluralistic universe in which there are an infinite variety of forces contending with one another to determine the future shape of reality. And in such a pluralistic universe God is but one, even if the most important, of the many forces influencing the course of life.

This conception of a finite deity, limited "either in power or in knowledge, or in both," was somewhat disturbing to James's predominantly Christian audience. James's God was subject to real gains and losses, unlike the static Absolute which most Americans—even those who didn't believe in a Supreme Being at all—understood the word *God* to mean. On rational grounds alone, James's insistence upon a finite deity remains unconvincing. It was ultimately ethical, not psychological, insight that guided his metaphysical argument. In a pluralistic universe other forces besides God—the most important of which is human effort—play a part in determining the final shape of things. As James put it, a pluralistic universe makes "the salvation of the world dependent upon the success with which each unit does its part."[59] In this way James made his aesthetic spirituality supportive of moral commitment. James not only emphasized the ways in which religious inwardness enriches personal existence but also showed how this revitalization must eventuate in a willingness to forgo certain forms of self-satisfaction in favor of strenuous activity on behalf of the larger whole. James's ethical position thus centered upon the individual's capacity both to perceive and identify with the claims posited by the whole of present and future humanity. It followed that the functions performed by the unconscious are indispensable to self-sacrificing moral conduct. Only insofar as we become aware that the inner reaches of our own being connect us with a transpersonal sphere can we experience the urgency of moral demands.

James described the world view that he came ultimately to embrace as "a pluralistic panpsychic view of the universe."[60] It was pluralistic in that it demanded moral action on the part of each and every one of us; it was panpsychic in that it asserted that nature contains a spiritual depth linking all of material creation—including humans—with an immanent, divine power. In this metaphysical scheme, the notion of a covenant between God and humankind can be expressed in psychological terms: "We and God have business with each other; and in opening ourselves to his influence our deepest destiny is fulfilled."[61]

This psychological interpretation of the covenant made religious belief compatible with the experimental character of modern intellectual thought. It also provided new conceptual resources for arguing against the two determinisms that were ever endangering American spirituality. On the one hand, strict humanism is seen as a distorted version of the empirical method. Humanism's emphasis upon the rational ego fails to acknowledge the resources available at the farther reaches of our psychological nature and hence fails to do justice to the full range of our capacities for creativity and environmental transcendence. At the other extreme, James's insistence upon the finite character of God provided a bulwark against theological determinisms that attribute all power and sovereignty to a Supreme Being. Responsible moral conduct is not only spiritually significant, but is the only means by which our open-ended, evolving universe can fulfill its highest possibilities.

James confessed that only through faith in this religious

vision could he keep himself "sane and true." He had, moreover, formulated the nature of religious commitment in a way that would help a great many individuals to find their religious bearings in an age dominated by scientific reason. In making psychology the focus of metaphysical considerations of the self's "wider connections," James gave his contemporaries a scientific vocabulary with which to describe God's presence in the universe. The "fact" that God can be approached through our own unconscious minds suggests that only a self-imposed, psychological barrier separates us from an immanent divinity. The cultivation of receptivity to the unconscious is thus a spiritually as well as psychologically regenerative act of the whole personality. James had now given an explicitly psychological formulation to the spiritual regeneration of personality that Edwards had attributed to holy affections and Emerson to the presence of the Over-Soul in nature.

The Jamesian synthesis of psychology and religion elevated the unconscious to the status of a modern symbol of the relationship of human beings to their creative source. But even as James was putting the finishing touches on the "American unconscious," an assault on its metaphysical underpinnings had been launched from across the Atlantic.

Five

Assimilation and Accommodation:
American Interpretations
of Psychoanalysis

IT was especially difficult for early psychotherapists to establish a distinct professional identity. Experimental psychologists conducted their research in mechanically equipped laboratories; therapists, however, observed and treated their patients in various uncontrolled settings such as bedsides and private offices. Moreover, they had to rely upon the introspection and self-reports of their patients as opposed to empirically derived statistical results. Their theories necessarily lacked the antiseptic quality of other scientific enterprises. Therapeutically oriented psychologists were seeking to establish a professional identity which aligned them more with the medical than the academic community. Unfortunately, medical models did little to establish the credibility of this fledgling field. Because the science of the period tended to classify psychopathology as belonging to the general category of neurophysiological disorders, psychiatry was mainly limited to the search for organic abnormalities such as tumors or lesions. Any symptom without a neurological basis was therefore dismissed as malingering, hypochondria, or evidence of a lack of firm resolve. When early practitioners in this field did try to demonstrate the role of strictly "psychological" factors in mental illness, their theories differed little from those of the mind-curists and positive thinkers.

It was thus a highly charged intellectual atmosphere into which psychoanalysis would introduce its theories concerning the unconscious.[1] Freud's writings were immediately seized upon as ammunition in the many theoretical battles then polarizing the emerging schools of psychological thought: determinism versus teleology, instinct versus learned response, mechanism versus vitalism, nature versus nurture, and "hardheaded" versus "softheaded" approaches to the study of human nature. Ironically, psychoanalytic theory was invoked by combatants on all sides of these disputes. Some Americans saw in psychoanalysis a means of establishing psychotherapy along the lines of a positivistic and deterministic science. A. A. Brill, Ernest Jones, and James Jackson Putnam were among those who interpreted Freud's work as having liberated psychotherapy from neurology while preserving the kind of precise causal language that differentiates science from armchair philosophy. The technical subtleties of the Freudian lexicon imparted the stamp of professionalism to the work of therapeutic psychologists and clearly distinguished it from the eclectic and haphazard theories of the mind-curists and positive thinkers. As we shall see, however, the efforts of American psychoanalysts to obtain scientific endorsement for their theories proved largely fruitless, particularly within the academic community. Appearing as it did in the heyday of objectivism in psychological method, psychoanalysis became a favorite whipping boy for American psychologists eager to preserve the narrow strictures that they had fought so hard to impose upon their fledgling discipline.

On the other hand, psychoanalysis appealed to some American psychologists as a tool for combatting mechanistic interpretations of the mind. The rich inner life uncovered by Freud contrasted sharply with such static conceptions of the mind as Titchener's structuralism or Watson's behaviorism.[2] Those who appropriated Freud to this end fated his theories to be accommodated to preexisting patterns of American cultural and intellectual thought. Anti-structuralist and anti-behaviorist sentiments in American psychology were found largely in the functionalist school—particularly as articulated in the writings of William James. Freud was thus being called upon to give psychological support for a vision of human nature heavily indebted to indigenous intellectual propositions: the evolutionary and progressive character of nature; the preexisting harmony between the individual and the wider community; the free and morally responsible individual; the democratic vision that all have equal access to the resources necessary for achievement; and the power of individual effort to influence our personal and collective destinies. These fundamental postulates of the (non-behaviorist) American psychological tradition destined psychoanalysis to be interpreted superficially and often assimilated to viewpoints at considerable variance with those of Freud.

Freud's ideas made their appearance in popular American culture at the same time as they began to gain currency in professional circles. This too had important consequences for the subsequent interpretation of his work.[3] The process by which psychoanalytic theory filtered into American thought is a good illustration of the interplay between popular and professional psychology; or, for that matter, between middlebrow and highbrow American culture. One of the factors in this complex interaction was the virtual nonexistence of reliable English translations of Freud's difficult and subtle German works. Many American psychologists alluded to Freud's views, but few discussed them at any length. Secondary sources that purported to review Freud's theories were unsystematic and rarely reconstructed clinical evidence on the basis of which Freud had arrived at his novel conclusions. In the 1924 issue of the *Psychological Review* which was devoted to "Contributions of Freudism to Psychology," it is notable that eminent psychologists like L. L. Thurstone, James Leuba, K. S. Lashley, and Joseph Jastrow fail to cite the relevant literature with any degree of consistency or expertise.[4] As late as 1932, Jastrow published a volume on Freud without including a single direct quotation. Readers had to accept on faith Jastrow's assertion that psychoanalytic theory is riddled with glaring fallacies, manifold errors, and gross exaggerations.[5]

Most Americans—including professional psychologists—were first introduced to Freud's work in popular literature that extolled the powers and attributes of the unconscious. James made a habit of dropping the names of Breuer, Janet, Charcot, and Freud in popular works such as "Energies of Men," "The Gospel of Relaxation," and "The Hidden Self." This was in the same context in which he praised the mind-curists and psychical researchers for their discoveries of the "higher" reaches of the unconscious. Nor was James the only distinguished psychologist whose views of the unconscious were shaped in large part by non-academic writers. The founding fathers of American psychotherapy, Boris Sidis and Morton Prince, unapologetically gave credit to the psychic research of Edmund Gurney and F. W. Myers for having aroused their initial interest in the study of the unconscious. By the time Sidis and Prince encountered psychoanalysis, they had long since incorporated Myers's insights into their "scientific" research.

This mingling of popular and professional interests had a profound influence upon the ways in which psychoanalytic theory was appropriated in America. As historian Nathan Hale has observed, "There is a distinctively American interpretation of psychoanalysis—optimistic, superficial, eclectic, far more environmentalist than Freud himself."[6] The American assimilation of psychoanalysis is a telling example of the role played by cultural factors in shaping the interpretation of psychological ideas.

Anticipations of Dynamic Psychiatry

Mesmerism and its various offspring predisposed Americans to perceive psychoanalysis in very specific ways. Nathan Hale documents this influence in a chapter in his *Freud and the Americans* entitled "Mind Cures and the Mystical Wave: Popular Preparations For Psychoanalysis, 1904-1910." If anything, Hale underestimates the pervasiveness of this preparation. By making a psychological doctrine of the Transcendentalist belief in the ordinary individual's inner light, the mesmerists had effectively laid out the agenda of questions to which all subsequent theories of the unconscious would be expected to furnish answers.

The most enduring and ultimately significant legacy of the various mind-cure groups was the ready equation of the unconscious with the phenomena associated with the trance state. Significantly, when in 1898 Boris Sidis published the results of his research into "the subconscious nature of man and society," he called it *The Psychology of Suggestion*. Sidis followed the mindcurists and psychical researchers in making the entranced subject's vulnerability to "suggestions" the basic paradigm for understanding the activities of the subconscious. Sidis's dependence upon nonacademic and nonmedical sources of psychological knowledge is revealed in his statement that "psychology is especially indebted to the genius of Myers for his wide and comprehensive study of the phenomena of the subconscious, or of what he calls the manifestations of the subliminal self."[7]

Although Sidis acknowledged that the "secondary self" is most directly observable in subjects under hypnotic trance or engaged in such behavior as crystal gazing or automatic handwriting, he believed that it is always present in every individual and exerts a continuous influence upon the normal waking consciousness. The principal characteristic of the secondary, or subconscious, self is suggestibility (i.e., total susceptibility to environmental influences). Impressions received by the subconscious form the substratum of all mental activity and thus profoundly affect the individual's interaction with both the natural and the social environment. "The psychology of suggestion" had implications that went far beyond the diagnosis and treatment of mental disorders. It gave new support to the long-standing American belief in the potential utility of the unconscious. Sidis carefully disassociated himself from Myers's interest in the religious and metaphysical significance of the so-called higher levels of hypnotic trance. He did, however, use the phenomena of the trance state to argue that the unconscious was essentially malleable and hence potentially amenable to programs of reeducation and self-improvement.

William James, Sidis's Harvard mentor, also linked interpretation of the unconscious with the phenomena associated with hypnotic trance. When, in 1890, James introduced the work of the French psychiatrist Pierre Janet to the readers of *Scribner's* magazine, he condemned Janet as insufficiently concerned with the "higher" regions of the unconscious. After reviewing Janet's theories of the subconscious origins of psychoneuroses, James noted:

> My own decided impression is that M. Janet's generalizations
> are based on too limited a number of cases to cover the whole
> ground. He would have it that the secondary self is always a
> symptom of hysteria, and that the essential fact about hysteria
> is the lack of synthesizing power and consequent
> disintegration of the field of consciousness into mutually
> exclusive parts. . . . But there are trances which obey another
> type.[8]

James felt that those activities which characterize the "lower" regions of the unconscious should not be made the exclusive basis for a psychology of "the hidden self." The "other type" of trance he had in mind was the clairvoyant state he had observed in the much-studied medium Mrs. Piper. The capacity of the mind to open up to transpersonal realms was, for James, the ultimate fact to which a theory of the unconscious must address itself. James was arguing that the scientific and medical communities were by no means the sole authorities on psychological matters. The mind-curers and psychical researchers, to the extent that they are open to the phenomenal experience and reality of mystical states of consciousness, are actually more likely to make significant contributions to psychological knowledge.

The Jamesian vision of the unconscious as the mediating term between religion and science was institutionalized in the Emmanuel Movement of the Reverend Elwood Worcester.

Worcester, the rector of Boston's prestigious Emmanuel Church, inaugurated a ministry that combined psychological science and Christian faith. Worcester established working relationships with several medically trained neurologists including Isador Coriat and James Jackson Putnam, and soon became a leading spokesman for the cause of psychotherapy. His steady stream of publications awakened in the general reading public a new interest in the healing powers of unconscious mind. A single article in the *Ladies' Home Journal* elicited more than five thousand responses. Worcester, along with Boris Sidis and Morton Prince, played a major role in convincing the American medical profession to take nervous disorders seriously and in their own terms.

To a greater extent than James, Worcester recognized the antisocial and even amoral tendencies of the unconscious. But he, too, tended to gloss over these negative attributes in his eagerness to extol its redemptive powers. For Worcester, the unconscious regulates instincts, coordinates vital body functions, stores memories, and impels the organism toward growth-oriented activities. It also contains reserve energies that can be summoned for the purpose of inner healing and mental creativity. It is, in short, the seat of all that preserves harmony in life. Worcester added that the "most important fact which has yet been discovered in regard to the subconscious mind is that it is suggestible, i.e., it is subject to moral influence and direction."[9] Indeed, his psychotherapeutic ministry was premised on this property of suggestibility. Worcester's Emmanuel Movement helped its clientele to cultivate proper mental habits and, in so doing, to take advantage of their own malleable psychic structures. Drawing upon well-known mind-cure authors, Worcester assured his own clients that the key to personal happiness and success lies in "the discovery and use of those inexhaustible subconscious powers which have their roots in the Infinite."[10]

The Emmanuel Movement's inspirational message was characteristic of American psychotherapy during the first decade of the twentieth century. In 1909, a journal entitled *Psychotherapy* appeared as a forum for "a course of reading in sound psychol-

ogy, sound medicine, and sound religion."[11] Among the contributors to its twelve issues were James R. Angell, Isador Coriat, A.
A. Brill, James Jackson Putnam, Joseph Jastrow, Paul Dubois,
Robert S. Woodworth, and numerous clergymen affiliated with
the Emmanuel Movement. The first volume alluded to a forth-
coming piece by Sigmund Freud, but no such article ever
appeared. In fact, Freud was referenced in only four of the eighty-
three articles included in the short-lived series. Given the journal's stated interest in linking medical, religious, and psychological perspectives on human personality, it should not be surpris-
ing that the authorities most often cited were James, Emerson,
and the philosopher of creative evolution, Henri Bergson.

Despite an amorphous array of titles, which ranged from
"Healing in the Old Testament" and "The Clergyman's Place in
Psychiatry" to "Obsessions and their Treatment by Suggestion,"
the contributions were strikingly uniform in tone and general
outlook. If one were to nominate a consensus voice among the
contributors, it would probably be that of Richard C. Cabot, a
Harvard Medical School professor who contributed papers to all
but one issue. In his "The American Type of Psychotherapy,"
Cabot made the telling observation that it was "not until the
translation in 1905 of Dubois's epoch-making book that the
American medical public became aware that there was such a
thing as scientific mind cure."[12] The fact that Cabot attributes
such importance to Dubois is revealing of the general tone of
American psychotherapy at the time when the writings of Freud
were first becoming available here. Dubois, a Swiss neurologist,
was very appealing to American physicians; he advocated the
same suggestive, educational, and inspirational tactics as the
mind-curists, but gave them a professional gloss. A review of
Dubois's *Psychic Treatment of Nervous Disorders* that appeared
in the *Psychological Bulletin* singled out for praise his emphasis
upon helping patients acquire a robust philosophy of life.[13] The
review further noted that Dubois's methods perfectly comple-
mented James's valuable suggestions concerning cultivation of
the hidden energies of the unconscious.

Cabot built upon Dubois's insights in an article entitled "Creative Assertions." Like the mind-curists, Cabot variously compared the therapeutic powers of our unconscious minds to positive thinking, electricity, and the telepathic transmission of mental energies. Through the proper use of autosuggestive techniques, he urged, we can activate our inner resources and set into motion "sympathetic vibrations" that will accomplish any desired result.[14] In a later issue he compared the nervous system to an electric trolley car powered by "currents of energy supplied from without by our fellow men, by nature, and by God."[15] Cabot's romanticized view of the unconscious predisposed him to dismiss Freud's belief in the sexual nature of the psyche as an "inconclusive idea" which falls short of the "all-encompassing fundamental principle that he considers it to be."[16]

The pull of American culture is also evident in the writings of Boris Sidis and Morton Prince, the two most respected and influential authorities on abnormal psychology in the early part of this century. Sidis's principal works,—*The Psychology of Suggestion* (1898), *Multiple Personality* (1904), and *The Foundations of Normal and Abnormal Psychology* (1914)—for the most part recapitulated the views of the French psychiatrist Pierre Janet. Janet had been a pioneer in the study of hypnosis. His studies eventually led him to conclude that the symptoms of mental pathology are caused by a "fixed idea" buried in the patient's unconscious mind. Janet eventually traced the origin of these "fixed ideas" to troublesome incidents in the patient's past. This discovery gradually led to a theory of the psychological origin of mental disorders and suggested goals and methods of psychotherapy (e.g., reconstruction of the patient's past, gaining of insight, and reeducation). Janet's writings found a receptive audience among American psychologists and physicians, for whom his essentially cognitive or transactional characterization of the psychoneuroses would contrast favorably with Freud's model of a closed, intrapsychic energy system.[17]

When Sidis appropriated Janet's work, he made at least three important innovations which became part of the generally accepted American "knowledge" of the unconscious. First, Sidis's experiments with hypnosis had convinced him that the subconscious plays an important role in the normal as well as the abnormal personality. The unconscious is essentially a mechanism that helps an individual successfully adapt to the environment; pathology reflects an unfortunate—but avoidable—disruption of the communication between the conscious and unconscious components of the mind. Second, Sidis expanded upon Janet's environmentalism by emphasizing fear or anxiety as the salient underlying factor in the origin of the neuroses.[18] This more situational, even existential, view of our psychological vulnerability meant that the psyche is more amenable than Janet's theory suggested to cognitive restructuring through what Sidis called "thought therapy." It also enabled American psychologists to rescue the unconscious from the intrapsychic determinisms of psychoanalytic theory. And, third, Sidis tailored Janet's psychiatric theory to suit the indigenously American pursuit of "higher energies." Following James, Sidis described at length the value of hypnotic-like states of consciousness for gaining access to the stores of reserve energy that reside in the unconscious:

> The hypnoidal state helps us to reach the inaccessible regions of dormant energy, it helps to break down inhibitions, liberate reserve energies, and repair the breaches of mental activity. The painful systems become disassociated, disintegrated, and again transformed, reformed, and reintegrated into new systems full of energy and joy of life. . . . The patient feels the flood of fresh energies as a "marvelous transformation," as a "new light," as a "new life," as "something worth far more than life itself."[19]

Morton Prince, like Sidis, developed his theory of the unconscious with little or no reliance upon Freud. Heavily indebted to the insights of Janet, Bernheim, and Charcot, Prince's theory shows striking similarities to Pavlov's theory of associative learning. According to Prince, the unconscious "is the great storehouse of neurograms which are the physiological records of our mental lives."[20] Past experiences are stored in what Prince called our "dormant consciousness." These can join together in clusters or complexes that are capable of erupting into consciousness as psychopathological symptoms. Prince's emphasis upon the "learned" character of so much of our unconscious implied that it is eminently reeducable. By making patients aware of the source of their emotional difficulties and teaching them to take a new point of view toward themselves, the unconscious can again be rendered beneficent.

Another aspect of Prince's work with consequences for Americans' appropriation of Freud's theories was his attribution of cognitive powers to the unconscious.[21] The unconscious, according to Prince, has an "intelligent, purposive, volitional character."[22] He therefore vehemently opposed Freud's theories, dismissing them as unwarranted inferences from insufficient data. Freud's view of dreams as wish-fulfilling fantasies of the unconscious was for Prince woefully inadequate in that it neglected the positive contributions of the unconscious to logical analysis, ethical reflection, intellectual curiosity, and the resolution of mental uncertainty.[23]

The ideas of Prince and Sidis traveled far beyond scientific circles. In three articles appearing in 1910, H. Addington Bruce summarized and highlighted their work for the readers of *The American Magazine* and *Forum*.[24] The work of Drs. Prince and Sidis, he wrote, proved that "'mind cure' has come to stay, and that it has at last been put on a soundly scientific basis."[25] Bruce did not burden his audience with technical discussions of medical psychiatry. It was apparently sufficient for the public to know that science had at last confirmed the mind-curists' discovery of "the existence of an amazing 'underground' mental life—or strong 'subconscious' realm with powers transcending those of the ordinary consciousness."[26] Bruce's review of the current literature predictably focused on the practical utility of works by the likes of Dubois, Annie Payson Call, and the Emmanuel Movement. They, along with Sidis, Prince, and "a little band of scientists, working mainly in France," had begun to formulate a scientific scheme of mental healing. Bruce explained that scientific mental healing was based upon the newly discovered principle that a properly phrased suggestion "sets in motion the hidden power, the 'latent energy' possessed by every human being and enabling one, when it is properly directed, to overcome many grievous diseases, notably diseases of the nervous system, such as hysteria, neurasthenia, psychasthenia."[27] Of the four great leaders in the development of scientific mental healing (Prince, Sidis, Janet, and Freud), Bruce found it necessary to sound a note of caution about the work of only one—Freud. Freud, he explained, was not only attempting to devise a new system of psychotherapy, but an entirely new psychology. "Thus far," Bruce observed, "it must be said, no other leading psychotherapist has accepted his sweeping, audacious theory."[28]

Thus, in 1909, when Freud first came to America to discuss his theories at a conference celebrating the twentieth anniversary of Clark University, it might fairly be said that Americans possessed very little precise information concerning the unconscious and its activities. But in a more fundamental way they had long since decided what they were interested in learning. As Maurice Green and R. W. Rieber have noted, for psychoanalysis to attract any sizeable following, it had first "to be shaped in its American assimilation to conform to this pre-existing pattern."[29]

Early Patterns of Assimilation

In 1908 a New York psychiatrist by the name of A. A. Brill returned from Zurich, where he had spent a year studying psychoanalysis under Bleuler and Jung. That same year the brilliant psychoanalytic proselytizer Ernest Jones left London for a teaching position at the University of Toronto. Within a few months' time the two had brought Freud's work to the attention of some of the most respected physicians and psychologists in America, including Isador Coriat, Morton Prince, Hugo Munsterberg, and

James Jackson Putnam. Brill and Jones would continue to be the most capable of Freud's followers on this continent during the first two decades of this century. Their articles, presentations at professional meetings, and organizational leadership helped preserve Freud's teachings from being irrevocably lost amidst a myriad of misinterpretations by friends and foes alike.[30]

In 1909 G. Stanley Hall invited Freud to deliver a series of lectures at a conference held at Clark University. The Clark Conference was the first formal introduction of psychoanalysis to an American professional audience. It was here that Freud both solidified the base of support already gained through Brill's endorsement and won the enthusiastic support of Edwin B. Holt and James Jackson Putnam. Both Holt and Putnam would eventually become successful (if not entirely faithful) popularizers of the psychoanalytic cause.

Freud's lectures were published in the *Journal of American Psychology* the next year, coinciding almost exactly with H. Addington Bruce's pieces on Freud in *Forum* and *The American Magazine* as well as with an excellent introductory article which Ernest Jones submitted to the *Psychological Bulletin*.[31] This essay by Jones was perhaps a better, more readable introduction to psychoanalysis than Freud's Clark lectures, and thus warrants review. Jones tended to sketch with broad strokes the distinctive shape and boundaries of the psychoanalytic forest rather than examine a few isolated trees in laborious detail, as Freud was wont to do. Psychoanalysis was, Jones forthrightly declared, a rigorously deterministic approach to mental life. It views the mind as a complex system of reflexes that operate exclusively according to the "motive" of maximizing pleasure and avoiding pain. To the psychoanalyst, there is no qualitative difference between normal and abnormal psychological processes, nor is there any distinction to be made between children's desires and affective states and those of adults; the more or less archaic and asocial instinctual needs of the infant remain as the permanent foundation of mental processes throughout the course of life. Finally, Jones informed his readers that Freud's clinical observations proved that our conscious personality is little more than a puppet manipulated by the aims and purposes of an infinitely richer and more complex psychical system—the unconscious.

Psychoanalysis stands or falls on the validity of Freud's fundamental postulate that "every mental process belongs in the first place to the unconscious psychical system."[32] "The unconscious," he instructed, "is a special realm, with its own desires and modes of expression and peculiar mental mechanisms not elsewhere operative."[33] The desires and mental mechanisms that Freud predicated of the unconscious were, of course, inferences from his clinical observations.[34] The unconscious, moreover, is the psychological datum on the basis of which Freud thought himself justified in using the biological language of instinctual energy in the context of discussions of purpose and meaning.[35]

Freud was committed to Darwinian principles and he saw the unconscious as the primary carrier of instinctual biological drives; he compared it to a seething caldron of instinctual energy. Since gratification of instinct is biologically speaking "the true purpose" of the individual organism's life, the unconscious is thus the primary source of our motives and drives. Freud often compared the activity of the unconscious to the operation of a hydraulic system—a closed energy system driven by the need to discharge pent-up pressure. The psyche's energies thus do not serve any progressive purpose; they do not in any way further the development either of the individual or the species. They are, rather, governed by the urge to return the system to a state of inertia or quiescence. The unconscious is, in short, an intractable agent acting solely on its own behalf, oblivious and even antagonistic to the practical necessities of our physical and social surroundings.

The immediate satisfaction of instinctual desire (for which the unconscious insistently presses) would often imperil the organism by bringing it into violent conflict with either natural or social "dangers." The ego must therefore impose restraints and restrictions upon their immediate expression. In Freud's terms, the rational ego must oppose the untamed passions arising in the unconscious and substitute the "reality principle" of moderation and delay for the "pleasure principle" of instantaneous gratification. The ego is thus saddled with the responsibility of keeping the promptings of the unconscious at bay. To this end, it must seek "the most favorable and least perilous method of obtaining satisfaction, taking the external world into account."[36] The ego and the superego (the internalized image of parental authority which harshly monitors the demands arising from the unconscious) inhibit instinctual drive mainly through repression. Repression results, however, in an intrapsychic network of insufficiently gratified desires. As these repressed desires seek expression, they utilize what Freud termed the "peculiar mental mechanisms" of the unconscious. The unconscious is thus entrusted with the biological task of disguising primitive biological urges so that they can escape detection by the "censor" lurking at the threshold of consciousness.

For this reason, even the most common mental event—a slip of the tongue, a joke, an ambition, a moral scruple—can be fraught with deeper psychological significance. For Freud, psychoanalysis is first and foremost detective work. The analyst traces a patient's dreams, free associations, or symptoms back to their origins in the repressed material of the unconscious. It was Freud's genius to discover the way in which the "peculiar mechanisms" of displacement, condensation, and symbolization disguise our primitive urges and traumatic memories from the rational ego. Psychoanalytic interpretation reveals that much of what humans consider to be "high" in life—artistic creation, moral values, religious belief—are in reality circuitous attempts to satisfy what is "low"—our unconscious instinctual passions.

The psychoanalytic vision of human nature perceived ceaseless tension and conflict between the individual and society and among the various components of the individual's own psyche. Driven by instinctual forces which if unrestrained would lead to murder, incest, and unmitigated egotism, the individual must be coerced by society into renouncing his innermost desires. The very existence of culture is therefore predicated upon society's ability to encroach upon and impose authority over our deepest wants and wishes. Society develops at the expense of the individual, who pays in terms of psychic frustration, repression, and eventually neurosis. But Freud, while drawing attention to the coercive character of social authority, simultaneously worked to undermine it. The entire enterprise of psychoanalysis encourages individuals to liberate themselves from externally imposed suppression. Given Freud's assumption that the amount or quantity of libidinal energy is fixed, it follows that our ability to achieve personal pleasure and fulfillment is a function of how effectively we can defend ourselves against society's attempts to channel instinctual gratification into more innocuous, but less satisfying, activities. Psychoanalytic insight fosters the pursuit of enlightened self-interest. Directed by shrewd, calculating rationality, the prudential ego learns to avoid any and all emotional attachments that could threaten the person's free pursuit of pleasure-giving activities. What Phillip Rieff calls "psychological man" is therefore characterologically suspicious and detached; he is wary of the false promises of institutions—familial, political, or religious—whose very existence demands the suppression of his individual interests.[37] Resigned to the tragic character of life, psychological man pursues whatever limited measure of personal fulfillment he can obtain while stoically accepting the inevitable compromises and renunciations imposed upon him in the course of everyday life.

Despite the valiant efforts of early converts to the psychoanalytic cause such as Brill and Jones, Freud's writings failed to make much of an impression upon the accumulated stock of psychological "knowledge" in America. Psychoanalytic literature was not a commercial success. As Nathan Hale has documented, neither the translations of Freud's major texts nor the works of his American followers ever sold as much as 10 percent of the number of copies needed to qualify a book as a best-seller in that period.[38] The exception, of course, would be the popularized versions of psychoanalysis that appeared in *McLure's, Ladies' Home Journal, Good Housekeeping, Forum,* and *The American Maga-*

zine. These popular tracts simplified psychoanalysis to the point of dissipating its internal consistency and explanatory power. They directed attention away from the primary instincts of sexuality and aggression, emphasizing instead our innate capacity for sublimation. They also neglected the more radical implications of the pleasure principle and the central aim of the unconscious to return the organism to homeostasis. And certainly they ignored the Freudian doctrine that the unconscious was utterly unresponsive to the dictates of logic or social prudence. The reasons for this were many; but perhaps the most important is the problem posed for American religious beliefs by Freud's reductionistic view of the psyche. For as Hale remarks, the American popularizations of psychoanalysis "suggest a search for a new moral guide and a new style of ethic, perhaps, indeed, for a new substitute for religion."[39]

Even the most "scientific" of Freud's early American followers appropriated from psychoanalysis only in ways that could support a new moral and religious outlook. William A. White, Edwin Bissell Holt, and James Jackson Putnam became the most influential champions of the psychoanalytic cause largely because they self-consciously minimized its dissonance with indigenous cultural attitudes. Chief administrator of the prestigious St. Elizabeth's Hospital for the Insane in Washington, D.C., William Alanson White displayed reasonable dexterity in conveying both the substance and spirit of Freud's theory. To help sensitize his readers to the inevitability of psychological conflict, White explained:

> We lead two more or less distinct and conflicting psychic
> lives. One rich in emotion but submersed beneath the region
> of clear consciousness, is the home of our crude, untamed
> desires of which the sexual is the most prominent. The other
> is the fully conscious life, the psychic veneer of civilization.[40]

The aim of psychoanalysis, White proclaimed, is to assist us to recognize our "untamed" desires, or what he termed the "first principles" of psychic life, en route to arriving at more realistic values and commitments.

But if White understood Freud on one level—that of the necessity of bringing unconscious motives into the clear light of critical reflection—he clearly did not grasp the wider philosophical outlook engendered by the psychoanalytic theory of human nature. White had a far more transactional or environmentalistic understanding of the individual's relationship to society than did Freud. By emphasizing the extent to which our innermost drives and motivations are the product of the natural and social environments, White thought of himself as anchoring psychoanalysis in the evolutionary science of the period. In practice, White's environmentalist outlook rescued the unconscious from total domination by the intrapsychic determinisms described by Freud. White further implied that the psyche was as fluid and open to change as nature itself. His therapeutic methods manifested his belief in the psyche's openness to external influence; they emphasized the importance of reeducation and self-suggestion in a manner similar to that of Dubois in the volume he had translated back in 1905.[41]

White's faith in the progressive character of natural law was hardly compatible with the detached objectivity with which Freud had pursued his clinical investigations. To White, studying the laws which govern the mind was nothing short of a moral and spiritual mission. Moreover, by increasing our knowledge of those factors which govern mental development, we augment and accelerate the progressive drift of evolution.[42] White's thinking here expresses the "progressivist" sentiment which dominated programs for economic, judicial, medical, and political reform at that time. Progressivism believed in improving social conditions steadily through the systematic use of science and technology. White, for example, championed the cause of more enlightened treatment for criminals and the insane. But White's progressivism was not the same as that of the bureaucratically minded political reformers, who thought in terms of organization

and increased efficiency. He espoused a highly Romantic evolutionary faith cut from the same cloth as the liberal Protestantism
of individuals such as Henry Ward Beecher, whose sermons
White had listened to in his youth. Any activity that opens up the
psyche to its own internal depths can be seen as a way of furthering the progressive manifestation of an immanent divinity.
Thus, although White could agree with Freud on the need for a
strictly deterministic psychology, his notion of determinism was
very different from that of Freud's. White's determinism was that
of Bergson's *élan vital.* Human actions and desires express not so
much our repressed past as the forward-propelling impulse
innate within the human soul.[43]

White's philosophical commitment to Bergson's evolutionary faith was reflected in his appropriation of psychoanalysis. A
review of his *Mechanisms of Character Formation* perceptively
observed:

> Where the European followers of Freud emphasize the point
> that the formation of the symbol is indicative of a
> "renunciation of reality," the American disciple sees it as a
> "carrier of energy" exquisitely fitted for increasing man's
> control over his environment.[44]

Edwin Bissell Holt's *The Freudian Wish and Its Place in Ethics* showed none of White's aesthetic spirituality, but did share
his progressivist enthusiasm. Holt, a student of James's pragmatism, insisted that observable actions are the only reality.
Believing that the "future of psychology . . . [lay] in the hands of
behaviorists," Holt was interested in Freud's theories solely insofar as they might serve his post-Deweyan, behaviorist understanding of social utility.[45] Holt thought that the social sciences
should be called upon to supply factual foundations for a more
efficient, realistic ethical philosophy. If Freud's theories could
shed light on those factors that influence human motivation, they
should be incorporated into social and educational reforms
designed to build a more ethical culture. Holt wrote that because

Freud had shown that the instinctual drive or "wish is the unit of conduct, it is clear that ethics ought to take the wish as the fundamental unit of discourse."[46]

Holt's progressivism was grounded upon a firm belief in objectivism, behaviorism, and realism. The adversary against which he and so many of his contemporaries were struggling was Protestant moralism. Freud buttressed Holt's conviction that moral absolutism was not only ineffective, but actually stifled individual motivation. Psychoanalysis was, then, a kind of scientific prolegomenon to ethical philosophy. By revealing that we do not naturally act in pursuit of fanciful ideals but rather in the attempt to satisfy biologically based "wishes," psychoanalysis had revealed that the only workable ethics was

> an ethics "from below." The ethics "from above" are a very
> different story. There someone exhorts or obliges us to
> suppress our wishes. . . . Ethics from above come indeed from
> above, from the man or institution "higher up." And for this
> there is a very frail and human reason, which no one need go
> very far to discover. According to the ethics from below, the
> unassuming ethics of the dust, facts are the sole moral
> sanction; and facts impose the most inerasable moral
> penalties.[47]

The progressivist interest in psychoanalysis was part and parcel of what historian Robert Wiebe calls the "search for order" among early twentieth-century intellectuals who felt the need for new guidelines to reality. The emergence of the social sciences can in fact be attributed in large measure to this widespread interest in developing more concrete, if less grandiose, programs for the improvement of the human condition.[48] As John C. Burnham points out, early American psychologists "tended to be lay preachers who sought to reform the world by means of reeducation and retraining."[49] Though less dogmatic than clergymen in their understanding of right and wrong, early psychoanalysts and psychiatrists were equally eager to utilize their knowledge in the service of such traditional goals as fostering moral responsibility, the pursuit of self-improvement, and social conscience.[50] As Burnham observes, "By means of sublimation man's evil would be turned into good . . . even the grossest sexual perversions would become artistic creations and love for fellow men."[51]

James Jackson Putnam also approached psychoanalysis with an agenda of progressivist concerns but, unlike Holt, did not confine himself to objectivist definitions of reality. On the contrary, Putnam found resources in the aesthetic strain of American intellectual thought to expand our definition of reality to include nature's deeper energies.[52] And it was this vision that led him to discover the importance of Freud's "discovery" of the unconscious.

Putnam's endorsement of psychoanalysis was a pivotal event in the introduction of Freud's theories to American audiences. His reputation as an esteemed Harvard neurologist gave psychoanalysis the aura of scientific respectability it needed if it was to secure a fair hearing among serious scholars. Freud appreciated Putnam's support and averred that "he was able to do perhaps more than anyone for the spread of psychoanalysis in his own country."[53] Freud was very well aware, however, that Putnam's endorsement was a mixed blessing. Putnam's writings were prime examples of what Freud described as the dangerous tendency among American analysts to force psychoanalytic theory into "the service of a particular philosophical outlook on the world . . . and urge this upon the patient in order to enoble him."[54]

Putnam, too, recognized that there were important ideological differences between him and Freud. Describing Freud's theory of repression and its implications for a fuller understanding of human motive, Putnam interjected, "I accept Freud's definition and merely assert that psycho-analytic doctrines, like all scientific doctrines, are valid only within certain definite limits."[55] In other words, Putnam agreed with Freud that behavior is largely determined by unconscious drives; it was, rather, the philosophical framework onto which Freud forced his observations that Putnam objected to. Particularly objectionable was Freud's insistence that there is a fixed quantity of mental energy. This fundamental postulate of psychoanalytic theory struck Putnam as denying the mind's known progressive and creative tendencies. Putnam argued his case before the International Psychoanalytic Association in a paper entitled "A Plea for the Study of Philosophic Methods in Preparation for Psychoanalytic Work." The reason for revising psychoanalytic doctrines was more ideological than scientific; for, as Putnam lamented, "in such a world as [Freud's], thought and will would have, of course, no power to create anything new. . . . No one really accepts such a world as this."[56]

Putnam continued his revision of the nonprogressive Freudian concept of the unconscious in a series of articles. He argued that the full significance of instinctual forces in the larger evolutionary scheme of things "can be adequately expressed only in metaphysical terms."[57] More specifically, Putnam thought that the unconscious drives must be interpreted as the psychological counterpart of Bergson's *élan vital*. The unconscious exerts a dynamic influence which goes well beyond the expression of instincts and repressed desires and is more properly understood as the psychological faculty that channels life's progressive impulses into conscious activities. Putnam was convinced that among the instinctual energies contained in the unconscious are "the expansive forces that make for a more spiritual life."[58]

> The mind contains a real, permanently abiding element which
> partakes of the nature of the real, permanently abiding energy
> of which the life of the universe is made. From the standpoint
> of the nature of his mind, a man belongs to the eternal and
> immortal realities of the universe.[59]

Viewed in their proper biological and evolutionary context, instinctual energies are seen to embody the creative impulse of the Life Force. Instinct is therefore not solely an agent of adaptation; it is also a "modifier and creator of structure."[60] The human psyche, by imagining a more ideal environment, can become the agent that brings that new reality into existence. Citing Emerson and Bergson, Putnam asserted that the mind's hidden depths furnish it with the means to transcend existing structures and bring novel additions into the world.

The unconscious was thus for Putnam—as it had been for the mesmerists, James, and so many of the early functionalists before him—the psychological mechanism that made it possible to give scientific credibility to willed freedom and creative adaptation to the environment. In effect, Putnam was saying that the distinction between the "lower" and "higher" reaches of the unconscious implied a similar distinction between the "lower" and "higher" motivational tendencies present in human nature.[61] To the extent that the psyche draws upon the lower energies of instinctual urge and egocentric defense, the individual is essentially at the mercy of existing determinisms. Yet, insofar as the unconscious also draws upon the "infinite world of spirit," the individual is endowed with higher motivational energies which receive expression in such environment-transcending attributes as creative genius, disinterested love, and consciously directed adaptations.[62]

Putnam's dogged efforts to recast psychoanalysis to conform to a preexisting ideology did not escape his contemporaries. H. Addington Bruce, in his preface to *Human Motives,* called attention to the ways in which Putnam's analysis would bring "encouragement to all oppressed by the seeming impossibility of reconciling the intuitions of religious faith with the dictates of modern science."[63] In a review for the *Journal of Abnormal Psychology,* L. Pierce Clark wrote that Putnam's efforts "to elevate psychoanalysis to the highest planes of philosophical speculation ... [and bring it] in unison with the eternal verities is deserving of the highest commendation and illustrates his deep faith in the nobility of this new resource for understanding the spiritual side of man."[64]

Putnam had apparently succeeded in persuading others to share his harmonial faith that, properly understood, psychoanalysis reconfirms the religious individual's belief "that there is something in him akin to the creative energy of the universe."[65]

It seems that Freud was thoroughly justified in writing to the American analyst C. P. Oberndorf that "the popularity of the term psychoanalysis in America is no evidence of a friendly attitude toward the subject or a particularly broad dissemination of, or profound understanding of its teachings."[66]

Objections Sustained

Few American psychologists had theoretical questions to which Freud's work on the unconscious provided acceptable answers. The presiding "deans" of American psychology at the time when Freud's ideas were first being discussed, G. Stanley Hall and William James, damned psychoanalysis with their faint and guarded praise. Hall, as president of Clark University, hosted the conference designed to showcase Freud's theoretical discoveries, and Hall's own study of child development had convinced him of the heuristic value of psychoanalysis. But Hall had studied child development for the purpose of ascertaining what is true and pure in human nature. He was prepared, and only prepared, to appropriate a "Freudism, ridded of its excessive stress on sex and broadened into a philosophy of life."[67]

James, like Hall, often gave polite recognition to Freud as the harbinger of great discoveries and is even reputed to have told Freud that "the future of psychology belongs to your work." Privately, however, James harbored grave reservations about the merits of both Freud and his theories. In a personal communication he commented that "Freud has condemned the American religious therapy (which has had such extensive results) as very 'dangerous because so unscientific.' Bah!"[68] James's impatience with the narrowness of Freud's philosophical outlook reflected the difference in their respective interpretations of nature. Freud viewed nature in the fairly static terms of Newtonian and Helmholtzian physics. James, on the other hand, subscribed to what he called a piecemeal supranaturalism which—à la Emerson, Swedenborg, Myers, and Fechner—permitted higher metaphysical energies to enter into and produce regenerative effects within the physical universe.

Not all of the psychologists who embraced James's functionalism also shared his metaphysically charged conception of the farther reaches of the unconscious. But most American functionalists exhibited the Jamesian tendency to view the unconscious as a sort of link or shunting valve connecting the conscious mind with nature's adaptive forces. Freud's insistence that libidinal energies are essentially nonprogressive thus cut directly across the grain of one of the most pervasive schools of American psychological thought. American psychologists thus denounced Freud's emphasis upon the sexual character of our fundamental drives not solely out of moral prudery but also because of their faith in the providential character of natural law. William McDougall, for example, resembled Freud to the extent that he, too, championed an instinctive and dynamic psychology and opposed the rising tide of behaviorism. Yet McDougall wanted it known that

> I do not delay to criticize in detail the popular Freudian
> dogma that all love is sexual. I reject it, not because it offends
> my "moral sense," but because it is so obviously untrue and is
> based upon implicit reasoning which is so obviously
> fallacious.[69]

The obvious truths to which McDougall appealed were, apparently, equally obvious to a good many of his contemporaries. Articles published in highly respected professional journals brushed Freud's theories aside without challenging their empirical foundations; it was rather their philosophical implications that were unacceptable. R. S. Woodworth based his criticisms of psychoanalysis at least partially upon the ad hominem charge that analysts were bent on belittling and debasing the high motives of others.[70] Because Freud's theories were based upon his observations of patients suffering from psychological illnesses, Bernard Hart classified Freud's work as "morbid psychology."[71] In an article entitled "Sigmund Freud, Pessimist," E. E. Southard insinuated that if one wished to know the practical consequences of Freud's theories, one need look no farther than the brutality and cruelty exhibited by the Germans in World War I.[72] Joseph Jastrow insisted that "a safe and sane Freudianism is not only possible but imperative," and implied that the original was neither.[73] And the reason?

> Freudianism when weighed in the scales of science is found
> seriously wanting. The cardinal defect is the false rendering of
> the "unconscious" phases of the psychic economy. . . . The
> second defect is the gross sexualization of libido.[74]

Those who shared Freud's conviction that psychology should be predicated upon a thoroughgoing determinism nevertheless rejected his theory of the unconscious. As early as 1909, Walter O. Scott found psychoanalytic theory of the subconscious origin of mental illness inconsistent with the spirit of scientific inquiry: "The subconscious, as is well known, is not open for introspection, but is assumed as an explanatory hypothesis. The hypothesis has no justification unless it explains the facts better than any other theory."[75]

The tendency toward positivism that characterized the early professionalization of American psychology dictated both Henry Woodburn Chase's early interest in Freud's work and his final repudiation of it. Chase approved the role of psychoanalysis in overturning the Wundtian dictum that mental activity below the threshold of consciousness could never be studied by psychology. He did not, however, endorse Freud's "theory of the structure of the psyche." Chase faulted Freud for drawing unwarranted inferences in his attempt to stretch his clinical observations into a complete psychology:

> The collection of phenomena in which the unconscious has
> been traced most keenly and with most insight is undoubtedly
> that given by Freud in his various works. But in attempting to
> account for them he has been led to conceptions which have
> at least this objection, that they are cumbersome and
> psychologically crude.[76]

Frederick Lyman Wells's "Critique of Impure Reason" and Knight Dunlap's *Mysticism, Freudianism and Scientific Psychology* sustained Chase's indictment of psychoanalytic theory as unscientific. Wells and Dunlap portrayed psychoanalysis as a thoroughly unreliable set of speculations that defied the accepted canons of both logic and scientific method.[77] A review in *The Nation* found Freud's theories so lacking in scientific rigor as to be downright "depressing" and concluded that Freud "portrays himself as one whose scientific judgment cannot be trusted."[78] Nearly three decades later the influential historian of psychology Edna Heidebreder felt justified in dismissing Freud's theories with the facile assertion that they had been offered without compelling evidence and were consequently "unsuitable to scientific verification and use."[79]

Without arguing the merits of these charges, one thing was certain: Academic psychology largely closed its doors to psychoanalytic doctrine. An unsigned editorial in a 1924 issue of the *Journal of Abnormal Psychology* bemoaned the endless stream of writings on the unconscious by European psychologists and dismissed them wholesale as possessing "no more worth than the German mark."[80] Not surprisingly, the number of articles on psychoanalytic theory accepted for publication in this prestigious journal subsequently declined dramatically.

What seems to have escaped the attention of the critics of psychoanalysis is that no one had eliminated Freudian theory as a helpful interpretation of psychopathology. In fact, no one really attempted to refute Freud on clinical grounds. Most American psychologists dismissed psychoanalysis and its implications on the same essentially philosophical grounds as McDougall, that psychoanalytic theory was "obviously fallacious." Noted psychological historian Joseph Adelson has hypothesized that the ideological incompatibility between Freud's tragic view of life and the optimistic bent of the American mind was sufficient to account for the reluctance of academic psychologists to give psychoanalysis a more serious reading: "Freud's mode of thought . . . his way of viewing the human situation, runs counter to attitudes deeply entrenched in the American disposition."[81] Adelson contends that a set of "implicit premises which guide our way to reality" makes it well nigh impossible for Americans to view the psyche as composed of dark and archaic components. American psychology is the creation of a cultural tradition which esteems vigor and flexibility; it consequently resists trammeling the self with a complex inner structure. American psychology tends to depict the individual as governed by malleable ego functions capable of devising ever new strategies for adapting to the environment. In the final analysis, psychoanalysis as a system of thought fails even to describe, much less strengthen, the psychological mechanisms with which Americans encounter their world.

Neo-Freudian Accommodations

In spite of the fact that psychoanalysis has by and large remained peripheral to academic psychology (medical psychiatry notwithstanding) a good portion of the Freudian lexicon has made its way into the stock of ideas with which Americans interpret their lives. Terms such as *fixation, projection, regression,* and *transference* are part of common American parlance. In fact, there seems good reason to believe that Freud's theories have been more widely disseminated in America than in any other nation.[82] The ways in which most Americans employ these Freudian terms, however, continue to be largely those prescribed by the likes of Holt, Putnam, and Bruce. Popular culture continues to accept the "fact" that the unconscious—though powerful and bent on the gratification of self-serving instincts—can be tamed and put into the service of actualizing inner potentials. The unconscious is generally considered to be present in all persons as the source of power and success; its energies can be unleashed to break down humdrum routines and restore the self to its natural condition of vitality and exuberance.

This entanglement of psychoanalytic terminology with an

inspirational reverence for the self's inner resources is partly attributable to the ubiquitous self-help books that describe "techniques for using your unconscious power."[83] Yet in no small measure the responsibility must rest with theoretical developments within psychoanalysis itself. The neo-Freudian movement of the 1950s and 1960s produced a revised version of psychoanalytic theory that bore the imprint of a distinctive American psychological tradition going back as far as Emerson. In his insightful reconstruction entitled "The Americanization of Sigmund Freud: Adaptations of Psychoanalysis before 1917," F. W. Matthews concludes that only by accommodating its theories to indigenous intellectual habits was psychoanalysis able to attract its following in the United States:

> That Freudian ideas were assimilated to a persistent native ideology (while themselves causing changes within it) is suggested by the similarities between Putnam's and Holt's interpretations of Freud and the later . . . schools of psychotherapy associated with Harry Stack Sullivan, Erich Fromm and Karen Horney [which] were largely developed in the American environment, and achieved their great popularity there.[84]

Dissatisfied with the Freudian doctrine of the instinctual nature of all psychic energy, Robert White and Heinz Hartmann laid the first plank of the neo-Freudian platform by arguing for the existence of a "conflict-free ego sphere."[85] Hartmann and White drew attention to the noninstinctual character of many ego functions such as play, experimentation, and the quest for competency. This innovation drastically altered the philosophical tone and implications of psychoanalytic theory. For one thing, "ego psychology" depicts the psyche as essentially purposive and progressive. Furthermore, the idea that the ego possesses independent, noninstinctual energies defuses Freud's tragic vision of the inevitable conflict between the individual and society. There is, argued Hartmann and White, in every individual an inborn adaptation to the "average expectable environment" which, under proper conditions, provides the foundations for harmonious interaction throughout the course of life.

During the 1940s, Karen Horney published a series of influential books and articles that gave quasi-official sanction to the emerging environmentalist, progressivist, and existentialist trends in American psychoanalytic thought.[86] Horney argued that neurosis is the product of social rather than intrapsychic factors. The aggressive or antisocial behaviors that Freud had thought basic to human nature are, she countered, understandable psychological defenses. Horney progressively denuded the unconscious of the baser associations which it had acquired in psychoanalytic theory, and instead pictured our deepest tendencies as directed toward affiliation, personal creativity, and the pursuit of moral and intellectual meaning.

Of all the neo-Freudians, Erich Fromm has unquestionably been the most influential. Virtually every theme that distinguishes the "American psyche" from its Freudian predecessor appears in Fromm's writings: the importance of the present (or existential) situation of the individual rather than his or her past; consciousness and willed freedom rather than intrapsychic determinisms; the continuing openness of the personality and its responsiveness to new experiences as opposed to fixed character structures; and rejection of the biological homeostasis in favor of belief in the forward-moving progressive tendency of the unconscious. Importantly, Fromm's psychoanalytic orientation prevented him from following his social and environmentalist ideas to their logical conclusion. The unconscious became for him a psychological bastion defending the individual from total domination by outer forces. Fromm asserts that authenticity, freedom, and personal creativity derive from an order of psychological activity which lies beneath the subject-object level of mental activity. Describing this deeper mental life, he repeatedly draws upon such patently mystical language as the Zen account of satori, Meister Eckhart's depiction of union with the Godhead, and Paul Tillich's description of the psyche's ontological participation in the "ground of being." Fromm's metaphysically charged doctrine of the unconscious has permitted him to turn psychology once again to the task of depicting humans' higher nature.

The aesthetic metaphysics of Emerson, Tillich, and Teilhard de Chardin, which guided Fromm's efforts to liberate psychoanalytic insights from Freud's stoic outlook, played an even greater role in the further extension of neo-Freudianism into the Transactional Analysis school of Eric Berne and Thomas Harris. Harris wrote of himself and Berne: "We are deeply indebted to Freud for his painstaking and pioneering efforts to establish the theoretical foundation upon which we build today."[87] Berne and Harris believe that the time has come for Freud's "theory that the warring factions [of human nature] existed in the unconscious" to be reexpressed so as to "reach people where they live."[88] Where their American readership lives, apparently, is in a world where individuals are far less determined by intrapsychic forces than Freud would have it. The translation of the id, ego, and superego into the Americanese of Child, Adult, and Parent simplified not merely the language of self-analysis, but the psyche itself. The ego, in becoming an "adult," acquired the ability freely to choose its own direction in life, unimpeded by either internal or external determinisms. The id, transformed into a "child," sprouted "a bright side ... creativity, curiosity, the desire to explore and know, the urge to touch and feel and experience."[89]

The Americanization of psychoanalytic language is nowhere more discernible than in Harris's bold proclamation that "we can change." Harris celebrates the optimistic consequences of his and Berne's revisions of psychoanalysis by showing how they support a philosophy of self-reliance. Interspersing his words with literally dozens of uplifting quotes from Emerson, Bergson, Tillich, Teilhard de Chardin, and process theologians of kindred spirit, Harris reminds us that "returning man to his rightful place of personhood is the theme of redemption, or reconciliation, or enlightenment, central to all of the great world religions."[90]

It is also the stated objective of Transactional Analysis. Harris understood that one implication of the philosophies of Bergson and Chardin is that the only barrier separating a power from an immanent spiritual power is an unnecessarily imposed psychological one. Transactional therapy restores individuals to psychological well-being even as it enables them to become vehicles through which an immanent spiritual force progressively manifests itself. In other words, Berne and Harris have altered psychoanalytic theory sufficiently to make "the rightful place of personhood" more a metaphysical or even religious condition than a psychological one.

This final transformation of neo-Freudianism into an optimistic philosophy of self-improvement reveals the most prominent recurring theme in the assimilation of Freud's theories into American psychological thought. The process of Americanization had—from Putnam to Fromm—been a movement away from Freud's own Enlightenment conceptions and toward the Romantic individualism of Emerson and James. Rejecting the monodimensional vision of humanity's relationship to nature characteristic of psychoanalytic theory, Freud's American interpreters displayed a remarkably consistent tendency to endow the psyche with a point of access to deeper orders of Being.

The neo-Freudian accommodations of psychoanalysis to American culture marked the end of what might be called the formative period in the shaping of a distinctively American interpretation of the unconscious. From the mesmerists to the functionalists to the Freudian revisionists, the unconscious has acted as a symbol of the fundamental harmony between the individual and an indwelling spiritual agency. It appears that many American psychologists have embraced the concept of the unconscious because of its symbolic and religious salience. This same religious salience was fated to evoke the professional wrath of those psychologists committed to establishing psychology along the lines of a "hard" natural science. And it has been their self-appointed task to attempt to extirpate the unconscious from academic psychology once and for all.

Six

Excising the Psyche: American Behaviorism

MANY academic psychologists were alarmed by the unscientific character of prevailing theories of the unconscious. The prestige of their discipline was at stake. In 1910 Joseph Jastrow of the University of Wisconsin published a book entitled *Fact and Fable in Psychology*. Jastrow believed that a great disservice had been done to psychology by the activities of a group of "men and women of philosophical inclinations, for whom an element of mysticism has its charm, and who are intellectually at unrest with the conceptions underlying modern science and modern life."[1] Unlike James, Jastrow was not prepared to countenance metaphysical speculation at the expense of established scientific method. A few years later he published another volume in continuation of his crusade to demystify the psychological term most subject to abuse by the general public—the subconscious.

> The word *subconscious* has a dubious sound. . . . The word, in
> company with others of analogous origin, *has been made the*
> *symbol* of an inner mystery . . . and capable, if only excursions
> could be followed, of overthrowing the limitations of sense
> and of discounting our most accredited psychological
> currency.[2]

Jastrow thought that the unconscious was merely a convenient term for those physiological activities of which we are not directly aware. He wanted to strip the unconscious of its metaphysical connotations so that his readers could differentiate between scientific and unscientific psychology. Psychology was having enough difficulty earning scientific recognition without being burdened with terminology that implicitly associated it with spiritualism, psychical research, or religious mysticism.

Turn-of-the-century psychologists were constantly under attack for their lack of methodological clarity and experimental rigor. Especially sensitive to criticism from their colleagues in the natural sciences, they became increasingly concerned with their scientific credentials.[3] Many turned their attention toward the one field of psychology that already emulated the more established sciences, the study of animal behavior. As Pavlov's study of conditioned and unconditioned reflexes demonstrated, animal psychology could provide this new discipline with a method for deriving precise experimental procedures.[4] The objective nature of animal psychology served to strengthen the growing connection between American experimental psychology and the positivistic philosophy derived from the British (Lockean) empirical tradition. The categories of positivistic analysis sharply altered the general tone of American psychological thought. The introspective techniques relied upon by the early functionalists could no longer be relied upon to deliver "objective" psychological knowledge. As a consequence, the functionalists' principal subject of study—private consciousness—was methodologically excluded from the province of scientific psychology.

Thus, by the second decade of this century the character of academic psychology had changed fundamentally. External observation and philosophical positivism had replaced the introspective examination and thinly veiled vitalism of the functionalists. This change in viewpoint drastically altered the relationship of psychology to Darwinian biology. Functionalists like James and Angell had given as much importance to the psychological implications of Darwin's theory of spontaneous or free variation as to those of his theory of environmental selection.[5] For them, mind or private consciousness is continuously supplying the acting individual with the psychological counterpart of genetic spontaneous variations; the creative activities of the mind thus play an originating role in shaping human behavior. Functionalist efforts to describe this supposed interaction between mind and body inevitably bogged down in fuzzy, subjectivist terminology. Hence, as increasing importance was placed upon the use of objectivist language in psychological description, American psychologists came to ignore the psychological analogues of free variation and, instead, focused their attention almost exclusively on environmental influences.

The acceptance of complete environmental determinism promised to help psychology take its place as an undisputed natural science. John Broadus Watson became the leading spokesman for this exciting new direction in psychological research when, in 1913, he published his epochal "Psychology as the Behaviorist Views It."[6] Watson contended that the principal error of psychology in the past was its misguided use of an imprecise method, introspection, to study a nonexistent entity, consciousness. The functionalists' methods had led psychology into the quagmire of metaphysics and mysticism. What was signified by the term *consciousness* was simply a disguised version of the theological idea of the soul and contributed nothing to a rigorously functional understanding of man's interaction with his environment. It seemed clear to Watson that

> the time seems to have come when psychology must discard all references to consciousness. . . . we advance the view that behaviorism is the only consistent and logical functionalism.[7]

The Empty Psyche

Watson's leadership in the behaviorist revolt was more symbolic than instigative. With his youthful appearance and bold manner, he infused added vigor into a movement that already had begun to dominate psychological journals. We have noted, for example, that the "Consciousness and the Unconscious" section of the *Psychological Bulletin* was troubled by the awkwardness and imprecision of both terms. By turning over the editorial responsibilities for this section to proponents of objectivist psychology, the journal helped to impugn the scientific credibility of these concepts as well. H. W. Chase and A. P. Weiss managed this column between 1912 and 1920; both used it as a forum for discrediting subjectivist language. As early as 1910 Chase asserted that the psychoanalysts' theories about the unconscious lacked scientific rigor.[8] Two years later he pronounced that "the conception of the subconscious has the same pragmatic justification as the ether of the physicist."[9]

Weiss was professionally committed to the excision from psychological literature of such words and phrases as *consciousness* and *the unconscious mind.* He contended that a behavioristic approach to psychology was called for because functionalism had failed to indicate the manner in which a conscious process could be regarded as controlling behavior.[10] Nor would it ever. Weiss argued that the term *consciousness* refers to physiological sensations which *follow* neuromuscular activity, and hence describes a result rather than a cause of behavior. Mentalistic terminology thus can have no justifiable standing in scientific psychology. The unconscious, one step further removed from objectivist language, belongs wholly to "the realm of poetry or mythology, not science."[11]

Dissatisfaction with mentalistic terminology spread into almost every area of psychological discourse. When, in 1923, K. S. Lashley published a lengthy article entitled "The Behaviorist Interpretation of Consciousness," he merely provided an epitaph for a concept that had already died out of the vocabulary of experimental psychologists. Lashley's objective was to demonstrate that each and every characteristic which had been assigned to consciousness (e.g. the property of awareness, the self-ordering of sensory impressions, the organizational unity of perceptions) could be more succinctly explained in terms of physical reflex mechanisms. In contrast to the pristine clarity of behaviorist terminology,

> the subjective systems . . . [give us] such self-contradictory expressions as co-conscious, foreconscious, subconscious, and unconscious mind. These are assumed to have all the attributes of consciousness except that of being known. They involve, as do the atomistic theories, the self-contradictory conception of unconscious consciousness. For this *the behaviorist may substitute* the conception of systems of varying degrees of complexity, from *the isolated reflex* to the activation of the entire mechanism.[12]

As Lashley's statement suggests, the neuro-muscular reflex had become the building block of behavioral analysis. The "reflex" gradually replaced the "instinct" in psychological description of human behavior. Because of the vitalism implicit in many functionalists' understanding of nature, instincts were often seen as the source of a kind of intuitive wisdom. This was particularly true in William McDougall's "hormic psychology." Throughout the second and third decades of this century, McDougall clung to his notion of the organism's hormic, or urging, tendencies against the growing behavioral tide in academic psychology. McDougall argued that instincts supply the individual with an innate drive toward the selection of appropriate, purposive behavior. As he wrote in his *An Introduction to Social Psychology,* "every instance of instinctive behavior involves a knowing of some thing or object, a feeling in regard to it, and a striving towards or away from that object."[13] Such vitalistic interpretations of instinct were fast becoming an intellectual scandal among experimental psychologists.[14] When, in 1924, McDougall and Watson met to debate the role of instinct theory in scientific psychology, the outcome was a foregone conclusion. For, even though McDougall undoubtedly "won" the debate on philosophical grounds, Watson's proposition that instincts ought to be redefined as "a series of concatenated reflexes" had already been ratified by the majority of academic psychologists.[15]

Watson's aversion to the kind of "inner man" terminology used by McDougall reflected his understanding of the limits of the scientific study of human behavior. The opening sentences of his early behaviorist manifesto clearly state his conviction that scientific psychology is solely concerned with observable and quantifiable phenomena: "Psychology as the behaviorist views it is a purely objective experimental branch of natural science. Its theoretical goal is the prediction and control of behavior."[16]

"Purely objective" methods boiled down to research techniques pioneered in animal psychology applied to the analysis of human behavior. As Watson put it, behaviorism "recognizes no dividing line between man and brute."[17] Here Watson clearly reveals that his psychology rejected not only the functionalists' introspective methods but the whole image of human nature which their subjectivist language struggled to defend. The functionalists insisted that human consciousness, especially insofar as it is rooted in some kind of biological or instinctual *élan vital,* enables individuals to engage in goal-seeking, meaning-oriented behavior. Watson contended that behavior could be more precisely explained in terms of environmental determinants. The older psychology of James, Angell et al. was in this view not a science so much as "a subtle religious philosophy."[18] Watson believed that functionalism's ascription of active properties to the brain was animistic and mystical. The term *consciousness,* he argued, was the stuff of monk's lore and had no more scientific merit than the mumbo jumbo of medicine men in primitive tribes:

> Behaviorism claims that "consciousness" is neither a
> definable nor a usable concept; that it is merely another word
> for the "soul" of more ancient times.[19]

Among the primary casualties of humankind's sudden loss of consciousness was the ability to think. Watson contended that thought is nothing more than the internalization of learned speech behavior. In his own words, "language habits ... when exercised implicitly behind the closed doors of the lips we call thinking."[20] Thus, "thought is in short nothing but talking to our-selves. The evidence for this view is admittedly largely theoreti-cal, but it is the one theory so far advanced which explains thought in terms of natural science."[21]

Once conscious thought had been reduced to implicit speech, the unconscious became an almost comical figment of the meta-physical imagination. Watson maintained that the only possible reference which the word *unconscious* might have is to behaviors learned without verbal correlates. The psychoanalysts' depiction of the unconscious as a repository of repressed childhood mem-ories, in this view, merely reflected their misapprehension of the fact that a great deal of behavioral conditioning takes place before the child is old enough to master language skills. "Thus infancy, where the process of 'repression' is supposed to bury so many unconscious treasures which come to light under the prestidigi-tation of the analyst, turns out to be a wholly natural kind of state."[22] Watson believed that neuroses, too, could be explained according to behaviorist principles—in this case, by the laws of approach and avoidance behavior. He confidently concluded that "the whole of Freud's 'unconscious' can be adequately accounted for along the lines I have indicated."[23]

The same methodological strategy that defined subjectivity out of existence made it possible for Watson to develop a science for the prediction and control of behavior. A radical environ-mentalism places the variables affecting human growth and development neatly before our eyes. In sharp contrast to the inef-fectual psychologies of the past, Watson was now in a position to boast:

Give me a dozen healthy infants, well-formed, and my own specified world to bring them up in and I'll guarantee to take any one at random and train him to become any type of specialist I might select—doctor, lawyer, artist, merchant-chief and, yes, even beggar-man and thief, regardless of his talents, penchants, tendencies, abilities, vocations, and race of his ancestors.[24]

By the 1960s B. F. Skinner had assumed Watson's role as the unrivaled champion of behaviorism's melioristic, even utopian, promise. And, while Skinner's interpretation of behaviorism differs from Watson's, it is no less relentless in its antimentalism:[25]

> A small part of the universe is contained within the skin of each of us. There is no reason why it should have any special physical status because it lies within this boundary, and eventually we should have a complete account of it from anatomy and physiology.[26]

According to Skinner, the language of subjectivity has, since Plato, borne almost no relationship to reality. The most conspicuous fictional entities "are the 'thought processes' called thinking and reasoning."[27] Skinner believes that language behaviors are the only thing separating human behavior from that of other species. This observation somewhat ironically led Skinner to say that behaviorism is almost exclusively a psychology of the unconscious.[28] Skinner maintains that consciousness is purely a social product and that "without the help of a verbal community all behavior would be unconscious."[29] The only difference between acts that are performed unconsciously and those which are executed consciously is the mediation of language. In either case the individual's behavior is completely shaped by environmental determinisms and there is consequently no need to postulate the existence of an inner self. "What behaviorism rejects is the unconscious as an agent, and of course it rejects the conscious mind as an agent, too."[30]

Skinner assumed an even more prophetic stance than Watson in envisioning the benefits of behavioral psychology. Watson had expanded upon his "Give me a dozen infants" motif in numerous popular works on child-rearing practices, but Skinner in his nonscientific writings launched an ambitious assault on anachronistic mentalisms of every stripe. Both his utopian novel, *Walden Two,* and his much-celebrated treatise *Beyond Freedom and Dignity* castigate his contemporaries for their belief in some hypothetical inner self. Skinner writes that for too long we have assumed that the locus of control and self-determination lies within the individual. We have thus ignored the environmental conditions that in fact totally and inexorably shape our behavior. The consequences have been disastrous. Our society has grown without thought for the necessity of systems of rewards and punishments designed to bring fully under control the otherwise anarchic behavior of its citizens. Crime, pollution, industrial inefficiency, and war are but a few of the unfortunate and unnecessary consequences of our persistent belief in the existence of an autonomous, inner man. Because philosophy and theology have conspired to perpetuate this fiction, their attempts to influence human behavior have been necessarily futile. It has finally come time to replace them with a scientifically based technology of behavior control. Then, and only then, will it be possible to build a truly humanistic culture in which the behavior of the individual can be shaped to the benefit of the general welfare of the wider community. Skinner is thus arguing that behaviorism "does not dehumanize man, it de-homunculizes him. . . . Only by dispossessing him can we turn to the real causes of human behavior. Only then can we turn from the inferred to the observed, from the miraculous to the natural, from the inaccessible to the manipulable."[31]

Behaviorism and the Search for Order

The shift occurring within academic psychology mirrored a pervasive cultural trend. Behaviorism was in many respects a reflection of the Progressivist movement then popular in American social and political thought.[32] It gave psychological expression to the Progressivists' belief that human nature is malleable and can be steadily improved through scientifically conceived programs of management and control. What Watson and others stressed most about behaviorism was its social usefulness. Theirs was a concrete program for the establishment of order and control in a society whose major institutions were no longer keeping

pace with rapid cultural change. Behaviorism was in fact as much
a crusade as it was a science; and foremost among the outmoded
institutions it sought to displace was religion.

The staunch antimentalism of behavioral psychology reflects
the temper of a generation eager to dispose of increasingly dys-
functional religious tradition. For example, Weiss's argument
that "consciousness" is incapable of exerting any real influence
upon our behavior was at least partially motivated by his understanding of how psychology must serve practical uses.

> If, as the functionalists assume, consciousness can modify
> behavior, then to bring about socially acceptable behavior . . .
> *the problem* then becomes *one of teaching "ideals."* . . . The
> behaviorist maintains that it is better to disregard the concept
> of consciousness altogether and the pedagogical *problem then
> becomes* one of determining exactly *how socially acceptable
> behavior is developed* directly from the properties of the
> neuro-muscular system.[33]

Academic psychologists were apparently finding it difficult to
define exactly "what should be" and turned instead to the less
ambitious task of identifying what can and cannot be controlled.

The connection between behaviorism and the breakdown of
an older, theological world view is particularly evident in the
development of Watson's thought. David Bakan has convinc-
ingly demonstrated a link between Watson's personal transition
from rural to urban life and his growing commitment to the tenets of behavioral psychology.[34] Born in rural South Carolina,
Watson was raised in the pietistic milieu of Christian fundamen-
talism. Watson's mother encouraged him from an early age to
pursue the ministry and had indeed named him after the most
prominent revivalist preacher in the area, John Albert Broadus.
For whatever reason, Watson resisted conformity to this strict,
moralistic environment. In his autobiographical reflections he
recounts that "I was lazy, somewhat insubordinate and, so far as
I know, never made above a passing grade."[35] Opting for a path
of overt rebellion against the rigid moralistic ethos of his com-

munity, Watson became increasingly delinquent and was arrested twice on charges of "nigger fighting" and firearms violations.

After a lackluster college career, Watson enrolled in graduate school at the University of Chicago. Watson went to Chicago to study psychology, specifically the pragmatic functionalism of John Dewey. He quickly lost interest, however, and later would say that "he never knew what [Dewey] was talking about."[36] Conversely, the research on animal reflexes being conducted by the biologist Jacques Loeb struck Watson as a more useful approach to the study of behavior. He decided that laboratory experiments with animals were far more rewarding than the introspective exercises required of students of functional psychology. Watson later wrote, "At Chicago, I first began a tentative formulation of my late point of view. . . . I hated to serve as a subject [in introspective exercises]. I didn't like the stuffy, artificial instructions given to subjects. I always was uncomfortable and acted unnaturally. With animals I was at home."[37]

To Watson, introspection was a fruitless "grieving over one's past sins."[38] Focused attention on one's state of mind inevitably gives rise to feelings of guilt and anxiety. Watson seems to have been especially sensitive to the way in which scrupulosity impedes confident and spontaneous action. In an impersonal and alienated modern society, inwardness not only feels uncomfortable and unnatural, but can produce indecision. The trauma of his religious upbringing had, it would seem, predisposed Watson to a view of human nature which bypasses such counterproductive considerations.

Behaviorism offered Watson a strategy with which to confront and ward off the problems he associated with subjectivity. It made possible what Bakan describes as "a kind of ruthless suppression of affective responses."[39] Moreover, the deliberate impersonality of behavioral analysis enhanced Watson's ability to control and manipulate others. By denying other persons' claims to "depth," we can escape the guilt which might otherwise deter us from such intentionally manipulative behavior.

In the preface to one edition of *Psychology From the Standpoint of a Behaviorist,* Watson noted that behaviorism meets the dominant need of modern man, the need to master an increasingly complex social environment:

> Civilized nations are rapidly becoming city dwellers, with this increase in the concentration of homes there come changes in our habits and customs. Life becomes complex, the strain of adjusting ourselves to others increases daily. . . . Fortunately, psychology is prepared to help us. The past ten years have seen the development of new points of view in psychology— points of view that have grown up partly to meet our ever changing social needs and partly because the very existence of these needs has made a new viewpoint necessary.[40]

The popularity of this "new viewpoint" was, as Robert S. Woodworth noted long ago, chiefly due to its "unlimited faith in the ability of science to take charge of human affairs."[41] So utopian had Watson and others become that they were, in effect, proselytizing for "a religion to take the place of religion."[42] Watson, of course, believed that by embracing the Darwinian belief that humanity is completely under the dominion of the laws of nature he had repudiated of the Wesleyan piety that permeated the fundamentalist culture in which he had been reared. Yet, at a deeper level, Watson had confirmed one of its basic tenets: the absence of any innate worth in human nature and the consequent need for methodical programs of self-discipline.[43] Again like Wesleyan asceticism, it was "the simplicity and severity" of behaviorism that recommended it to Watson as a guide to the control of human behavior. Unlike the fanciful world of introspective psychologies, behaviorism offered a method by which Americans might "manipulate, hold up, examine and change" their world.[44]

Watson had, in effect, simply transmuted the traits of what had traditionally been viewed as the "higher" spiritual life into their "lower" physical correlates.[45] He thus laid the foundations of an ascetic program of his own aimed at what Edna Heidebreder described as "the secular salvation of the race."[46] The vision Watson sets before us in *Behaviorism* rivals the biblical book of Revelation in its eschatological outlook.

> I wish I could picture for you what a rich and wonderful individual we should make of every healthy child if only we could let it shape itself properly and then provide for it a universe in which it could exercise that organization—a universe unshackled by legendary folk-lore of happenings thousands of years ago; unhampered by disgraceful political history; free of foolish customs and conventions which have no significance in themselves, yet which hem the individual in like taut steel bands. . . . The universe will change if you bring up your children, not in the freedom of the libertine, but in behavioristic freedom. . . . Will not these children in turn, with their better ways of living and thinking, replace us as society and in turn bring up their children in a still more scientific way, until the world finally becomes a place fit for human habitation?[47]

Watson's rejection of pietism and moralism in favor of a radically positivistic view of human nature was an understandable response to the decline of rural, revivalist Protestant culture. As Peter Homans points out, "In commending what is, in theological language, a 'kenotic' evacuation of the psyche in favor of the behavioral field, Watson sought a methodological solution to the psychic problem that religious piety seeks to resolve through the experience of conversion. In this sense, behaviorism may be seen as a methodological flight from the superego."[48] Watson's behavioral psychology eliminated the major obstacle with which he and millions of other Americans had had to contend in their attempt to take control of their lives—subjectivity. By defining our psychic depths out of existence, Watson freed us to set about rearranging our lives unshackled by a punitive religious conscience.

Behaviorism's repudiation of the unconscious as a normative source of human conduct seems to have been intimately connected with a widespread dissatisfaction with a particular type of religious thinking. As B. F. Skinner has confessed, "My position as a behaviorist came from . . . [my attempt] to resolve my early fear of theological ghosts. Perhaps I have answered my mother's question, 'What will people think?' by proving that they do not think at all."[49]

In their eagerness to exorcise their personal theological ghosts and through excision of the psyche, the behaviorists lost sight of the possibility that religious consciousness might not be exhaustively defined by the haunting guilt born of ascetic Protestantism.[50] Dismissed as irrelevant was the aesthetic spirituality that had enabled Americans, since Emerson, to believe that the self is inwardly connected to a power capable of healing the conflicted personality.[51] It is ironic that behaviorism's methodological exclusion of subjectivity fated it to assume the cultural role formerly held by ascetic Protestantism and its cultural counterpart, the work ethic. Having rescued modern individuals from an oppressively restrictive conscience, behaviorism equipped them for nothing more than the relentless pursuit of efficiency and self-control for their own sake.

The Dilemmas of Determinism

Behaviorism touted itself as the very epitome of efficiency and methodical control. George Santayana quipped that it "is evident that what recommends this science especially is its use in organizing work and in getting as much work as possible out of everybody."[52] In a behavioral utopia we could decide how many workers are needed, how many singers, and so on, and then churn them out at a predictable rate. Santayana mused that for a behaviorist, the millennium would consist of a society in which there was "no such thing as fatigue, only efficiency temporarily reduced, and easily restored after short intervals of organized rest."[53]

The secular successor to Puritan asceticism, behaviorism pursued the goal of personal efficiency with a vengeance. Its programmatic vision of human conduct neatly captured almost every characteristic that Max Weber discerned in ascetic Protestant culture: uniformity, regularity, the eschewing of mystery, distrust of the intrapersonal realm, the repression of sociality and spontaneity. And, as Daniel Shea points out, the historical lineage of B. F. Skinner's deterministic philosophy can be traced all the way back to early American Puritanism:

> But viewed as a product of the American culture, B. F.
> Skinner emerges as the continuator of a very special strain in
> it. That strain cannot be called Puritanism as such, because
> the historical phenomenon of Puritanism was itself diverse
> and contained extremes difficult to reconcile. There is nothing
> in Skinner, for instance, of the antinomian thrust of much
> Puritan piety, which Edwards carried forward with qualified
> enthusiasm and which reappears in the transcendentalism of
> Emerson and Thoreau. . . . Skinner's Puritanism is moralistic,
> deterministic, and pragmatic.[54]

The methodology of behaviorism effectively excluded the aesthetic strain in American religious thought. The result was a dramatic exaggeration of American Protestantism's inherent urge to master the environment.[55] Absent is any recognition of the need, or even ability, of individuals to become receptive to a supersensible reality. Behaviorism consequently makes religious discourse highly problematic. Although behavioral psychology, qua psychology, is not necessarily atheistic, it does insist that it is superstitious to believe that there are immaterial forces influencing human behavior. Thus, in the behavioral version of the work ethic divine influence is not only superfluous, but psychologically impossible.

Behaviorism's highly secularized and reductionistic explanation of human motivation has been the subject of a steady stream of critical essays. One continuing strand of this polemic concerns itself with the logical dilemma faced by behavioral psychologists when they try to persuade others to accept their theory. From Arthur O. Lovejoy's "The Paradox of the Thinking Behaviorist" to Noam Chomsky's critique of Skinner in his *For Rea-*

sons of State, behaviorism has been attacked as philosophically indefensible.[56] Behaviorists' efforts to convince others of the correctness of their position seem quixotic if their own determinist views are justified. Santayana argued that behaviorism is predicated upon a spurious idealism and fails to acknowledge its own presupposition of "an antecedent wakefulness or lucidity on our part. . . . We must be minds, if we can come to the conclusion that we are only habits in matter."[57]

As early as 1913, in an address delivered at a meeting of the American Psychological Association, James Angell lamented that the "term 'consciousness' appears to be the next victim marked for slaughter [after the 'soul'] and as one of the claimants for its fading honors we meet the term 'behavior.' "[58] Angell knew only too well why experimental psychologists were dispensing with mentalistic terminology. The functionalists had not, as yet, adequately explained how mental processes are converted into physical acts. The functionalists' belief that consciousness could exert an original influence upon material processes had opened a "Pandora's box of intellectual plagues whose ravages one is powerless to stay."[59] Yet Angell maintained that psychology could not secure its scientific status simply by defining its conceptual problems out of existence. "We must be cautious therefore that in seeking for bettered means of knowing human nature in its entirety we do not in effect commit the crowning absurdity of seeming to deny any practical significance to that which is its chief distinction—the presence of something corresponding to the term mind—the one thing of which the fool may be as sure as the wise man."[60]

It is worth noting that Angell did not ground his antibehaviorist sentiments upon empirical data ignored by objectivist psychologists. Instead, he appealed to the cultural vision that he and others had hoped psychology would uphold: "What becomes, in such a program, of psychology as the science of self? What becomes of the entire system of moral and spiritual values and experiences?"[61] The early functionalists had lived in the hope that psychology would yield empirical evidence on which to base a distinct metaphysical outlook. With their theories of human-kind's psychic depth, they tried to forestall the further erosion of the principles historically central to American identity. James, Hall, and Baldwin saw the "farther reaches" of human consciousness as the locus of humanity's inner connection with a wider, spiritual universe. They preserved the vision of a multidimensional reality in which the individual has access to motivational energies that make it possible to transcend social, historical, and even psychological determinisms.

Behaviorism, by denying the scientific validity of the concepts of consciousness and the unconscious, bequeathed to psychology what Karl Mannheim has called a "trained incapacity" to help men and women find a meaningful orientation to life. According to Mannheim, the mechanistic assumptions of behavioral psychology have

> contributed very much to the general insecurity of modern man. The acting man must know who he is, and the ontology of psychic life fulfills a certain function in action. To the extent that mechanistic psychology and its parallel in actual life, the social impulsion towards all-embracing mechanization, negated these ontological values, they destroyed an important element in the self-orientation of human beings in their everyday life.[62]

Mannheim, founder of the discipline of the sociology of knowledge, pointed out the consequences of the mechanistic assumptions of modern psychology for society and culture. He believed that the most important function of thought is to provide guidance for the acting individual. By eliminating the mind or psyche, behaviorism rendered psychology irrelevant to persons concerned with finding answers to such fundamental questions as, What is right or wrong? and, What is the meaning of life? No matter how valuable behavioristic theory may be in conducting psychological research, it thus inevitably fails "when it is placed in the total context of life experience because it says nothing concerning the meaningful goal of conduct, and is therefore unable to interpret the elements of conduct with reference to it."[63]

> A psychology without a psyche cannot take the place of an ontology. Such a psychology was itself the outcome of the fact that men were attempting to think in the framework of categories which strove to negate every evaluation, every trace of common meaning, or of total configuration. What may be valuable for a specialized discipline as a research hypothesis may, however, be fatal for the conduct of human beings.[64]

Behaviorism had left the individual in an inherently meaningless universe, for, unless it is grounded in some intrinsically purposeful reality, the psychological apparatus is abandoned to innumerable, and equally arbitrary, external determinisms.

Advocates of behaviorism contend that the problems of modern society can all be traced to the spurious conviction that humanity is somehow free and capable of self-determination. We fail to take cognizance of, or control over, the real environmental influences that shape human behavior. The only solution to our many social problems is to banish all talk about the "inner man" and set about constructing institutions that will so distribute positive and negative reinforcements as to bring all behavior under the control of a rationally planned environment. Here, however, we bump into another facet of the dilemma of psychic determinism. The behaviorist theory of human nature seems to rule out the possibility that we can liberate ourselves from past conditioning to do anything new or different.[65] If the behaviorist maintains his deterministic point of view, he logically can neither approve nor deplore any course of conduct whatsoever. And the dilemma gets worse. The behaviorist cannot tell us why we should want to improve the world, particularly if it would require even the slightest self-sacrifice. The "empty organism" view of human nature implies that it is psychologically impossible for us to experience ourselves as immediately and integrally linked with others. The behaviorist model of human nature is, in short, antithetical to the fostering of moral conduct.

Skinner has time and again resisted the suggestion that behaviorism is inconsistent with ethical philosophy.[66] As a natural scientist, he believes it is perfectly permissible for him to identify the survival of humankind as an ultimate value. However, the dilemma created by behaviorism's "metapsychology" when the attempt is made to postulate an "ultimate" anything is apparent when he adds:

> Do not ask me why I want mankind to survive. I can tell you why only in the sense in which the physiologist can tell you why I want to breathe. Once the relation between a given step and the survival of my group has been pointed out, I will take that step. And it is the business of science to point out just such relations.[67]

Skinner's faith that individuals will always and automatically sacrifice self-interest for the good of either society or the future is precisely that, faith. Moreover, it is not nearly so consistent with the Darwinian natural science tradition as he implies. Skinner's contention that individual behavior is determined by its consequences is certainly the psychological counterpart to Darwin's theory of natural selection. But Darwin's theory ultimately rests upon the spontaneous occurrence of "free variations" by which the organism generates novel variations within its own structure. Behaviorism, because of its methodological exclusion of "inner" processes, can offer no counterpart to this vital component in the creation of adaptive behavior. And thus, as Mannheim observed, no matter how valid behavioral psychology may be as a research stratagem, it is inherently incapable of serving as a vehicle of cultural meaning.

It was William James who first recognized and sought to redress the dilemmas of deterministic psychology. James said that it was an egregious error to represent Darwinian theory as consonant with a view of the mind as a passive, reflexive mechanism. On the contrary, James believed that psychology must also consider the ways in which the individual's inner life continuously brings novel contributions or "free variations" to its experience of the environment. At the core of mental life is a rich supply of instincts, needs, and interests that give the individual the ability to search out and even create an environment conducive to personal fulfillment. And thus, although James agreed with behaviorists in advocating "the strenuous life" of discipline and control, he insisted that such a life was conditional upon our possession of passional, even vitalistic, inner resources.

As we saw in Chapter 4, James believed that an ethical commitment to the ultimate survival of humankind such as Skinner professes is possible only insofar as we first become receptive to the energies and promptings of our unconscious selves. And, importantly for purposes, it was his psychology of the subliminal self that enabled him to elude the dilemmas of deterministic psychology. The unconscious gave James an explanation of the mechanism by which environment-transcending energies flow into, and become an original force in, our motivational system. It also provided the psychological mechanism through which individuals might come to experience themselves as participants in a transpersonal reality. James believed that without such intimate relations with a wider psychic reality it is impossible for most individuals willingly to sacrifice their personal gratification in favor of the moral claims of others. William Barrett has observed that it is precisely this reluctance to exclude the dimension of psychic depth in the name of scientific method that makes James so relevant to the modern reader:

> James was in his own way a kind of forerunner of
> behaviorism: He championed the extension of the methods of
> the laboratory to psychology, and he always insisted on the
> essentially behavioral nature of consciousness. But throughout
> his varied scientific interests, James never—and this is the
> point to be stressed—never lost sight of the fact of the human
> person, in all its complexity and concreteness, as the ultimate
> subject and center of psychological research. The difference
> between James and Skinner, then, seen in its proper context,
> is a sign of how far our culture, or one very influential

segment of it, has moved toward the reduction of human personality.[68]

With its denial of psychic depth, behaviorism severed the cord that had linked academic psychology to the American aesthetic appreciation of nature's spiritual depths. Commenting upon the one-sidedness of Skinner's appropriation of Puritanism, Daniel Shea reminds us that "for either Edwards or Thoreau, the boundary one crossed in prosecuting an inward exploration divided the world of fact from the world of value, the world of limitation from the vast territory within, the world of appearances from the world of ultimate reality."[69] Insofar as behaviorism has succeeded in replacing this metaphysical vision of the inner self with an empty, reflexive organism, it has stripped American culture of one of its most powerful traditional symbols of our participation in a larger, spiritual universe.

Seven

Rediscovering the Unconscious: Humanistic Psychology

IN the early 1960s, Abraham Maslow announced the emergence of a new orientation in American psychology:

> The two comprehensive theories of human nature most influencing psychology until recently have been the Freudian and the experimentalistic-positivistic-behavioristic. All other theories were less comprehensive and their adherents formed many splinter groups. In the last few years, however, these various groups have rapidly been coalescing into a third, increasingly comprehensive theory of human nature, into what might be called a "Third Force."[1]

For the purpose of accelerating the coalescence of these "various groups," Maslow joined forces with Anthony Sutich to establish the *Journal of Humanistic Psychology*. Sutich drafted a statement of purpose for the journal in which he described this third-force psychology as "primarily an orientation toward the whole of psychology rather than a distinct area or school . . . [and which] finds expression in the writings of such persons as Allport, Angyal, Asch, Buhler, Fromm, Goldstein, Horney, Maslow, Moustakas, Rogers, Wertheimer, and in certain of the writings of Jung, Adler, and the psychoanalytic ego-psychologists, and existential and phenomenological psychologists."[2] Improbably eclectic as this list appears, it accurately represents the historical and ideological lineage of humanistic psychology.

Jung had little discernible impact upon American psychology in the early part of this century. His association with Freud as well as the esoteric nature of his writings caused American psychologists to suppose that his work did not deserve serious scientific attention.[3] By the late 1950s and early 1960s, however, many theorists began to recognize Jung as an important ally in their fight against psychological reductionism.[4] Jung's distinction between the personal and the collective unconscious seemingly avoided the pitfalls of either a psychoanalytic or a behavioral interpretation of human nature; it credited individuals with a dynamic inner life but made the personal unconscious subordinate to the collective unconscious which connects the individual to a transpersonal sphere of symbolic meanings and creative forces.

Other Freudian revisionists, notably Adler, Horney, and Fromm, were also important to the new American humanistic psychology. These three had jettisoned Freud's rigid determinism and his commitment to the principle of homeostasis. And, importantly, they maintained that there is in the psyche an innate drive toward the fulfillment of individual potentials.

The phenomenological and existential psychology referred to by Sutich represented broad attitudinal dispositions of many American psychologists rather than distinct schools of thought. Both viewpoints were initially developed by European philosophers (e.g., Husserl, Kierkegaard, Heidegger, and Sartre) and then expanded by psychological theorists such as Medard Boss, David Katz, Karl Buhler, and Ludwig Binswanger.[5] In general, American psychologists associated the word *phenomenology* with the concern to represent an individual's experience with as little distortion as possible. The word *phenomenology* was thus often used as a rallying cry in the antibehaviorist and antipsychoanalytic camps. Both behaviorism and psychoanalysis were accused of superimposing predetermined theories upon, and therefore distorting, the experience of human beings. The implication was that a properly phenomenological psychology would reveal human behavior as irreducible to either environmental or instinctual determinisms.

The term *existentialism* was also associated with commitment to understanding the individual's subjective experience of the world. In this usage, phenomenology and existentialism were virtually synonymous. Each entailed the repudiation of psychological models that excluded the "lived" quality of human experience. And, furthermore, each tended to be used less to define humanistic psychology than to elicit partisan commitment. Carl Rogers proselytized for the humantistic school of thought by characterizing behaviorism and psychoanalysis as "impersonal," "logical-positivistic," and "instinctual." The third force, by contrast, was associated with "terms such as phenomenological, existential, self-theory, self-actualization, health-and-growth psychology, being and becoming, science of inner experience."[6] Rogers apparently thought that such terms denoted a psychology that manifestly sought to realize humanity's highest potentials.

The approach to psychological science now being labeled as phenomenological and existential is, of course, virtually the same as that taken by William James, G. Stanley Hall, and other early functionalists.[7] Humanistic psychology to a large extent represents the resurgence of the indigenous American functionalist orientation. Its major goals have been to refocus attention on the individual's internal frame of reference, to rid psychological theory of reified abstractions, and to use psychology to describe—and enhance—the individual's capacity for meaningful acts of self-determination. As Rollo May explained, the third force in American psychology has made it possible to "unite science and ontology" and to recapture "the American genius for combining thought and action (as shown so beautifully in William James)."[8]

The theoretical construct that has had the greatest influence on humanistic psychologists is a biologically grounded concept of organismic growth based upon Kurt Goldstein's studies of brain-damaged soldiers. Goldstein's studies support the view that an organism, unless impaired by illness or injury, seeks "to actualize itself in further activities, according to its nature."[9] Goldstein believed that his research invalidated Freud's tension-reduction model of human motivation. The individual, he countered, is motivated "toward activity and progress." Goldstein explained that the fundamental drive of human existence is to achieve the realization of all of his or her innate potentials. Goldstein's concept of self-actualization fit perfectly into humanistic psychologists' larger agenda. It supplied them with the nonreductive theory of psychological causation they needed to account for the individual's inherent orientation toward growth. As the *Journal for Humanistic Psychology* explains, the third force in American psychology is defined by its concern with the study of "human capacities and potentials that have no systematic place either in positivistic or behavioristic theory or in classical psychoanalytic theory, e.g., creativity, love, self, growth, organism, basic need-gratification, self-actualization, higher values, ego-transcendence."[10]

Humanistic psychology thus differs both from psychoanalysis and from behaviorism in its interpretation of what constitutes a psychological "cause." Freud, Watson, and Skinner all insisted that psychological science was defined by its ability to specify the material (i.e., neurophysiological) and efficient (i.e., environmental) causes of behavior. Humanistic psychology, however, postulates what might be called a "final cause" explanation of behavior—the organism's inherent tendency toward self-actualization. This is really an explanation of ultimate purpose rather than of immediate cause and so fails to conform to the criteria of positivistic science. It serves, however, to redefine the very nature of psychological science in such a way as to make it compatible with an ontology or world view that acknowledges the reality of nonphysical entities and forces.[11] It is important to note that humanistic psychologists disagree among themselves about the precise nature of the "final cause" of human behavior. Albert Ellis and Gordon Allport, for example, carefully restrict their theories to the explanation of the individual's capacity for gaining rational control over environmental determinisms and instinctual drives.

Most humanistic psychologists, however, have given their theories of self-actualization ontological rather than purely psychological significance—that is, they refer to the structures governing the life process itself rather than properties distinct to an individual mind. This is especially true of Rollo May, Abraham Maslow, and Carl Rogers, who describe the individual's preconscious participation in an order of creativity and expressiveness intrinsic to the universe. Their version of the ontology, or even metaphysics, of self-actualization testifies to a remarkable continuity in American psychologists' conception of the unconscious core of personality. At the deepest level of human nature, they maintain, is a "higher" psychological force that gives to the individual an innate potential both for self-enhancement (i.e., successful adaptation to the physical and social environments) and self-transcendence (i.e., adaptation to some supranatural environment). Thus, for many humanistic psychologists, just as it was for American psychological thought "from Edwards to Emerson to James," the unconscious is the aesthetic medium through which the individual can align himself with an immanent life force.

Reclaiming the Unconscious

The expressed purpose of humanistic psychology is to counter the reductionism of both behaviorism and psychoanalysis. It is, consequently, difficult for humanistic psychologists overtly to embrace the idea of a separate compartment of the mind known as "the unconscious." Such an entity would, almost by definition, lack those qualities which are distinctively human: deliberation, sustained attention, goal-setting, and conscious valuation of experience. Yet humanistic psychology can add precious little to behavioral or psychoanalytic perspectives on human potential unless it can specify ways in which the mind engages reality at a deeper or more fundamental level than ego rationality.[12]

Humanistic psychologists are thus in a quandary very similar to that faced by the early functionalists. They, too, want to invest preconscious psychic functions with normative psychological significance while avoiding any suggestion that these functions are in any way subhuman or primitive. Rollo May was among the first explicitly to recognize the fact that an adequate doctrine of the unconscious is essential to any psychological account of humanity's higher potentials:

> The existential analysts are correct, in my judgement, in their criticisms of the doctrine of the unconscious as a convenient blank check on which any causal explanation can be written or as a reservoir from which any deterministic theory can be drawn. *But this is the "cellar" view of the unconscious* and objections to it should not be permitted to cancel out the great contribution that the historical meaning that the unconscious had in Freud's terms. . . . I would propose, rather, to agree that being is at some point indivisible, that unconsciousness is part of any given being, that the cellar theory of the unconscious is logically wrong and practically unconstructive; but that the meaning of the discovery, namely the *radical enlargement of being,* is one of the great contributions of the day and must be retained.[13]

This distinction between a lower and higher interpretation of the unconscious enabled May to speak of the individual's point of contact with a higher spiritual reality. His point was that such phenomena as self-actualization and self-transcendence were not simply psychological faculties but, more importantly, testified to a distinct ontological or metaphysical conception of reality. Thanks to the "radical enlargement" of our psychological being, that is, the discovery of the unconscious, we can avail ourselves of "far-reaching possibilities for freedom in self-development, freedom in directing our minds, and freedom in enjoying the ecstatic possibilities of intellectual exploration."[14] The unconscious, while itself a part of our psychological nature, is also the point at which we have access to and participate in a nondetermined order of being. It was for this reason that May deemed it appropriate to describe the unconscious with terminology borrowed from Eastern mystical philosophies. Personal fulfillment comes from within rather than without. We must therefore develop a life-style that will facilitate openness to this inner reality. Sounding much like James and his "The Gospel of Relaxation," May advises, "One cannot avail oneself of the richness of preconsciousness or unconsciousness unless one can let oneself periodically relax, be relieved of tension. It is then that the person lets silences speak."[15]

Walter Weisskopf, a member of the editorial board of the *Journal of Humanistic Psychology,* presented one of the most lucid discussions of the role played by the concept of the unconscious in carrying forward the larger scientific and cultural missions of the third force.[16] Weisskopf attributed the spiritual crisis of modern Western culture to the fact that urbanization and industrialization had combined to repress certain dimensions of human experience. Much of what belonged to the inner life had gradually succumbed to the materialistic attitudes spawned by our technological era. To his credit, Freud helped to reclaim much of our lost inner world through his discovery of the unconscious. Unfortunately, however, psychoanalysis permits only a partial liberation of the repressed dimensions of human nature. Psychoanalysis restricts its concept of the unconscious to the activity of those physiological drives which humans share with lower species. As a consequence only the animalistic aspects of human nature are considered to be essential, real, or authentic. Everything that distinguishes humans from the rest of creation is reduced to and derived from the animalistic and in Weisskopf's view is thereby devalued. And thus Weisskopf believes that instead of fully liberating modern individuals, psychoanalysis has contributed to our alienation.[17]

Weisskopf believed that psychology needed to reconceptualize the unconscious in such a way as to restore humans' "higher" nature. The unconscious, he explained, is the "source and ground of experience."[18] It represents the state of dreaming innocence that exists before the development of a distinct sense of individuality. It is a level of experience in which the individual and his or her world are fused into a single ontological reality. Weisskopf maintained that the spiritual crisis of Western culture is the direct consequence of our having lost touch with this deeper psychic level. Our emphasis upon utilitarian reason has led to the repression of intuitive modes of thought and, consequently, of our ability to recognize our essential unity with the whole of creation. As a result we feel isolated, alienated, and bereft of spontaneity.

The primary mission of humanistic psychology should be to respiritualize Western culture by teaching the value of inner receptivity to our unconscious depths. Weisskopf thought that we need to learn to develop completely different life-styles so that we can remain continuously in touch with our ontic source. We must learn that deep within ourselves resides the source "of everything normative, of everything higher, of the good; it is the inner judge, the conscience, and the ideal, the inner voice which drives us toward the higher things."[19]

Weisskopf made it clear that his interest in the unconscious was not motivated by the desire to derive self-help formulas for success in the secular world. He believed that the intellectual and cultural integrity of scientific psychology depended on the rediscovery of the "higher" unconscious. A psychology that fails to acknowledge the unconscious source of our higher mental capacities "knows only *causae efficentes,* not *causae finales,* only causes and not ends and goals."[20] Such a psychology is inherently incapable of giving meaning to our existence. If psychology is to become a culturally relevant force, it must be committed to "the rediscovery of a lost reality, a reality which has been thought and talked about so far in religious, theological, and metaphysical categories."[21]

> At stake is, indeed, the re-conquest of the meaning of our existence, which has become meaningless. At stake is the reconstruction of an objectively meaningful world in which everything, including the transcendental dimensions of human existence, finds a meaningful place. The old religious concepts

have to be modernized by existential psychology and philosophy and their meaning lighted by encompassing reason.[22]

The Farther Reaches of Human Nature

The restoration of freedom and dignity to human behavior was no simple task. It required that humanistic psychologists develop a theory of human nature that adequately accounts for the individual's ability to act in free and undetermined ways. Abraham Maslow's contributions to this effort have made him one of the premier spokesmen for the third force. It was Maslow's conviction that there is a "biologically based and instinctoid" core to the human personality which continuously orients the individual in the direction of growth, integration, and synergistic functioning.[23] Because of its essentially biological or organismic character, "much of this inner, deeper nature is . . . unconscious."[24] Each individual possesses an inner source of spontaneity, initiative, and valuation. The unconscious and organismic nature of this inner core of selfhood protects it from the impact of environmental conditioning. Maslow believes that the most fundamental psychological drive is neither the pleasure principle of Freud nor the operant conditioning of Skinner; it is the innate tendency of the organism to seek self-actualization, which he describes as the "ongoing actualization of potentials, capacities, talents, as fulfillment of mission (or call, fate, destiny, or vocation)."[25]

Maslow's studies of individuals who exhibited a great deal of self-actualizing behavior led him to assert that "man has a higher and transcendent nature, and this is part of his essence."[26]

> We have seen that there is not an absolute chasm between man and the reality which is beyond him. He can identify with this reality, incorporate it into his own definition of his self, be loyal to it as to his self. He then becomes part of it and it becomes part of him. *He and it overlap.*[27]

The existence of this point of overlap, which Maslow calls "the farther reaches of human nature," made it possible to speak of a psychology of transcendence. Maslow's studies revealed that when humans are most free from environmental restraints, their whole way of viewing the world tends to undergo dramatic changes. It seems that when adults have almost entirely satisfied their basic physiological and social needs, they spontaneously begin to have what Maslow called "peak experiences." These experiences are especially intense moments in which an individual is enveloped by the sensations of ecstasy, wonder, and awe. Peak experiences take the individual beyond his or her accustomed way of viewing life and impart a vivid perception "of the whole cosmos or at least the unity and integration of it and of everything in it, including his Self."[28]

Likening the peak experience to the aesthetic spirituality of William James, Ralph Waldo Emerson, Walt Whitman, and the Zen philosopher D. T. Suzuki, Maslow describes it as an intrinsically religious state of consciousness. Peak experiences awaken individuals to life's intrinsic meanings and give rise to the conviction that the sacred is somehow present in the here and now of everyday life. They are the source of the life-altering insight that "religion's Heaven is actually available in principle all through life. It is available to us now, and is all around us."[29] Taking a position similar to that espoused by James Mark Baldwin some sixty years earlier, Maslow maintained that the final stage in psychological development is the attainment of states of consciousness in which we can "see the universal in and through the particular and the eternal in and through the temporal and momentary."[30]

His study of self-actualization led Maslow to the conclusion that individual consciousness, at its farther reaches, has access to a higher realm and can become receptive to its creative powers. He believed that humanistic psychology was pioneering new areas of research which would provide a common ground between science and religion. Maslow reasoned that "if, as actually happened on one platform, Paul Tillich defined religion as 'concern with ultimate concerns' and I then defined humanistic psychology in the same way, then what is the difference between a supranaturalist and a humanist?"[31] Indeed, humanistic psychologists were pursuing lines of inquiry that were bringing them into agreement with liberal theologians; both groups, Maslow noted, have come to define God "not as a person, but as a force, a principle, a gestalt-quality of the whole of Being, an integrating power that expresses the unity and therefore the meaningfulness of the cosmos, the 'dimension of depth.' "[32] Defined in this way, God is the ontological presupposition of Maslow's psychology of self-actualization.

Viktor Frankl joined Maslow in arguing that a psychological theory of human fulfillment must take into consideration the "farther reaches of human nature." Trained as a psychoanalytically oriented psychiatrist, Frankl eventually became convinced that individuals are not, as Freud had theorized, primarily motivated toward instinctual gratification. Frankl's clinical experience convinced him that man differs from lower species mainly in that man is "a being whose main concern consists in fulfilling a meaning and in actualizing values."[33] Frankl chose the term *logotherapy* to differentiate his theories from those of psychoanalysis. Logotherapy postulates that psychological health consists of finding the fundamental meaning (or logos) of one's life. Frankl was not suggesting that humans arbitrarily invent or create meanings. Human fulfillment comes not so much from making values as from "discovering" them.[34] Psychological health seems to require that we lay hold of meanings that are in some way supranatural. Frankl writes that our lives are grounded in an "ultimate meaning [which] necessarily exceeds and surpasses the finite intellectual capacities of men; in logotherapy, we speak in the context of supra-meaning."[35]

Frankl was not the least bit bashful about the metaphysical and religious overtones of his psychological theories. He believed that "the trend is away from religion conceived in such a strictly denominational sense . . . if religion is to survive, it will have to be profoundly personalized."[36] Because logotherapy assists individuals to experience that which transcends them, it is clearly a form of religious belief well suited to the modern, scientific age. In *The Doctor and Man's Soul* and *The Unconscious God* Frankl has argued that "there is not only an instinctual unconscious but a spiritual unconscious as well."[37] Frankl explains that this spiritual or transcendent unconscious is the source of all environment-transcending activities and impulses such as art, love, and moral conscience. The spiritual unconscious is in fact the very foundation from which individuality and consciousness itself have emerged. Finally, it is the fact that our psyche "reaches down into an unconscious ground" which makes religious experience possible, for it is here, and here alone, that we can come to experience "a relationship between the immanent self and a transcendent thou."[38]

Ira Progoff is yet another third-force psychologist committed to the task of describing "the possibilities hidden in the depths of man."[39] Heavily influenced by Jung, Progoff maintains that the unconscious is the psychological source of the "patterns of development that are inherent in the human organism ... [and provides] the directive principle in the human being which guides its growth from the moment of conception forward."[40] Self-actualization, then, is little more than the process whereby the unconscious progressively manifests itself. Thus for Progoff, as for Frankl and Maslow, the farther reaches of the unconscious reveal not so much the psychological as the ontological or metaphysical realities that make for our well-being and fulfillment.

Maslow, Frankl, and Progoff illustrate how far humanistic psychology has gone in repudiating positivistic interpretations of mental life. They describe the unconscious as a conduit through which supraindividual energies flow into and exert causal influences within the psychological realm. To this extent, third-force psychologists are spokesmen for a particular world view as much, or even more, than they are promulgators of a distinct set of psychological doctrines.

Gardner Murphy, one of the founding fathers of the movement, was among the first to draw attention to the fact that the metaphor of self-actualization symbolized the commitment of humanistic psychologists to a "soft determinism": " 'Soft' determinism says that man is himself a part of the system of cosmic forces and these forces, so to speak, flow through him."[41] For humanistic psychologists, psychological variables are necessary but not sufficient causes of self-actualizing behavior. The ultimate cause of creativity in life transcends the psychological dimension and is thus literally meta-physical in nature. Murphy believed that for this reason the most important task of psychological research was the study of those states of consciousness which best facilitate the flow of "cosmic forces" into our individual lives. Much like Emerson and James a century before, Murphy and other humanistic psychologists are calling for a new vision of reality in which concepts like "correspondence" and "influx" replace our current scientific understandings of causality. "The scientific challenge to create a kind of field theory sufficiently open to provide a place for the main parapsychological findings still stands. . . . It would make use of a monism . . . according to which all reality is both physical and mental."[42]

Third-force psychology's doctrine of reality as "both physical and mental" was, as it had been for the early functionalists, a means of explaining the causal efficacy of nonphysical forces such as consciousness. It is consequently no surprise that humanistic psychologists are so attracted to Eastern mystical philosophies and to the process philosophy defended by Whitehead, Smuts, Teilhard de Chardin, and others. Both Eastern metaphysics and Western process thought envision reality in ways that allow for interpenetrating realms of causality. Such concepts as Teilhard's "noosphere," Whitehead's "ingression of eternal aims," and Hindu descriptions of the Atman-Brahman state of consciousness all support the view that, under proper psychological conditions, directive energies from higher metaphysical planes can enter into and exert an actualizing power within human personality.[43]

This tendency among humanistic psychologists to interpret the farther reaches of human consciousness as the point of connection between the individual and higher ontic powers shows that secularization has not so much eradicated religious beliefs among the educated populace as it has turned them away from conventional theology. The rediscovery of the "higher" unconscious has made a kind of religious discourse possible for individuals to whom the idea of a Supreme Being "up there" or "out there" is untenable. By making it possible to speak about our relationship to nonphysical dimensions of reality, humanistic psychologists have helped make the unconscious one of the most powerful religious ideas of the twentieth century.

From Emerson to James to Rogers

Humanistic psychology's explanation of the nature and utility of the unconscious is further evidence of a remarkable continuity in American psychological thought. With the important exceptions of behaviorism and physiological psychology, American psychology has characteristically maintained that the mind's unconscious depths defy reduction to the categories of positivistic science. Since it was "discovered" by the mesmerists, the unconscious has been interpreted as supplying mental life with adaptive energies that originate "beyond" the psychological dimension per se; furthermore, this concept of the unconscious reveals American psychology to be a far more complex cultural force than is usually recognized.

Most studies of American psychology assume that it emerged as a secular successor to theology. Phillip Rieff, Christopher Lasch, Martin Gross and Peter Berger have all supported the contention that psychology has from the outset understood itself as in an adversary role to religion and religious belief. Psychology induces individuals to think in both humanistic and individualistic ways, and is thus partly responsible for the gradual decline of the Western religious tradition. Martin Gross writes, "When educated man lost faith in formal religion, he required a substitute belief that would be as reputable in the last half of the twentieth century as Christianity was in the first. Psychology and psychiatry have now assumed that special role."[44]

Gross further suggests that psychology has profoundly altered the moral and spiritual tenor of modern society. Ours, he writes, is a "psychological society . . . a civilization in which, as never before, man is pre-occupied with Self."[45] Christopher Lasch similarly bemoans what he takes to be the fact that "the contemporary climate is therapeutic, not religious. . . . People today hunger not for personal salvation, but for the feeling, the momentary illusion, of personal well-being, health and psychic security."[46] In other words, because psychological theories are inherently skewed toward the personal and immediate, it logically follows that they cause us to regard religious ideas about the ultimate or eternal as superfluous to human welfare.

These apprehensions are misplaced. A close analysis of the cultural context in which psychology attained such prominence shows that Americans appropriated psychological ideas in order to reinforce broader cultural and religious commitments. The intellectual problems confronted by religious faith have changed drastically in modern times. The contest between believer and nonbeliever is replaced by the believer's own internal struggle with the element of unbelief within himself. Many individuals no longer find traditional theological doctrines adequate to sustain belief in the existence of a supersensible, spiritual reality. In an age of empiricism, reason and logic are insufficient bases upon which to establish the intellectual foundations of theology. Religion, too, must establish its claims with reference to publically verifiable facts. The intellectual question now confronting religious thinkers is thus largely a psychological one concerning whether humans are in fact capable of experiencing any reality beside that apprehended through the physical senses. For unless humans are so psychologically constituted as to be able either to experience or be influenced by "higher" orders of being, religion will be irrelevant to the empirical study of human fulfillment.

It is in this cultural context that the symbolic functions of the "American unconscious" are best understood. This becomes especially apparent when we attempt to account for the career and popularity of humanistic psychology's single most influential theorist, Carl Rogers. The theories of Gordon Allport and Abraham Maslow may receive equal attention in college textbooks, but Rogers continues to dominate such fields as school guidance counseling, psychiatric nursing, marriage and family therapy, sensitivity training groups, and pastoral counseling. Because Rogers's theories dovetail so neatly with the conceptual needs of a widespread readership, an examination of his career can be particularly useful in our attempt to understand why Americans turn to psychology in their individual quests for wholeness and fulfillment.[47]

Rogers has on several occasions noted that his interest in psychology began with his gradual rejection of orthodox religious beliefs.[48] Like many of the pioneering figures in American psychology he was raised in a highly conservative Protestant family. His early socialization into religious thought had a twofold impact upon his subsequent career. On the one hand, having learned the importance of viewing personal life *sub specie aeternitatis,* he was sensitized to the limitations of scientific positivism. Yet, because of the narrowness of his parents' beliefs he became almost painfully aware that they could no longer serve most individuals as trustworthy guides to action in the modern world. Throughout his youth and young adulthood Rogers became increasingly hostile toward biblical absolutism and the rigid piety he associated with it. By the time he entered college his inherited faith no longer functioned as a commanding power in his life. In a term paper entitled "The Source of Authority in Martin Luther," he adduced historical evidence in support of the affirmation that "man's ultimate reliance is upon his own experience."[49] Just a few years later he made the more radical assertion that "perhaps Jesus was a man like other men—not divine."[50]

Whatever else one may infer from Rogers's early theological musings, they certainly reflect a growing conviction that it is possible to speak of human values without reference to a transcendent Supreme Being. For Rogers, meaning is found within human experience, not outside of it. His spiritual sensibilities, however, had not in any way been blunted. Upon graduating from college he entered Union Theological Seminary with the intention of pursuing a career in religious leadership. Union was at this time already known for its liberal leanings, and many of its faculty tended to equate religious commitment with involvement in programs for human betterment rather than with conformity to orthodox doctrine. Rogers had thus chosen an ideal environment within which to pursue his abiding interest in "the meaning of life and the possibility of the constructive improvement of life for individuals."[51]

At Union, Rogers first became acquainted with the methods and goals of psychological counseling. He had now reached a personal, theological, and professional crossroads. Deciding that it was "a horrible thing to have to profess a set of beliefs in order to remain in one's profession," Rogers promptly quit his studies at Union in order to enter "a field in which I could be sure my freedom of thought would not be limited."[52] He transferred into the child guidance program at Columbia University and soon became a practicing psychotherapist working with children and their parents. From there it was but a few more years before his "client-centered" approach to psychological counseling earned him both national and international renown.

Rogers's experience in counseling led him to develop a theory of personality based upon the interaction of two basic psychological structures. The first and developmentally more fundamental of these structures is "the organism." The organism is the moving force behind an individual's interactions with the physical and social environments. Rogers often uses the expression "organismic valuing process " to describe the dynamic way in which this inner core of personality guides the individual toward activities that maintain, enhance, and actualize its innate potential. The second basic structure of personality is "the self." The self, unlike the organism, is largely derived from the external environment. It consists almost solely of the ideas, opinions, and judgments of others which have been introjected into the person's developing identity.

Rogers says that psychological health exists whenever there is a fundamental congruence between the self and the deeper activity of the organism. Such congruence establishes a psychological condition in which the individual is fully functioning and acts in accordance with his own actualizing tendencies. However, when the values that have been incorporated into the self are incompatible with the individual's deeper organismic valuing process, psychological disturbance occurs. The functioning of the personality breaks down and becomes fragmented. Thought and behavior become constricted and rigid, ultimately resulting in various forms of psychopathology.

It follows that the goal of psychotherapy should be to establish congruence between these two psychological structures. The originality of Rogers's theory lies in his understanding of what types of therapeutic activity promote this kind of inner healing. His "client-centered" theory of psychotherapy rests on his conviction that every individual possesses within him- or herself the resources for self-integration and growth. Successful therapy therefore requires only that the therapist provide a safe emotional environment within which clients will be able to let go of their defenses long enough to be guided by the deeper, organismic valuing process. "As the individual perceives and accepts into his self-structure more of his organic experiences, he finds that he is replacing his present value system—based so largely upon introjections which have been distortedly symbolized—with a continuing organismic valuing process."[53]

In the warm, nonimpositional relationship between therapist and client, the client experiences renewed openness to his or her own valuing process. Rather than trying to force their experiences into the mold of socially acquired expectations and values, clients begin to place trust in the full range of their own experience. The freeing nature of the "client-centered" relationship enables individuals to trust their own inner feelings and to view their lives as fluid, ongoing processes.

Clearly, the humanistic psychology for which Rogers has been the preeminent spokesman is clearly not humanistic in the strict sense. It does not embrace the Enlightenment belief that the individual's basic dignity and capacity for self-improvement derive from his or her possession of the faculty of instrumental reason. Rogers's humanism more closely resembles Emerson's "romantic individualism."[54] That is, Rogers locates the ultimate source of humankind's growth-oriented potential outside of the psychological realm per se. His conviction that "our organisms as a whole have a wisdom and purpose which goes well beyond our conscious thought" presupposes the existence and causal efficacy of a psychic sphere that quite literally transcends the conditioned structure of empirical reality.[55] In contrast to the more or less Newtonian interpretation of nature underlying both psychoanalytic and behavioral psychology, Rogers's brand of humanism grants normative psychological status to "a flood of experiencing at a level far beyond that of everyday life."[56]

Rogers's belief in a preconscious, "organismic" actualizing tendency makes it possible for him to speak of the

> human organism as a pyramid of organic functioning, partly suffused by an unconscious knowing, with only the tip of the pyramid being fleetingly illuminated by the flickering light of fully conscious awareness . . . some of my colleagues have said that organismic choice—the nonverbal, *subconscious choice* of being—is *guided by the evolutionary flow.* I would agree and go one step further. I would point out that in psychotherapy we have learned something about the psychological conditions which are most conducive to self-awareness. With greater self-awareness a more informed choice is possible, a choice freer from introjects, a conscious choice which is even more in tune with the evolutionary flow. There is (to use Claudio Naranjo's term) an *organismic convergence* with that directional evolutionary process.[57]

Rogers's belief in the "organismic convergence" of individual consciousness with the directional tendency central to the universe reveals the fact that his often-quoted observation that "what is most personal is most universal" is far more than a useful clinical hypothesis; it is also a metaphysical belief. Among other things it has led him to "find definitely appealing the view of Arthur Koestler that individual consciousness is but a fragment of a cosmic consciousness."[58] The psychological sphere is, in other words, intimately connected with a transpersonal order. Thus, attuning ourselves to the psyche's deeper reaches also aligns us with the very forces that govern the universe. Rogers has written that the experience of fully and deeply entering into another person's inner world is like "listening to the music of the spheres, because beyond the immediate message of the person, no matter what that might be, there is the universal."[59]

In all of this Rogers recapitulates, chapter and verse, the aesthetic or harmonial world view behind American philosophies of self-reliance. Like Jonathan Edwards, Ralph Waldo Emerson, and William James, Rogers holds that authentic human action is a direct function of an inward identification with Being itself. According to the Rogerian notion of authenticity, no less than the Emersonian or Jamesian, by opening ourselves to the raw impressions of nature we can take hold of the spiritual principle of things. Thus "psychological congruence" is to Rogers what "consent to Being in general" was to Edwards, "divine influx" to Emerson, and incursions from the "subliminal self" to James. All point to the psychological process whereby individuals can apprehend, and become inwardly connected to, an immanent divinity.

Rogers, perhaps even more than James, went from nature to psychological nature in his articulation of an aesthetic spirituality. To Rogers, the orderly psychological laws which govern self-actualization are "aspects of the same order we find in the universe as a whole."[60] Paralleling Emerson's view of "correspondence" between various metaphysical planes, Rogers established his humanistic psychology on the thesis that "there appears to be a formative tendency at work in the universe, which can be observed at every level."[61]

Thus, when we provide a psychological climate that permits persons to be . . . we are tapping into a tendency which permeates all of organic life as a tendency to become all the complexity of which the organism is capable. And on an even larger scale, I believe *we are tuning in to a potent creative tendency which has formed the universe* . . . and perhaps we are touching the cutting edge of our ability to transcend ourselves, to create new and more spiritual directions in human evolution.[62]

Self-actualization can thus be considered not just a psychological but also a spiritual attainment. Like especially growth-producing moments in therapy, it is dependent upon the fulfillment of those psychological conditions that allow "the powers of the Universe to be present and operative in a very special way."[63] Rogers has even gone so far as to say that the boundaries between the psychological (personal) and spiritual (transpersonal) realms are the new frontiers of knowledge in psychology.[64] Rogers sees considerable scientific importance in recent experimental work with precognition, telepathy, psychic healing, out-of-the-body experiences, and psychedelic drugs. The findings of these parapsychological studies, he says, are placing psychology "on the verge of discovering a new type of lawful order."[65] This "lawful order" will disclose the intimate connection between our personal psychological growth and the fundamental meanings and values of the universe. Humanistic psychology, by helping individuals to make full use of their inner natures, is thus not only working toward more effective adaptations to the social and economic realms, but is also attempting to transform personal consciousness in ways that will enable individuals to "feel they are in touch with, and grasp the meaning of, this evolutionary flow."[66]

In the self-actualization theories propounded by Maslow, Rogers, and others, Americans are rediscovering ontological and metaphysical beliefs with deep roots in American cultural thought. Humanistic psychology appears to have been a major force in the American cultural awakening of the early 1960s as described by historian William McLoughlin. According to McLoughlin, older formulations of the core concepts of American intellectual thought had become culturally irrelevant. Social, economic, and even ecological changes had created a jarring disjunction between traditional norms and everyday realities. New visions of human existence have emerged in recent years that meet our need to "maintain faith in ourselves, our ideals, and our 'covenant with God' even while they compel us to reinterpret that covenant in the light of new experience."[67] As McLoughlin sees it, the widespread spiritual unrest reflected by the cultural awakening of the 1960s will only be satisfied by a new vision that can provide

> a new sense of the mystical unity of all mankind and of the
> vital power or harmony between men and nature. The
> godhead will be defined in less dualistic terms, and its power
> will be understood less in terms of an absolutist sin-hating,
> death-dealing "Almighty Father in Heaven" and more in
> terms of a life-supporting, nurturing, empathetic, easygoing
> parental (motherly as well as fatherly) image.[68]

Humanistic psychologists like Rogers, by giving a new vocabulary with which to describe our means of access to the "formative tendency of the universe," have simultaneously articulated a psychological perspective well attuned to the modern demand for a more actable world view. Rejecting the subject-object realm of experience as the ultimate referent of psychological analysis, they have revived a mode of self-understanding which, since Emerson, has bolstered the conviction that "getting right with God" and "being your own person" are one and the same act of self-reliance.[69] From the first adherents of mesmerism in the 1840s to the followers of humanistic psychology in the 1980s, Americans have found in the unconscious a powerful conceptual tool with which to reconcile their scientific and religious convictions. Whatever its strictly scientific contribution, the "American unconscious" has enabled psychology to assume a role of signal importance in contemporary American culture.

Eight

The Apotheosis: The Unconscious in Popular Psychology

THE unconscious has been a central theme in popular as well as academic American psychology. The term *popular psychology* refers to those writings specifically addressed to general reading audiences. What distinguishes a psychology as popular is thus its overt intention to help individuals symbolize and resolve problems that arise in the context of everyday life. And while a good many psychologies have attracted popular followings by promising solutions to isolated behavioral problems such as smoking or overeating, most are concerned with regenerating the whole person. From mesmerism in the 1840s up to and including contemporary groups such as est and Scientology, popular psychologies have responded to Americans' need for an all-encompassing philosophy of life. They have extended the theories and techniques of psychology well beyond their strictly scientific applications, and routinely address such matters as the purpose of life, the reason for human brokenness, and the secret for finding happiness and success. In other words, popular psychologies are important sources of Americans' beliefs about themselves and their world.

The distinction between popular and professional psychology is important to an understanding of the cultural significance of modern psychology. It draws our attention to the larger sociological and cultural forces that shape psychological ideas as they find their way into the vernacular of the general reading public. Sociologist Peter Berger has examined the development of psychology in this larger context. He concludes that psychology generally—and the concept of the unconscious in particular—developed in response to the disorientation caused by urbanization and industrialization. Modern individuals find it increasingly difficult to define themselves in terms of their social and economic roles and thus stand in need of new paradigms that can help them to establish an identity in the private rather than public sphere. Berger says that "a psychological model that has as its crucial concept a notion of the unconscious may be related to a social situation in which there is so much complexity in the fabric of roles and institutions that the individual is no longer capable of perceiving his society in its totality. . . . Society confronts the individual as a mysterious power, or in other words, the individual is unconscious of the fundamental forces that shape his life."[1]

Another related factor predisposing Americans to accept the idea of the unconscious is the Protestant ethic with its implicit tenet that each individual should systematically pursue success in the outer world. Those seeking to reinterpret the Protestant ethic in ways more befitting a modern, secular age have tended to embrace the unconscious as the source of virtue and success. By constituting what Martin Gross calls the "anticlerical equivalent of the soul," the unconscious has both caused and accompanied recent changes in the methods through which Americans seek control over their material and spiritual destinies.[2] Perfectibility once sought through the intervention of God's grace is now thought to be possible through the scientific adjustment of the psyche. The many self-help philosophies currently bedecking our televised talk shows and grocery store bookshelves have abandoned petitionary prayer in favor of techniques designed to activate the higher powers of the unconscious.

The concept of the unconscious is, as Berger and Gross suggest, well suited to help individuals better to relate to complex modern social and economic realities. This alone, however, does not account for the extent to which the concept of the unconscious pervades popular American culture. Clifford Geertz has cautioned that "the sociology of knowledge ought to be called the sociology of meaning, for what is socially determined is not the nature of conception but the vehicles of conception."[3] In other words, while a belief or idea may win popular support largely because of its practical utility, we should be aware that it is simultaneously related to the larger conceptual processes whereby individuals interpret the meaning of their lives. Berger and his colleague Thomas Luckmann have, for example, pointed out that every society has a "symbolic universe" which individuals draw on in their interpretation of everyday life.[4] Berger and Luckmann have shown that a scientific theory will gain wide acceptance only if it is compatible with these underlying assumptions about the nature and meaning of life. From this cultural point of view, then, scientific theories perform symbolic functions; they translate highly abstract assumptions about life into more concrete— and actable—categories. As Geertz warns, therefore, failure to probe "the system of meanings embodied in the symbol . . . [is] to take for granted what *most* needs to be elucidated."[5]

The fact that popular works on the unconscious continue to thrive suggests that academic psychology may be out of touch with the "symbolic universe" to which many Americans are deeply committed. Even as academic psychology intensified its efforts to effect a permanent divorce between scientific and religious considerations of the self, popular culture became ever more insistent upon bringing them together. The unconscious, precisely because it occupies the boundary between science and religion, has furnished popular culture with a powerful symbol of the ultimate harmony of the universe. The historical persistence of popular tracts on the unconscious would apparently testify to the fact that Americans have often appropriated psychological ideas for the purpose of supporting—not supplanting—the religious dimensions of self-understanding.

Popular Psychology and Unchurched Religiosity

Thomas Jay Hudson's *The Law of Psychic Phenomena* is representative of the many popular books on the unconscious that began appearing in the 1890s. Subtitled "a working hypothesis for the systematic study of hypnotism, spiritualism, mental therapeutics, etc.," it went through twelve editions in the first four years after its release in 1893. Americans learned from Hudson that they possessed "two minds, each endowed with separate and distinct powers."[6] The objective mind was said to coordinate our responses to the environment and direct higher reasoning processes. The subjective mind, on the other hand, has no connection with the outer world; it is closely associated with instinctual processes, emotions, and healing or regenerative functions like those discovered by the mesmerists. Among its potentials is the "power of transmitting intelligence to other subjective minds otherwise than through the ordinary sense channels."[7] Hudson believed that the ability of the subjective mind to act independently of the physical body was conclusive proof that human nature is "fitted especially for a Higher Plane of Existence."[8]

In a later volume, entitled *The Divine Pedigree of Man,* Hudson asserted that the psychological investigation of the unconscious "furnishes the data for the inductive study of religion."[9] Hudson believed himself to be addressing the "great majority of educated persons of all religious denominations [who] now recognize evolution as God's method of creation."[10] He assured these progressively minded readers that psychology could prove scientifically the scriptural doctrine that humans were created in the image of God. The existence of the unconscious, Hudson claimed, is empirical evidence of the fact that we are linked with God's creative spirit; its discovery has revealed the very real sense in which each and every one of us "is potentially divine."[11]

Equal to Hudson's contribution to Americans' early acquaintance with their unconscious depths was that of H. Addington Bruce. In addition to two successful books, *The Riddle of Personality* (1908) and *Scientific Mental Healing* (1911),

Bruce published numerous articles about the unconscious mind for *Good Housekeeping, Forum, Appleton's,* and *The American Magazine.*[12] Bruce was an exponent of William James's view that the unconscious opens onto metaphysical planes not yet recognized by the natural sciences. In "Religion and the Larger Self," for example, he urged his readers to recognize the unconscious as the divinely appointed medium though which we may avail ourselves of unlimited spiritual energies and powers.[13] And in a later piece, entitled "The Soul's Winning Fight with Science," Bruce demonstrated that the empirical fact of the unconscious made it possible to reconcile science once and for all with belief in the immortality of the soul.[14]

The themes championed by Hudson and Bruce have continued to dominate popular psychology well into the 1980s. Ira Progoff, Thomas Harris, Rollo May, Leo Buscaglia, and Wayne Dyer still reassure readers that they possess unlimited spiritual potential. M. Scott Peck's recent best-seller, *The Road Less Traveled,* reveals just how fully modern popular psychologies function as a source of American religious belief. Peck tells his readers that they ordinarily use a mere 5 percent of their minds; by exploring the other 95 percent "you will come to discover that this vast part of your mind, of which you now have little awareness, contains riches beyond imagination."[15] Warning that Freud's descriptions of the unconscious are misleading in that they are concerned only with the phenomenon of repression, Peck assembles innumerable anecdotes from his clinical experience to prove that the unconscious is "a benign and loving realm." The road to full personal development eventually leads us to the discovery that "our unconscious is God. God within us. We were part of God all the time."[16]

> I have said that the ultimate goal of spiritual growth is for the individual to become as one with God. It is to know with God. Since the *unconscious is God all along,* we may further define the goal of spiritual growth to be the attainment of godhood by the conscious self.[17]

The commercial success of books such as Peck's *The Road Less Traveled* or Maxwell Maltz's *Psycho-Cybernetics* reminds us of the important fact that Americans take their religious metaphors from a good many sources other than their churches. Of course, psychological ideas about our inner point of connection with higher spiritual realities have often made their way into mainstream religious denominations. The pastoral counseling movement has borrowed heavily from psychological sources ever since its beginnings in the Reverend Worcester's Emmanuel Movement.[18] Also, much of the recent interest in contemplative or mystical spirituality has been explicitly wedded to a specific view of the unconscious. The writings of Thomas Merton, Henri Nouwen, and Morton Kelsey all presuppose what Kelsey describes as the belief "that there is a depth in humankind called the unconscious through which one experiences the spiritual world."[19]

The fact that the churches have so readily appropriated and then "Christianized" the terminology of popular psychology does not diminish the significance of the unconscious as a religious symbol that emerged and continues to function outside of the church setting. Since its discovery by the mesmerists in the 1840s, the unconscious has been a common ingredient in the many innovative and experimental approaches to religious faith that have flourished in popular American culture. The various "New Age" groups spawned by the mind-cure movement, American followers of Eastern religious traditions, and those pursuing the mysteries embodied in paranormal or occult phenomena have all embraced the unconscious as a full-blown religious symbol of humanity's relationship to a higher world.

The Mind Cure Legacy

Phineas P. Quimby's teachings lived on through the work of his students. After Mary Baker Eddy, the most notable of these was a former Methodist Episcopal minister and ardent Swedenborgian enthusiast by the name of Warren Felt Evans.[20] Himself a former patient of the famed Yankee mesmerist, Evans followed in his mentor's footsteps, opening a healing office of his own in Boston. There for the next twenty years he spearheaded what is variously referred to as the Mind Cure or New Thought movement. Although a gifted healer, it was Evans's pen that brought Quimby's insights to the attention of the nation's large middle class. His *The Mental Cure* (1869) and *Mental Medicine* (1871) had, by 1875, gone through seven and fifteen editions, respectively. In these and numerous other books, with titles like *The Divine Law of Cure, Esoteric Christianity and Mental Therapeutics,* and *The Primitive Mind Cure,* Evans expounded the doctrine that the healing powers of the unconscious were nothing less than the psychological manifestation of Christian metaphysics.

Evans proclaimed that through their discovery of mental healing the mesmerists had recovered the kerygma of the early Christian church. The attainment of mental states in which we are receptive to subtle spiritual influences is essentially a sacramental experience. "In the impressible state, the patient comes under the action of the law of faith, the great psychological remedy in the Gospel system, the importance of which even the Christian world has never fully appreciated."[21]

Evans translated mesmerist psychology into a theological model, based entirely on mesmerist psychology, of humanity's true, spiritual nature. He said that the duality of the human condition is determined by the structure of our brains. One half of the brain, the cerebrum, controls voluntary functions, while the cerebellum is the seat of the involuntary nervous system. According to Evans, the cerebellum is also the psychic conduit through which God sends us life and guiding wisdom. If we have a conscious awareness of our total being, our vital bodily processes will maintain a continuous connection with a wisdom far superior to that of our conscious thoughts. By shifting awareness toward this deeper level of consciousness we can "come into direct and immediate communication with God [so] that His creative energy shall be added to our cognitive and volitional power."[22]

When, however, we become preoccupied with material conditions or indulge a false sense of self-importance, we effectively sever the conscious mind from its unconscious, spiritual source. Evans wrote that we can abolish this harmful inner duality by turning our attention inward, toward the magnetic or impressible plane of consciousness. By "turning the mind inward upon itself towards its divine center, man comes into such relations with his own immortal Self, the anima divina."[23] Here, in what Evans called the preconscious life of the soul, the two hemispheres of the brain are united and "the right relationship of mind to the potent active forces of the universe" is restored.[24]

Evans's vision of human nature is evocative of the introspective and ascetic paths espoused by the gnostic traditions of the West and of the meditative paths of Hinduism and Buddhism. He wrote that the true self is covered over by several sheaths, or layers, of mundane identifications. These layers must be stripped away before we can achieve firsthand knowledge of our own divine nature:

> First is the outer court of sense, next, the inner sanctuary of
> the intellectual soul; and lastly, in the East, the most holy
> place, the spirit where like the high priest we may commune
> with God. This is the inmost region of our being, and our real
> self. It is included in the Christ, or the Universal Spirit. . . .
> The Summit of our being which is the real and divine man, is
> never contaminated by evil, nor invaded by disease.[25]

Mind-cure psychology rendered conventional theology more or less irrelevant. Mesmerist theories did away with the necessity for repentance or contrition as a means of reconciling oneself with God's will. Obedience to the laws of the mind, not to scriptural commandments, is what enables God's presence to manifest itself in our lives. Spiritual progress is achieved through systematic self-adjustment. Men and women should stop straining so hard in their efforts to get ahead in life. Preoccupation with outer conditions blinds the individual to the true causal principles governing the universe. It is far more beneficial to spend a few moments alone in silence for the purpose of activating the powers of the unconscious mind. Just beneath the threshold of waking consciousness there is what Evans termed "a battery and reservoir of magnetic life and vital force" ready to replenish the exhausted nervous system.[26]

Another New Thought author, Ralph Waldo Trine, provided perhaps the clearest exposition of the movement's harmonial piety:

> In just the degree that we come into a conscious realization of our oneness with the Infinite Life, and open ourselves to the Divine inflow, do we actualize in ourselves the qualities and powers of the Infinite Life, do we make ourselves channels through which the Infinite Intelligence and Power can work. In just the degree in which you realize your oneness with the Infinite Spirit, you will exchange dis-ease for ease, inharmony for harmony, suffering and pain for abounding health and strength.[27]

For Trine, mental healing was proof that "thoughts are forces." Thoughts generate a vibratory field of energy, which can be strengthened and amplified to exert causal influence upon natural conditions. Trine asserted that "in the degree that thought is spiritualized, does it become more subtle and powerful . . . this spiritualizing is in accordance with law and is within the power of all." Even more to the point: "Within yourself lies the cause of whatever enters your life. To come into the full realization of your awakened interior powers, is to be able to condition your life in exact accord with what you would have it. . . . This is the secret of all success."[28]

"As a man thinketh, so is he" was no mere aphorism for the New Thoughters. It was metaphysical law. Mind-cure psychology had taught Evans that "if we form the true idea of man and apply it to ourselves, and hold it steadfastly in the mind and believe in its realization, by one of the deepest and most certain laws of our nature, it will tend to recreate the body of the mental type."[29] When the New Thoughters said that "thoughts are forces," they meant just that. Many New Thought writers believed that by dipping into the subconscious and summoning up a state of mystical reverie they could acquire the power to influence events in the outer world. Properly spiritualized thoughts could be telepathically transmitted into the psychic ethers with full confidence that by the action of immutable psychological laws subconscious desires would be transformed into physical reality.

The New Thoughters encouraged Americans to take belief in the "power" of positive thinking quite literally. To some persons, access through the unconscious to unlimited powers seemed to promise the possibility of mastery of the otherwise risky world of business. By the late 1890s a new form of success literature appeared on the popular market, dedicated to the proposition that there must be some cash value in the unconscious mental forces touted by the mind-curists.[30] For example, in the early 1900s Frank Haddock edited a multivolume "Power Book Library" which included such titles as *How to Get What You Want, Practical Psychology, The Personal Atmosphere,* and *Power for Success.* And, as another think-your-way-to-success pundit put it, the mind-curists had discovered that the individual's "own thought power is a force, the intentionality and utility of which has been almost undreamed of."[31] The significance of this discovery was unmistakable: "We may grasp and wield its divine forces, and through them assert our supremacy over the kingdom of our rightful domain."[32]

Mind-cure psychology was also the cause of the extension of positive thinking into institutionalized religion. Mary Baker Eddy's Christian Science was, of course, a direct descendant of Quimby's healing practice.[33] The many New Thought groups that have sprung up over the past one hundred years also exemplify the infiltration of mind-cure beliefs into American religious life. These organizations, scattered throughout the country and usually short-lived, have understood themselves as supplements rather than competitors to established religious institutions. As a consequence, their informal study groups and ubiquitous literature have done far more than Christian Science to introduce harmonial imagery and self-help techniques into the devotional lives of churched and unchurched Americans. Groups such as Unity School of Practical Christianity and Ernest Holmes's Divine Science as well as the inspirational literature from writers such as Eric Butterworth, Emmet Fox, and Marcus Bach continue to this day to promulgate the message that peace, power, and material plenty are within the reach of all who learn to become receptive to the spiritual powers within.

It is, however, the Reverend Norman Vincent Peale who has been most successful in converting Americans to the gospel of the unconscious. In his phenomenally popular *The Power of Positive Thinking,* Peale infected millions with the harmonial belief that "by channeling spiritual power through your thoughts . . . you can have peace of mind, improved health, and a never-ceasing flow of energy."[34] Self-consciously borrowing from both Emerson and James, Peale has time and again insisted upon the essentially religious, even Christian, character of his belief that our unconscious minds have continual access to the spiritual power which flows throughout the universe:

> Years ago Emerson said there are unexplored chambers of the
> human mind which some day will be opened to release
> unrealized spiritual powers. A French psychiatrist says that
> there is another element present in the mind beyond the
> conscious and the subconscious. This element he terms "the
> superconscious." The characterization is interesting. Perhaps
> it was to this "superconscious" that Christ referred when He
> said, "If you have faith . . . nothing shall be impossible unto
> you."[35]

Teaching us to envision God as an "electrical energy" invisibly enveloping the material universe, Peale has labored ceaselessly to drive home his message that God helps those who activate their own unconscious minds:

> In the unconscious are all the forces which make for our
> success or failure, our misery or our happiness. These forces,
> according to their strength, control the mind, determining our

choices and decisions. In the unconscious lie hidden energies which can defeat us if not understood and properly used but which wisely used can endow us with great power.[36]

In his proselytizing zeal, Peale has introduced some compromises and inconsistencies into his system. For example, coaching readers in practical self-help strategies, Peale often fell back on forms of autosuggestion indistinguishable from those of the most banal of the positive thinkers in the New Thought movement. The rationale behind his prescription of a rigorous regimen of personal thought control was that "the unconscious can only send back what was first sent down."[37] If we stuff the right orders down into the unconscious, it will attend to their faithful execution. This sort of tenuous reasoning prompted Donald Meyer's accusation that Peale had made the unconscious into a passive, empty cubicle merely awaiting instructions from the conscious personality. The aim of Peale's program, says Meyer, is ultimately "not that of inducing contemplative states of Oneness nor of advancing self-insight nor of strengthening conscious will, let alone sensitizing people to their world."[38] Peale's system merely helps weak people to imagine they are strong.

There is some validity to Meyer's indictment. By tailoring his message to meet the self-help needs of a popular reading audience Peale inevitably compromised his system. Instead of consistently confronting persons with the radical option of opening themselves to what James called the MORE of psychic existence, Peale can often be read as offering little more than a new set of terms to apply to the continued pursuit of middle-class comforts. But it is wrong to insist upon seeing either Peale, or his popularity, entirely in this light.[39] Although he may have encouraged the tendency of modern Americans to think of nothing beyond themselves, Peale also challenged individuals to pierce through material appearances to some deeper source of meaning and value. He, no less than Emerson or James, has exhorted his readers to learn to live in "harmony with nature and in contact with the Divine energy."[40] And to Peale should go a great deal of credit for equipping his contemporaries with a terminology to make religious faith credible in a modern, scientific world.

The Oriental Connection

From Emerson on, the aesthetic strain in American religious thought has often called upon the metaphorical and symbolic language of Eastern mystical traditions. The Hindu monistic philosophy, which establishes a fundamental unity between the Atman (individual consciousness) and Brahman (the Over-Soul or world consciousness), supplied both Emerson and Thoreau with the psychological underpinnings of self-reliance. New Thoughters such as Warren Felt Evans also used Eastern terminology to explain the individual's connection with creative spiritual energies. Their writings extol Eastern metaphysical traditions for nurturing belief in the psyche's spiritual depths in ways that the Christian tradition does not. The pantheistic theologies and meditative psychologies of the Orient supply a ready-made vocabulary for expressing the harmonial conviction that inward journeys lead to higher, spiritual worlds.

American appropriation of Eastern metaphors for the successive layers of the unconscious mind is perhaps not as meaningful as it seems at first glance. Most American adherents of Eastern traditions actually know precious little about the cultural or historical origins of the symbols they so avidly embrace. American versions of Zen, Theosophy, Vedanta, and Yoga are little more than a repackaging of indigenous spirituality.[41] Individuals whose aesthetic rather than doctrinal approach to religion prompts them to sever ties with the Judeo-Christian scriptural tradition find in Eastern religions a ready-made vocabulary for articulating their profoundly incarnational and sacramental view of the universe. In Eastern teachings they find reassurance that the deepest realms of their own unconscious minds provide a portal through which a transcendent spiritual power can enter into and illuminate their lives.

Almost nowhere in American versions of Eastern metaphysics does one find ideas that contradict the substance or style of Yankee optimism. For example, never do Americans embrace the cosmic fatalism that belief in the immutable law of karma entails for Hindus. On the contrary, Americans see invariant cosmic law in much the same light as the promise of a covenant linking God with His creation in a lawful, dependable way. The Atman-Brahman model of our unconscious depths reaffirms the religious assumptions underlying a great many American philosophies of self-reliance. It lends metaphysical authority to the idea that by cultivating our inner or unconscious selves we can avail ourselves of God's creative powers.

The Eastern language of self-discovery has been carried into the vernacular of the American public in a variety of ways. D. T. Suzuki's writings on Zen, Alan Watts's advocacy of meditative states of consciousness, Huston Smith's defense of the "perennial psychology," and the works of beat generation authors like Snyder, Kerouac, and Ginsberg have all invited Americans to view Eastern religions as replete with psychological concepts relevant to modern self-understanding. Eastern descriptions of humanity's unconscious connection with higher spiritual worlds pop up everywhere in the twentieth-century's many "New Age" religious movements. Theosophy, Anthroposophy, the Self-Realization Fellowship founded by Paramahansa Yogananda, Elizabeth Claire Prophet's Summit Lighthouse, and Eckankar have all attracted followers who learn to view the unconscious as the royal road to enlightenment. And, too, such humanistically inclined psychologists as Fromm, May, Maslow, Buscaglia, Peck, and Rogers repeatedly connect their doctrines of self-actualization with the pantheistic beliefs of Eastern religious traditions.

Americans became so accustomed to Eastern philosophies of the "sacred unconscious" that the 1970s saw hippies, business executives, and housewives alike taking up Transcendental Meditation to "learn the way to individual joy and peace through the simple, popular method of deep meditation."[42] With its decidedly less self-sacrificing understanding of traditional Hindu spiritual exercises, Transcendental Meditation teaches its members meditative techniques for piercing through their personal unconscious minds to achieve inner harmony with Divine Mind. The movement's founder, Maharishi Mahesh Yogi, writes that his meditational techniques "may be defined as turning the attention inwards towards the subtler levels of a thought until the mind transcends the experience of the thought. This expands the conscious mind and . . . brings it in contact with the creative intelligence that gives rise to every thought."[43]

Practitioners of Transcendental Meditation come to redefine their conception of psychological health. "Cosmic consciousness should not be considered as something far beyond the reach of normal men. . . . Any state below cosmic consciousness can only be taken to be subnormal human consciousness."[44] In this view the purpose of "true" psychology is more or less identical with that of "true" religion; in both cases the goal "is to set the life of an individual in tune with the laws of nature and set it so that it naturally flows in the stream of evolution."[45]

Even while academic psychology has been busily purging itself of metaphysical overtones, popular culture has thus drawn upon the "Oriental connection" to preserve the unconscious as a symbol of the individual's harmony with the universe.

From Spiritualism to Parapsychology

In his seminal study of nineteenth-century American religious life, Whitney Cross remarked that "mesmerism led to Swedenborgianism, and Swedenborgianism to spiritualism, not because of the degree of intrinsic relationship between their propositions but because of the assumptions according to which their American adherents understood them."[46] Although the process did not always follow the order of progression suggested by Cross, his perception of a common core of assumptions underlying American interest in these offbeat metaphysical systems is fundamentally correct. As we have already noted, many believed that mesmerism supplied a scientific explanation of humankind's higher, spiritual nature. Swedenborgianism supplemented the mesmerists' theories by describing the metaphysical laws and principles that govern the connection of psychological inwardness to higher, spiritual realms.

Emanuel Swedenborg's (1688–1772) influence on American religious and psychological thought can hardly be overstated. Swedenborg was himself a kind of symbol of the unity of science and religion. An eminent scientist in his day, he had already made significant contributions to such varied fields as physics, astronomy, and anatomy when he dedicated his life to the study of Christian mysteries. Granted "perfect inspiration" during a moment of mystical reverie, Swedenborg went on to write more than thirty volumes purporting to uncover the hidden meaning of Christian doctrines.

Swedenborg thought that his revelations freed the Christian message from its bondage to traditional formulations. Both religious and scientific interests were accommodated in his explanation of the universe as composed of several interpenetrating dimensions—physical, mental, spiritual, angelic, etc. Each of these dimensions was in some invisible way connected with every other. It followed that complete harmony in any one dimension of life depends upon establishing rapport, or "correspondence," with other dimensions of the cosmic scheme. Since all true progress has its source in influences received from above, mental, emotional, and spiritual growth depends upon the degree to which we become inwardly receptive to "psychic influx" from higher planes of reality.

Swedenborg's fervent belief in the soul's limitless capacity for development exerted an influence in philosophical circles as varied as Transcendentalism, the communitarian movements, and the drawing room discussions of wealthy dilettantes like Henry James, Sr. Ultimately, however, it was spiritualism that would prove to be the most effective vehicle for the popularization of Swedenborgianism in America.[47] Nineteenth-century spiritualism supplied vivid demonstrations of the existence of a hierarchy of spiritual realms with which we may make psychic contact. And, in so doing, spiritualism provided further warrant for believing that the claims of religion might be put to an empirical test.

The gaudy seances and shoddy deceptions for which spiritualism is best known have unfortunately obscured the aesthetic spirituality that permeated the movement in its early phases. Two leading spokesmen for the spiritualist cause, Thomas Lake Harris and Andrew Jackson Davis, viewed the mediumistic trance state as an avenue through which to discover one's true divinity. According to Harris, spiritualism taught individuals to become receptive to the "spirit of Christ, which descends to be immanent in the heart."[48] True religious faith is not intellectual but experiential in character. "To believe in God," Harris wrote, "is but to believe that the spirit which we feel flowing into ourselves flows from an Infinite Existing Source."[49] Harris turned to what he called "the spiritualist state of consciousness" not to contact departed relatives but to consecrate his senses and thereby discover the Divinity within."

Andrew Jackson Davis was an apprentice cobbler in 1843 when the famed mesmerist J. Stanley Grimes passed through his hometown of Poughkeepsie. During a lecture-demonstration, Grimes randomly selected the young Davis for a volunteer subject. Davis turned out to be an adept trance subject and was soon performing such standard mesmeric feats as reading from books while blindfolded and reporting clairvoyant travels to distant locales. After several months of repeated journeys into the inner recesses of his mind, Davis suddenly realized that the self-induced mesmeric trance state was one in which "mighty and sacred truths spontaneously gushed up from the depths of my spirit."[50] Davis insisted moreover that these truths were being communicated to him by departed spirits. Not the least of these discarnate entities was Emanuel Swedenborg, who from his vantage point in heaven now had even more lessons to teach.

As spirits dictated one metaphysical treatise after another through the entranced Davis, friends feverishly recorded every word. These lessons from the spirit world became a remarkable publishing success. In his major work, *The Harmonial Philosophy,* Davis and his spirit tutors wedded mesmerist psychology to Swedenborgian metaphysics. The text explains that human consciousness is arranged along a continuum, ranging from "rudimental" sensory awareness all the way to the "spiritual state," in which we may experience "a high reality, an expansion of the mind's energies, a subjugation of material to spiritual, of body to soul."[51] Davis painstakingly argued that the spiritual state is distinct from, and superior to, other realms of the unconscious, such as those achieved through ordinary hypnosis. In the spiritual state—and the spiritual state alone—the mind is able to "hold communion with the sanctified."[52]

With time the proponents of spiritualism became ever less concerned with the inner spirituality sought by its founders. They gravitated toward the staging of showy seances which offered a paying clientele palpable evidence that they had indeed made contact with the other side. The hopes generated by the early spiritualists for the reconciliation of science and religion consequently shifted elsewhere. The emerging field of parapsychology was one example.[53] The British Society for Psychical Research, and its American counterpart, attracted eminent scholars and wealthy "seekers" alike to their study of such phenomena as trance mediumship, telepathy, clairvoyance, ghostly apparitions, and life after death. William James put his finger on the underlying reason that he and others found themselves turning to parapsychology: "Science has come to be identified with a certain fixed general belief, the belief that the deeper order of Nature is mechanical exclusively, and that non-mechanical categories are irrational ways of conceiving and explaining such a thing as human life."[54]

The famed psychic researcher F. W. Myers said that the Society for Psychical Research had emerged out of the Weltschmerz felt by individuals in modern society. Science had undermined the factual basis of Christian belief, leaving the educated public bereft of a credible metaphysic. Myers, like his sometime collaborator William James, thought that parapsychology held out a promise of softening the outlines of nature so as to make faith possible again in a scientific age. "The search for new facts," he wrote, "is precisely what our Society undertakes."[55]

In his monumental work, *Human Personality and Its Survival of Bodily Death,* Myers amassed an overwhelming body of testimony about paranormal occurrences which had led him "to believe that there was truth in a thesis which at least since Swedenborg and the early mesmerists had been repeatedly, but cursorily and ineffectually, presented to mankind—the thesis that a communication can take place from mind to mind without the agency or the recognized organs of sense."[56] His investigations of paranormal phenomena prompted Myers to hypothesize the existence of what he called the ultramarginal or subliminal self. The self of waking consciousness, he argued, is but a fragmentary manifestation of a nonempirical, transcendental Self.

Such an extra-somatic field of consciousness would make otherwise mysterious phenomena like telepathy, clairvoyance, or, for that matter, life after death explicable in terms of psychological science. It could also be said to corroborate the truth of what Myers termed "the preamble of all religions"—the existence of an invisible spiritual reality.[57] Their belief in this transcendental Self provided Myers and his associates with a powerful symbol of *communitas* with which to oppose the encroachments of an industrialized society upon personal and communal vitality. As one review of *Human Personality* noted, "The conception of telepathy proves that the kinship between souls is more fundamental than their separation."[58] The psychology of the unconscious thus made it possible to affirm essential tenets of democratic faith despite the evidence of the senses to the contrary. The discovery that human consciousness opens up to a transpersonal realm revealed, moreover, that what is ultimate and unconditional about life exists on a continuum with what is mundane and conditioned. If we can somehow establish a more conscious relationship with this inner realm, even the most routine affairs of everyday life may be experienced as enveloped by a higher reality.

The interest in reconciling "head and heart" that motivated so many of the early American psychologists made them sympathetic toward the aims of the Society for Psychical Research. William James, Boris Sidis, Morton Prince, William McDougall, and J. G. Rhine all showed professional interest in the society and its investigations.[59] G. S. Hall, though ambivalent in his endorsement of the society, recognized its importance for clarifying the metaphysical assumptions of academic psychology and admitted that its existence was a sign of "the utter inadequacy of current psychology in dealing with the unconscious."[60]

The tendency of American academic psychologists to make a distinction between the subconscious (forgotten memories, the regulation of psychological processes, etc.) and a supraconscious (paranormal mental states like those involved in telepathy or psychic healing) was exaggerated in the writings of those who addressed the general reading public. Richard M. Bucke's *Cosmic Consciousness* (1901) was without question the most influential of the works that taught Americans to distinguish between the "lower" and the "higher" unconscious minds. Bucke, a physician, had devoted years to studying the phenomenon of religious illumination from a psychological point of view. His research led him to conclude that in addition to the "simple consciousness" which governs our organismic processes and the "self consciousness" of reflective thought, a higher state of "cosmic consciousness" was also within the range of human potential. "Cosmic consciousness," he wrote, "was the consciousness of the cosmos, that is, of the life and order of the universe"[61] Describing Walt Whitman's experience of such a state of expanded awareness, Bucke spoke of "ineffable light—light rare, intelligible, lighting the very light—beyond all signs, descriptions, languages."[62]

True, up to this stage in humankind's psychical evolution few had attained this lofty state of enlightenment; but, as Bucke's research suggested, incidences of cosmic consciousness were

occurring at an increasing rate, foreshadowing the onset of a New
Age. He prophesied that the faculty for cosmic consciousness
would eventually become universal. The psychic realm that Paul
had entered and called Christ, that Gautama had entered and
called Nirvana, that Whitman had entered and called Brahmic
Splendor, was on the fringes of ordinary consciousness and coming closer with every day. Bucke observed that cosmic consciousness could be brought on by drugs; but, he cautioned, the state
induced by drugs is an "artificial and bastard cosmic consciousness."[63] Besides exhorting his readers to learn to place themselves
"in the right mental attitude," however, Bucke unfortunately had
little to offer those who desired a personal glimpse of cosmic consciousness. He could but encourage them to emulate the biographical details of history's most enlightened souls and dream
of some future evolutionary epoch.

By the mid-twentieth century the appetites of the reading
public had grown more demanding. An increasing number were
not satisfied to postpone psychic awakening; they yearned for
techniques that would produce cosmic consciousness within
themselves. Human potential movements and various transpersonal psychologies emerged to meet this demand. Roberto Assagioli, in his avidly received *Psychosynthesis* (1965), asserted that
the distinguishing feature of his psychology was that it was primarily concerned with "the activation of superconscious energies
and the arousing of latent potentialities."[64] Assagioli cites such
authorities as Bucke and Jung in his effort to distinguish among
the lower unconscious, the middle unconscious, and the higher
unconscious. Unlike the lower two, the higher unconscious is neither the simple preconscious workings of our biological instincts
nor a by-product of our social development. It is, in fact, a level
of consciousness that transcends the physical self. The higher
unconscious can provide a locus for the unification and integration of the disparate elements of our various social roles. Contact
with the superconscious brings higher, psychic energies into the
service of our waking personality. With a logic recalling James's
pragmatic criterion of truth, Assagioli assured his readers that his

psychology was none the less scientific because it dealt with an entity like the higher unconscious: "May I emphasize the fact that the elements and functions coming from the superconscious, such as aesthetic, ethical, religious experience, intuition, inspiration, states of mystical consciousness, are *factual,* are real in the pragmatic sense (Wirklich to use the significant German word), because they are *effective* (Wirkend), producing changes both in the inner and the outer world."[65]

Assagioli's was an early voice in what soon became a litany of psychologies dedicated to the proposition that, through the unconscious mind, each of us participates in a transpersonal psychic realm. In 1969 *The Journal of Transpersonal Psychology* was created to weld the findings of psychologists such as Assagioli and Abraham Maslow into a full-fledged "fourth force" in American psychology. The stated purpose of the journal was to serve as a clearinghouse for studies in

> unitive consciousness, meta-needs, peak experiences, ecstasy, mystical experience, being, essence, bliss, awe, wonder, transcendence of self, spirit, sacralization of everyday life, oneness, cosmic awareness, cosmic play, individual and species-wide synergy, the theories and practices of meditation, spiritual paths, compassion, transpersonal cooperation, transpersonal realization and actualization; and related concepts, experiences and activities.[66]

The common denominator was interest in what are somewhat euphemistically referred to as "altered states of consciousness." Recently Charles Tart has emerged as the unofficial guru of the cult of any and all states of consciousness qualitatively distinct from the normal waking state. In a series of publications including *Altered States of Consciousness, Transpersonal Psychology,* and *States of Consciousness,* Tart champions the view that various altered states such as those induced by drugs, meditation, dreaming, and hypnosis are in many ways "superior" to the normal waking state as known in modern Western cultures.[67] Altered states not only promote personality integration, enrich our aesthetic appreciation of everyday life, and freshen perception, they hold the key to recovery of the long-neglected spiritual insights of both Eastern and Christian mystical traditions.

For Tart and others writing in post-Timothy Leary America, Bucke's admonition against drug-induced incursions into the unconscious seems to have lost its moral force. By the mid-1970s, Stanislav Grof's LSD-based research into the hidden "realms of the unconscious" was being hailed by American Jungians, humanistic psychologists, and proponents of transpersonal psychology. Grof's studies offer laboratory evidence suggesting that the unconscious consists of a series of successively deeper levels. From its beginnings in the lower Freudian-like personal unconscious, the unconscious extends into transpersonal realms in which telepathy, clairvoyance, and the experience of past lives are common and lawful occurrences.[68] Grof's research thus supports the parapsychologists in their belief that the unconscious is our point of connection with "the higher subtle and transpersonal realms of being."[69]

Americans' fascination with spiritualism and parapsychology is the sign of a pervasive concern to reconcile scientific method and religious belief. As parapsychologist Robert Monroe recently explained, the value of research into such manifestations of the "higher" unconscious as out-of-the-body experiences and extra-sensory perception is to be found in the empirical proof they furnish in support of the "belief that (1) man's Inner Self is neither understood nor fully expressed in our contemporary society; and (2) this Inner Self has capabilities to act and perform mentally and materially to a degree unknown and unrecognized by modern science."[70]

Whether we find them exploring inner selves through the writings of academic psychologists or through those of psychic researchers such as Edgar Cayce, Lawrence LeShan, or Stanley Krippner, it is hard to escape the conclusion that Americans' continuing interest in their unconscious mind is motivated by the compelling need to find evidence in support of religious faith. By depicting our capacity to experience an invisible spiritual reality, popular accounts of the unconscious supply ostensibly scientific proof for what F. W. Myers termed the "preamble of all religion." And although theologians might well object that persons should be helped to establish more than just the preamble of faith, it is nonetheless to the credit of our popular psychologies that they have so persistently done no less.

Epilogue

TO assess the validity of psychological concepts is a precarious enterprise. For one thing, it presupposes a commitment to some particular set of epistemological criteria. And this, of course, is precisely what is lacking in contemporary psychological thought. Furthermore, because all epistemologies are rooted in philosophical and metaphysical assumptions about the nature of the universe, any conclusions are destined to be the product of circular reasoning. Rather than judging the relative plausibility of competing psychological models, we are apt to find ourselves legislating a particular conception of reality and then picking the model that corresponds best to that conception.

A great deal depends on whether we understand psychological ideas as belonging to the natural sciences *(naturwissenschaften)* or the humanities *(geisteswissenschaften)*. A great deal of modern psychology rightfully belongs to the natural science tradition. Those psychologists who view their discipline exclusively in these terms are correct to restrict discussions of the unconscious to objectivist and positivist criteria of knowledge. This is not to say that psychological reality is itself so clearly delimited. Nor, as Karl Mannheim points out, does a psychological model's suitability as a research hypothesis entail equal usefulness as a guide to meaningful conduct.

The purpose of this book has been to draw attention to the fact that psychological concepts, while originating in the world of scientific discourse, perform many of the cultural functions traditionally associated with philosophy and theology. Psychological theories offer fully articulated interpretations of human nature, identify the sources of human suffering, and point the way to human betterment and progress. To the extent that psychological systems attempt to nourish our sense of identity and purpose, they conform to the pattern of the humanities, or sciences of the spirit. Indeed, psychology now constitutes the dominant cultural form through which Americans seek to understand the nonempirical "realities" that sustain and give meaning to human existence.

Modern culture's fascination with science has given the concept of the unconscious its salience as a symbol of humanity's higher nature. The unconscious is, after all, a direct inference from empirically verifiable facts of human behavior and consequently commands a certain intellectual authority.[1] But what has given the unconscious its religious salience is its affinity with what Perry Miller calls the continuities of American culture. The fact that the ontological and metaphysical assumptions associated with the aesthetic strand of American religious thought has persistently guided Americans' interpretations of the unconscious does not necessarily vitiate their social scientific validity. It does, however, enable them to perform the additional functions of myth and symbol.

As Paul Tillich repeatedly reminded us, authentic religious symbols are not created by ecclesiastical fiat but emerge spontaneously out of the "cultural situation." That is, they arise out of "a period's characteristic mode of self-interpretation" of the "cultural forms which express modern man's interpretation of his existence."[2]

> In the light of the twentieth-century's *rediscovery of the unconscious,* it is *now* possible for Christian theology to re-evaluate positively the sacramental mediation of the Spirit.

One could even say that a Spiritual Presence apprehended
through the consciousness alone is intellectual and not truly
spiritual.[3]

The function of religious symbols is to induce belief in the
existence of some nonempirical order of reality. Both logically
and experientially, symbols "precede" formal theology. The
validity of a religious symbol thus hinges upon pragmatic or psychological issues rather than theological ones. It is a simple historical fact that liberal Protestant thought has shown a tendency
to see the whole of religion as dependent upon the existence of a
sui generis mode of human experience in which the self becomes
aware of a spiritual MORE. Ever since Schleiermacher, the
defense of religious faith against the criticisms of its "cultured
despisers" has entailed articulation of its "preamble"—a prereflective, preconscious dimension of human personality in which
a higher spiritual reality is directly apprehended. Indeed, from
Emerson on, a good many Americans have been so convinced
that theology must commence with the study of consciousness
that they necessarily regard psychological discourse as pregnant
with religious meaning. That Americans should find psychological theories of the unconscious spiritually edifying is thus not
only understandable but perhaps even worthy of emulation.[4]

The discovery of the unconscious in the twentieth century in
many ways represents a refinement of themes long grown in liberal American religious thought. As a symbol of the spiritual core
of human nature, the unconscious has enabled modern individuals to embrace the categories of secular culture without capitu-
lating to them. That is, the "American unconscious" has served
to deflect facile attempts to reduce explanations of human behavior to the scientific categories of material (e.g., physiological) and
efficient (e.g., environmental conditioning) causation. Insofar as
the individual can be seen as unconsciously linked to a nondetermined motivational force, it is possible to view scientific categories as properly superceded by metaphysical considerations of
the ultimate (e.g., teleological or providential) cause of adaptive

behavior.[5] From the mesmerists in the 1840s to contemporary spokespersons for the humanistic branch of American psychology, the unconscious has symbolized this possibility of reconciling scientific and religious models of human nature in some kind of higher conceptual synthesis.

The unconscious has occupied a precarious position within American psychological thought. On the one hand, it has persistently threatened to thwart the discipline's scientific aspirations by equivocating the significance of precise causal terminology. This, in fact, is precisely why psychoanalysts and behaviorists alike have so adamantly resisted the incursion of the "American unconscious" into academic psychology. Yet, the unconscious has made it possible to recognize the role of final or ultimate causes—those that lie beyond the psychological dimension proper—in guiding human behavior. In so doing, the unconscious has enabled psychology to perform a variety of religious and cultural functions for which it would otherwise be ill equipped. It has fostered a renewed sensibility to a communal ground of reality that is both the depth out of which our individuality arises and the fund of meaning to which our lives contribute.[6] In an age in which individuals can easily become lost in the pursuit of external measures of worth, the unconscious has forced recognition of our participation in deeper metaphysical orders of reality and thereby made it possible to affirm life's intrinsic meaning. The psyche, as symbol of our spiritual depth, is thus a modern vehicle for the aesthetic spirituality which has beckoned Americans to behold the beauty of living in harmony with what Emerson called "the divinity which flows through all things."

Notes

Introduction

1. Martin Gross, *The Psychological Society* (New York: Random House, 1978), p. 4.
2. Gordon Allport, *Becoming* (New Haven: Yale University Press, 1955), p. 4.
3. Henri Ellenberger, *The Discovery of the Unconscious* (New York: Basic Books, 1970).
4. See also Lancelot Whyte's *The Unconscious Before Freud* (New York: Basic Books, 1960).
5. Paul Tillich, *The Theology of Culture* (New York: Oxford University Press, 1959), p. 5.
6. Paul Tillich, *Dynamics of Faith* (New York: Harper and Row, 1957), p. 42. Of interest is the fact that Tillich defined theology as the religious response to a "cultural situation," a term which he variously defined as "a period's characteristic mode of self-interpretation" or the "cultural forms which express modern man's interpretation of his existence" (see his *Systematic Theology,* 3 vols. (Chicago: University of Chicago Press, 1967), 1: 4, 5). Tillich went on to state, "In light of the twentieth-century *rediscovery of the unconscious,* it is *now* possible for Christian theology to re-evaluate positively the sacramental mediation of the Spirit. One could even say that a Spiritual Presence apprehended through the consciousness alone is intellectual and not truly spiritual" (*Systematic,* 3: 122, emphasis mine).

201

Chapter One

1. Perry Miller, *Errand Into the Wilderness* (Cambridge: Belknapp Press, 1975), p. 185.

2. Ibid., p. 192.

3. William Clebsch, *American Religious Thought* (Chicago: University of Chicago Press, 1973), p. xvi.

4. Ibid., p. xv.

5. Jonathan Edwards, *The Works of Jonathan Edwards,* 4 vols. (New Haven: Yale University Press, 1957), 2: 95.

6. Ibid., 2: 205.

7. Norman Fiering, in his *Jonathan Edwards' Moral Thought and its British Context* (Chapel Hill: University of North Carolina Press, 1981), cautions against the tendency of scholars who—following Perry Miller—interpret Jonathan Edwards as adhering to an essentially Lockean epistemology. Pointing out that Edwards did not share Locke's extreme positivism, Fiering correctly observes that Edwards was "a supranaturalist and a metaphysician all of his life" (p. 36). Fiering's qualifications should not, however, obscure the important fact that Edwards agreed with Locke's contention that sensation and direct experience are the basis of all knowledge; it was Edwards's special genius to construct a psychological theory of experience that included a special faculty for the sensing of divine things.

8. Edwards, *Works,* 2: 254–255.

9. Ibid., 2: 206.

10. Charles Feidelson offers an excellent discussion of Edwards's participation in the development of a distinctly American tradition of literary symbolism. Feidelson, agreeing with the central thesis of this chapter, contends that American literary symbolism is primarily rooted in the aesthetic as opposed to the moral or mechanistic strain of the Puritan tradition. See his *Symbolism and American Literature* (Chicago: University of Chicago Press, 1953).

11. Jonathan Edwards, *Observations Concerning the Scripture Oeconomy of the Trinity and Covenant of Redemption,* cited in Feidelson, p. 100.

12. Alexis de Tocqueville, *Democracy in America,* 2 vols., trans. Henry Reeve et al. (New York: Alfred A. Knopf, 1945), 2:31–32.

13. Miller, p. 197.

14. Ralph Waldo Emerson, *The Complete Works of Ralph Waldo Emerson,* 12 vols. (New York: AMS Press, 1968), 1: 62.

15. Ibid., 1: 62.

16. Since Perry Miller wrote his essay "From Edwards to Emerson," American intellectual historians have found it increasingly problematic to assert any easy line of continuity or direct link between these individuals. Yet, as Conrad Cherry points out in *Nature and Religious Imagination: From Edwards to Bushnell* (Philadelphia: Fortress Press, 1980): "Nevertheless Perry Miller's generalization captures an essential truth: there was, from early Puritanism to Edwards to Emerson, a persistent effort in New England to confront images of God within the physical universe" (p. 2).

17. Sydney E. Ahlstrom, *A Religious History of the American People,* 2 vols. (New Haven: Yale University Press, 1972), p. 605.

18. Emerson, *Works,* 1: 10.

19. Ralph Waldo Emerson, *The Journals and Miscellaneous Notebooks of Ralph Waldo Emerson,* 14 vols. (Cambridge, Mass.: Harvard University Press, 1960), 4: 28.

20. Ralph Waldo Emerson, *The Early Lectures of Ralph Waldo Emerson,* 3 vols. (Cambridge, Mass.: Harvard University Press, 1959), 2: 89.

21. Emerson, *Works,* 1: 27.

22. Ibid., 2: 282.

23. Emerson, *Journals,* 7: 450.

24. Emerson, *Works,* 4: 33.

25. Ibid., 4: 35.

26. Ibid., 1: 73.

27. Ibid., 3: 26. Emphasis mine.

28. Ibid., 1: 76.

29. Emerson, cited in Stephen Whicher's *Freedom and Fate* (Philadelphia: University of Pennsylvania Press, 1953), p. 87. Of further

interest is Emerson's response to Swedenborg's "On the Intercourse Between the Soul and the Body Which Is Supposed to Take Place by Physical Influx or By Pre-Established Harmony." Pondering the choice, Emerson sided with the influx theory and concluded that the human being is "an organ recipient of life from God." Unfortunately, Swedenborgian metaphysics did little to help Emerson clarify the psychological foundations of such a claim. See Kenneth Cameron's *Young Emerson's Transcendal Vision* (Hartford: Transcendental Books, 1971).

30. George Ripley, review of James Martineau, *The Rationale of Religious Enquiry, The Christian Examiner* 21 (1836): 254.

31. Emerson, *Works,* 1: 63.

32. Ahlstrom, p. 1019.

33. William G. McLoughlin, *Revivals, Awakenings, and Reform* (Chicago: University of Chicago Press, 1978), p. 103.

34. Miller, p. 55.

35. Charles G. Finney, cited in McLoughlin, p. 126.

36. Finney, cited in McLoughlin, p. 125.

37. Charles G. Finney, cited in William McLoughlin, *Modern Revivalism* (New York: Ronald Press, 1959), p. 84.

38. Ibid.

39. Whitney Cross, *The Burned-Over District* (Ithaca: Cornell University Press, 1950), p. 183.

40. Emerson, *Works,* 11: 486.

41. Herbert Hovenkamp, *Science and Religion in America, 1800–1860* (Philadelphia: University of Pennsylvania Press, 1978), p. 37.

42. Edward Hitchcock, *The Religion of Geology and Its Connected Sciences* (Boston: Phillips, Sampson and Company), p. 433.

43. Hovenkamp, p. 44.

44. McLoughlin, *Revivals,* p. 152.

45. John Fiske, *Through Nature to God* (New York: Houghton Mifflin, 1899), p. 191.

46. Lyman Abbott, *The Theology of an Evolutionist* (New York: The Outlook Company, 1925), p. 8.

47. Lyman Abbott, *Reminiscences* (Boston: Houghton Mifflin, 1915), p. 462.

48. John Bascom, *Evolution and Religion; or, Faith as a part of a complete cosmic system* (New York: G. P. Putnam's Sons, 1897), p. 201–202.

49. Horace Bushnell, *The Vicarious Sacrifice,* 2 vols. (New York: Charles Scribner's Sons, 1903), 1: 422. Interestingly, Bushnell once cited the mystic seer Emanuel Swedenborg and the enraptured ontologist Jonathan Edwards in a single breath extolling God's sustaining presence in nature, in *Nature and the Supernatural is Together Constituting the One System of God* (New York: Charles Scribner, 1858), p. 188.

50. Bushnell, *God in Christ* (Hartford, 1849), p. 74, and *Christ in Theology* (Hartford, 1851), p. 87, quoted in Feidelson, p. 155.

51. Henry Ward Beecher, *Evolution and Religion,* 2 vols. (New York: Fords, Howard, Hulbert, 1885), 1: 119.

52. Ibid., 1: 123.

Chapter Two

1. A more complete account of Poyen's lecture tour can be found in my *Mesmerism and the American Cure of Souls* (Philadelphia: University of Pennsylvania Press, 1982). This chapter is, in fact, constructed from materials presented in that book. The citation here comes from Poyen's personal account of his efforts on behalf of mesmerism, entitled *Progress of Animal Magnetism in New England* (Boston: Weeks, Jordan, 1837).

2. Franz Anton Mesmer, quoted in Ellenberger, *The Discovery of the Unconscious* (New York: Basic Books, 1970), p. 62.

3. Poyen, *Progress,* p. 63.

4. Ibid., p. 35.

5. William Stone, *Letter to Dr. A. Brigham on Animal Magnetism* (New York: George Dearborn, 1837), p. 81.

6. A Practical Magnetizer [pseud.], *The History and Philosophy of Animal Magnetism and Practical Instructions for the Exercise of Its Power* (Boston: 1843), p. 8.

7. Ibid., p. 9.

8. Ibid., p. 8.

9. A selected bibliography of the mesmerists' writings is included in my *Mesmerism and the American Cure of Souls.*

10. A Gentleman of Philadelphia, *The Philosophy of Animal Magnetism Together with the System of Manipulating Adopted to Produce Ecstasy and Somnambulism* (Philadelphia: Merrihew and Dunn, 1837.)

11. See Chauncy Townshend, *Facts in Mesmerism* (London: Bailliere Press, 1844).

12. Ibid., p. 222. Emphasis mine.

13. LaRoy Sunderland, *"Confessions of a Magnetizer" Exposed* (Boston: Redding, 1845), p. 22.

14. Joseph Buchanan, *Neurological System of Anthropology* (Cincinnati: 1854), p. 252.

15. George Bush, *Mesmer and Swedenborg* (New York: John Allen, 1847), p. 160.

16. Poyen, *A Letter to Colonel William Stone* (Boston: Weeks, Jordan., 1837), p. 6.

17. Ibid., p. 47.

18. From an unsigned article in *Buchanan's Journal of Man* 1 (1849): 319.

19. Poyen, *Letter to Stone,* p. 27.

20. Sunderland, *"Confessions,"* pp. 19–22.

21. J. Stanley Grimes, *The Mysteries of the Head and the Heart Explained,* 3rd ed. (Chicago: Sumner, 1881).

22. A Gentleman of Philadelphia, *Philosophy.*

23. Joseph Haddock, *Somnalism and Psycheism of the Science of the Soul as Revealed by Mesmerism* (London: Hodson, 1848), p. 4.

24. Buchanan, p. 195.

25. Ibid., Appendix I.

26. Poyen, *Progress,* p. 88.

27. Ibid.

28. A Gentleman of Philadelphia, p. 68.

29. Ibid., p. 71.

30. A Practical Magnetizer, p. 19.

31. John Dods, *The Philsophy of Electrical Psychology* (New York: Fowler and Wells, 1850), p. 57.

32. Theodore Leger, *Animal Magnetism, or Psychodynamy* (New York: D. Appleton, 1846), p. 18.

33. John Dods, *The Philosophy of Mesmerism* (Boston: William Hall, 1843), p. 137.

34. Dods, *Electrical Psychology,* p. 22.

35. Ibid., p. 28.

36. John Dods, *Spirit Manifestations Examined and Explored* (New York: DeWitt and Davenport, 1854), p. 92.

37. Dods, *Electrical Psychology,* p. 36.

38. George Bush, p. 47.

39. Ibid., p. 127.

40. Ibid., p. 13.

41. Ibid., p. 168.

42. Phineas Quimby, *The Quimby Manuscripts* (New York: Thomas Crowell, 1921), p. 30.

43. Ibid.

44. Ibid., p. 180.

45. Ibid., p. 319.

46. Ibid., p. 62.

47. Ibid., p. 243.

48. Ibid., p. 173.

49 Ibid., p. 210.

Chapter Three

1. William James, *The Varieties of Religious Experience* (New York: Collier, 1961), p. 100. James's appreciative analysis of the mind cure movement in the chapters under the title "The Religion of Healthy-Mindedness" remains the most illuminating account of mind cure to date. Other noteworthy discussions of the movement can be found in Gail Thain Parker's *The History of Mind Cure in New England* (Hanover: University Press of New England, 1975), Donald Meyer's *The Positive Thinkers* (New York: Doubleday and Co., 1965), and my *Mesmerism and the American Cure of Souls* (Philadelphia: University of Pennsylvania Press, 1982).

2. James, p. 102.

3. Henry H. Goddard, "The Effects of Mind on Body as Evidenced by Faith Cures," *American Journal of Psychology* 10 (1899): 432.

4. Ibid., p. 447.

5. Ibid., p. 498. Goddard is here citing the works of a Dr. Edes.

6. Ibid., p. 496.

7. Ibid., p. 497.

8. A. A. Roback, *History of American Psychology* (New York: Library Publishers, 1952), p. 121.

9. These dates, while only approximate, demarcate the period between the appearance of William James's *Principles of Psychology* (New York: Holt, 1890) and John Watson's *Psychology From the Standpoint of a Behaviorist* (Philadelphia, Pa.: Lippincott, 1919). While James's monumental volume was among the first self-consciously functional psychologies, Watson's shifted the emphasis from "mental functionalism" to "behavioral functionalism" and, in so doing, inaugurated a new era in American psychological thought.

10. See Duane Schultz, *A History of Modern Psychology* (New York: American Press, 1957), p. 154.

11. Edwin G. Boring, *A History of Experimental Psychology* (New York: D. Appleton-Century Company, 1929), p. 538.

12. Titchener's psychology is usually identified with that of Wilhelm Wundt. Wundt's system was, however, more in keeping with the philosophical tradition of Leibnitz, Spinoza, and Hegel. By recasting

Wundt's work into a Lockean mold, it is quite possible that Titchener did structuralism a great disservice. See Arthur L. Blumenthal's "Wilhelm Wundt and Early American Psychology: A Clash of Cultures," in R. W. Rieber and Kurt Salzinger, eds., *Psychology: Theoretical-Historical Perspectives* (New York: Academic Press, 1981), pp. 25–42.

13. James Rowland Angell, "The Province of Functional Psychology," *The Psychological Review,* 14 (1907): 61–91.

14. As Darnell Rucker observes, the functionalist view of human behavior was "at once biological, psychological, and ethical.... It involves the idea of an agent with a feeling, emotive, willing nature, and it implies an object or purpose toward which it is directed." Sech's *The Chicago Pragmatists* (Minneapolis: University of Minnesota Press, 1969), p. 5.

15. John Dewey, "The Reflex Arc Concept in Psychology," *Psychological Review* 3 (1896): 357–370.

16. James Rowland Angell, *Psychology* (New York: Henry Holt, 1904), p. 455.

17. Ibid.

18. Ibid., p. 456.

19. My decision to characterize Woodworth's psychology as functional will no doubt be challenged by some readers who are aware of his differences with the viewpoints of Angell and Dewey. Woodworth's psychology is, however, for the most part functional in orientation. I might refer the reader to Duane Schultz's discussion of this issue in his *A History of Modern Psychology* (New York: Academic Press, 1975), pp. 168–170.

20. Robert S. Woodworth, *Psychology: A Study of Mental Life* (New York: Henry Holt, 1923), pp. 561, 562.

21. Ibid., p. 562.

22. Ibid.

23. Ibid., p. 565.

24. In my opinion, the three most succinct analyses of this "watershed" are William McLoughlin's chapter entitled "The Third Great Awakening, 1890–1920," in his *Revivals, Awakenings, and Reform* (Chicago: University of Chicago Press, 1978); Arthur Schlesinger's "A

Critical Period in American Religion, 1875–1900," *Proceedings of the Massachusetts Historical Society* 64 (1932–33): 532–538; and Robert Wiebe's *The Search For Order: 1877–1920* (New York: Hill and Wang, 1967).

25. Wiebe, p. 42.

26. McLoughlin, *Revivals,* p. 152.

27. Angell, "The Province of Functional Psychology," p. 88. Emphasis mine.

28. James Mark Baldwin, *Mental Development in the Child and Race* (New York: Macmillan, 1895), p. 215.

29. Ibid., p. 202.

30. Angell, "The Province of Functional Psychology," p. 96.

31. Edwin Starbuck, "Religion's Use of Me," in Vergilius Ferm, *Religion In Transition* (New York: Macmillan, 1937), p. 260.

32. Historical surveys of this movement within academic psychology can be found in Benjamin Heit-Hallahmini, "Psychology of Religion, 1880–1930: The Rise and Fall of a Psychological Movement," *Journal of the History of the Behavioral Sciences,* 10 (January 1974): 84–90 and Orlo Strunk's *The Psychology of Religion* (Nashville: Abingdon, 1959).

33. It is important to note that Baldwin, Hall, Starbuck, Leuba, Woodworth, Judd, and Coe all at one time anticipated a career in the ministry before redirecting their energies to a more scientifically based means of studying and nourishing human natures. Hall, Starbuck, Baldwin, Leuba, and Coe each specifically attributed his career shift to the inability of his conversion experience to hold up under the pluralizing forces of university education and urban living. See their respective autobiographies in Vergilius Ferm's *Religion in Transition* and E. G. Boring and G. Lindzey, *A History of Psychology in Autobiography* (New York: Appleton-Century-Crofts, 1967).

34. With the possible exception of James Leuba, those who contributed to the movement were trying to purge, not supplant, religious thinking. All were convinced that Darwinian theory demanded a new religious view of reality, and their studies were somehow minor steps toward that goal. Edward Scribner Ames, for example, used the findings of developmental psychology to formulate his own

"Theology from the Standpoint of Functional Psychology" *(American Journal of Theology,* 10 [April 1906]: 219–232.

35. Edwin Starbuck, *The Psychology of Religion* (New York: Charles Scribner's Sons, 1901), p. 108.

36. Ibid., p. 105. Emphasis mine.

37. Ibid., p. 146.

38. Starbuck, "Religion's Use of Me," p. 204.

39. Ibid., p. 202.

40. Dorothy Ross, *G. Stanley Hall: The Psychologist As Prophet* (Chicago: University of Chicago Press, 1972), p. 45.

41. G. S. Hall, *Life and Confessions of a Psychologist* (New York: D. Appleton, 1923), p. 359.

42. G. S. Hall, "The New Psychology," pt. 2, *Andover Review 3* (March 1885): 248.

43. G. S. Hall, *Adolescence,* 2 vols. (New York: D. Appleton, 1904) 2: 342.

44. G. S. Hall, "The New Psychology," pt. 1, *Andover Review* 3 (February 1885): 133. Hall later wrote, "Deep down in every individual slumbers a racial soul which acts autistically and comes into the consciousness of the individual only in the most imperfect and fragmentary way" ("The Psychology of the Nativity," *Journal of Religious Psychology,* 7 [1915]: 458–460.

45. G. S. Hall, "The New Psychology," pt. 1, p. 133.

46. Ibid., p. 123.

47. G. S. Hall, "Why Kant is Passing," *American Journal of Psychology* 23 (July 1912): 421.

48. A number of essays appraising the significance of Baldwin's works can be found in a volume edited by J. Broughton and D. Freeman-Noir entitled *The Cognitive-Developmental Psychology of James Mark Baldwin* (New York: Ablex, 1982).

49. Baldwin's autobiographical essay is included in the first volume of Boring and Lindzey, eds., *A History of Psychology in Autobiography.*

50. Edwin Boring disdainfully notes Baldwin's highly philosophical style by commenting that his work "contained too much theory and too little experimental fact to make a lasting impression in the days

of the new psychology. Baldwin's felicitous literary style, surpassed only by James, gave a transient vitality to his ideas; but his effect was not permanent." Boring, *A History,* p. 516.

51. Among the more important of Baldwin's books are *Darwin and the Humanities* (Baltimore: Review Publishing, 1909), *Development and Evolution* (New York: Macmillan, 1902), *Elements of Psychology* (New York: H. Holt, 1893), *Genetic Theory of Reality* (New York: Knickerbocker Press, 1915), *The Individual and Society* (Boston: R. Badger, 1911), *Mental Development in the Child and Race* (New York: Macmillan, 1895), and *Social and Ethical Interpretations in Mental Development* (New York: Macmillan, 1897). Due to its more cohesive and encompassive treatment of developmental psychology, I will confine most of my commentary to issues in his relatively late volume, *Genetic Theory of Reality.*

52. Examples of this would be the eighth stage in Erik Erikson's theory of personality development and the sixth stage of moral and religious development advocated by Lawrence Kohlberg and James Fowler, respectively.

53. James Mark Baldwin, "The Limits of Pragmatism," *Psychological Review* 11 (January 1904): 53.

54. James Mark Baldwin, "Reply to Moore's Criticisms," *Psychological Review* 11 (1904): 428.

55. Baldwin, *Genetic Theory of Reality,* p. 236.

56. Ibid., p. 28.

57. Baldwin, "Reply to Moore," p. 428.

58. Baldwin, *Genetic Theory,* p. 309.

59. Baldwin noted that the aesthetic state was experienced as "ecstasy or trance" and could be likened to the hypnotic state. These were, however, unacceptable designations because they implied a disassociated rather than a fully unified state.

60. Baldwin, *Genetic Theory,* p. 303.

61. Ibid., p. 304.

62. See also Louis Brink's "How the Concept of the Unconscious is Serviceable," *Journal of Philosophy and Psychology* 15 (1918): 405–414.

63. Louis Waldstein, *The Subconscious Self and Its Relation to Education and Health,* 2nd ed. (New York: Charles Scribner & Sons, 1926), p. 21.

64. Brink, p. 408.

65. A similarly entitled article appeared in *The Psychological Review* 5 (1898): 650–652.

66. *Psychological Bulletin* 11 (1914): 7–10.

67. *Psychological Bulletin* 14 (1917): 7.

68. Ibid., p. 10.

69. William James, "Does Consciousness Exist," *Essays in Radical Empiricism* (New York: E. P. Dutton, 1971), pp. 3–22.

70. *Psychological Bulletin* 15 (1918): 10.

71. *Psychological Bulletin* 16 (1919): 9.

72. Wiebe, p. xiv.

73. See Klaus Riegel, "Influence of Economic and Political Ideologies on the Development of Developmental Psychology," *Psychological Bulletin,* 78 (1972): 129–141.

Chapter Four

1. Charles Jaekle and William Clebsch, in their *Pastoral Care in Historical Perspective* (New York: Jason Aronson, 1975), nominate James as the historical figure par excellence of the modern "era of religious privacy."

2. William James, "What Pragmatism Means," in *Pragmatism* (New York: New American Library, 1974), p. 61.

3. Ibid.

4. No less astute an observer of American intellectual thought than Ralph H. Gabriel notes the value-conserving nature of James's writings by observing that he "never lost his awareness of [life's] mystery and believed pragmatism to be a method whereby the values of the old supernaturalism could be preserved." *The Course of American Democratic Thought* (New York: The Ronald Press, 1956), p. 348.

5. The biographical dimension of James's professional career has been plenteously studied. The best analyses are to be found in Gay Wilson Allen's *William James* (New York: Viking, 1967), William Clebsch's chapter on "The Religious Humanness of William James" in his *American Religious Thought* (Chicago: University of Chicago Press, 1973), Ralph Barton Perry's *The Thought and Character of William James,* 2 vols. (Boston: Little, Brown, 1935), and Cushing Stout's "The Pluralistic Identity of William James," *American Quarterly* 23 (1971): 135–152.

6. Henry James, Sr., *The Literary Remains of Henry James*, ed. William James (Boston: James R. Osgood, 1885), p. 14.

7. Ibid., p. 341.

8. Henry James, Sr., quoted in Stout, p. 142.

9. Henry James once confided to his close friend Ralph Waldo Emerson that he ought to "learn science and bring myself first into men's respect, that thus I may better speak to them" (Perry, 1: 43). This assumption that metaphysics can, and should, be rooted in sound empirical knowledge prefigured the course of William's own transition from physiology to psychology, and finally to philosophy and religious reflection.

10. William James, *Principles of Psychology.* Quoted in Clebsch, p. 145.

11. Erik Erikson, *Young Man Luther* (New York: W. W. Norton, 1962), p. 67.

12. Henry James, Jr., ed., *Letters of William James* (Boston: Kraus Reprint Co., 1969), 1: 130.

13. Ibid., 1: 158.

14. From a diary entry on April 10, 1873, included in Ralph Barton Perry, *The Thought and Character of William James: The Briefer Version* (Boston: Little, Brown, 1935), p. 136. The entry goes on to profess that "it is not necessary to attack the universal problems directly, and as such, in their abstract form.... [and that he preferred] solving minor concrete questions" concerning the ways of nature.

15. James's functionalism was, however, of a particular kind. It differed from more popular versions such as Spencer's by emphasizing the phenomenon of free variation equally with that of natural selection.

I refer the reader to an excellent discussion of James's functional position in Don Browning, *Pluralism and Personality* (Lewisburg, Pa.: Bucknell University Press, 1981), pp. 64–86.

16. I would refer the reader who might wish to follow up on—or debate—this designation to either Joseph Adelson's "Still Vital After All These Years," *Psychology Today* 16 (April 1982): 52–58, or Browning's *Pluralism and Personality.*

17. William James, *The Principles of Psychology,* 2 vols. (New York: Henry Holt, 1890), 1: v.

18. Ibid., 1: 1.

19. Ibid., 1: vi.

20. Ibid., 1: 8.

21. William James, *Psychology: The Briefer Course* (New York: Henry Holt, 1892), p. 467.

22. Ibid., p. 468.

23. Ibid.

24. Discussions of the phenomenological themes in James's work and their influence upon Heidegger, Husserl, and Whitehead can be found in Bruce Whilshire, *William James and Phenomenology* (Bloomington, Ind.: University of Indiana Press, 1968), Hans Linschoten, *On the Way Towards a Phenomenological Psychology* (Pittsburgh: Duquesne University Press, 1968), and John Wild, *The Radical Empiricism of William James* (New York: Anchor Books, 1970).

25. William James, *The Varieties of Religious Experience* (New York: Collier, 1971), p. 387.

26. Ibid., p. 191.

27. Ibid.

28. Ibid., p. 193.

29. F. W. Myers, cited in William James, "What Psychical Research Has Accomplished," in *The Will to Believe* (New York: Dover, 1956), p. 316. James cites this passage again in *Varieties,* p. 396.

30. James, *The Will to Believe,* p. 321.

31. James, *Varieties,* p. 396, and *A Pluralistic Universe* (New York: E. P. Dutton, 1971), p. 264.

32. James, *Varieties,* p. 193.

33. James, "The Hidden Self," *Scribner's Magazine* (March 1890): 373.

34. James, *Pluralistic Universe,* p. 264.

35. Ibid., p. 224.

36. Ibid., p. 196.

37. James, *Varieties,* p. 401.

38. James, *Pluralistic Universe,* p. 266.

39. James, *Varieties,* p. 399.

40. James, *Pluralistic Universe,* p. 267.

41. Ibid., p. 266.

42. James, *Varieties,* p. 399.

43. Ibid., p. 172.

44. Ibid.

45. Ibid., p. 233.

46. Ibid., p. 405.

47. James, *Pluralistic Universe,* p. 267.

48. James, *Varieties,* p. 401.

49. James, *Pluralistic Universe,* p. 137.

50. James, *Varieties,* pp. 104 and 110.

51. Ibid., p. 396.

52. Ibid.

53. Ibid., p. 398.

54. Ibid., p. 393.

55. Ibid.

56. James wrote, "God is the natural appelation, for us Christians at least, for the supreme reality, so I will call this higher part of the universe by the name of God" (Ibid., p. 399).

57. Ibid., p. 400.

58. Ibid., p. 400, 407.

59. Ibid., p. 407.

60. James, *Pluralistic Universe,* p. 270.

61. James, *Varieties,* p. 399.

Chapter Five

1. Since Freud's theories concerning the unconscious are inseparable from the larger matrix of psychoanalytic doctrines, this chapter is necessarily linked with broader considerations of the history of psychoanalysis in America. I would like to acknowledge my indebtedness to several historical and interpretive studies of the reception which psychoanalysis has received in the United States. Nathan A. Hale, *Freud and the Americans: The Beginning of Psychoanalysis in the United States, 1876–1907* (New York: Oxford University Press, 1971), is the most comprehensive survey of the introduction of Freud's theories to American audiences. Helpful assessments of the impact of Freud's work on American psychology include David Shakow and David Rapaport, *The Influence of Freud on American Psychology* (New York: International Universities Press, 1964), and Gardner Murphy, "The Current Impact of Freud in American Psychology," in Benjamin N. Nelson, ed., *Freud and the 20th Century* (New York: World Publishing, 1957). Three excellent interpretive essays are: F. H. Matthews, "The Americanization of Sigmund Freud: Adaptations of Psychoanalysis before 1917," *Journal of American Studies* 1 (1967): 39–62; Maurice Green and R. W. Rieber, "The Assimilation of Psychoanalysis in America," in Rieber and Salzinger, *Psychology: Theoretical-Historical Perspectives* (New York: Academic Press, 1980), pp. 263–304; and Joseph Adelson, "Freud in America: Some Observations," *American Psychologist*, (1956): 467–470.

2. See, for example, Harry Woodburn Chase, "Psychoanalysis and the Unconscious," *The Pedagogical Seminary* 17 (1910): 281–327, and L. L. Thurstone, "Influence of Freudism in Theoretical Psychology," *Psychological Review* 31 (1924): 175–183.

3. Nathan Hale has observed, "In America popular and professional cultures are closely bound together, and, beginning with the Clark Conference, the reception of psychoanalysis occurred on both levels" (Hale, p. 20).

4. *Psychological Review* 33 (1924): 175–218.

5. Joseph Jastrow, *The House That Freud Built* (New York: Greenburg, 1932).

6. Nathan G. Hale, from a personal communication cited in Shakow

and Rapaport, p. 26. See also Hale's restatement on this thesis in *Freud and the Americans,* pp. 332, 363–364.

7. Boris Sidis, *The Psychology of Suggestion: A Research into the Subconscious Nature of Man and Society* (New York: D. Appleton, 1911), p. 22.

8. William James, "The Hidden Self," *Scribner's Magazine* (March 1890): 373.

9. Elwood Worcester, Samuel McComb, and Isador Coriat, *Religion and Medicine: The Moral Control of Nervous Disorders* (New York: Moffat, Yard, 1908), p. 43.

10. Ibid., p. 73. Nathan Hale has commented:

> The Emmanuel Movement functioned as a transition from the supernaturalism of the mind cure cults to scientific psychotherapy. When Worcester hinted that the subliminal self disposed of the infinite resources of the universe, he retained a strain of transcendentalism and of the hopes of psychic researchers, of whom he was one. . . . The Emmanuel Movement not only helped to prepare the way for psychoanalysis, but together with the enthusiasm for the mysterious subliminal self, also helped to compromise it. (Hale, pp. 248–249)

11. *Psychotherapy,* 3 vols. (New York: Centre Publishing Corporation of New York, 1909).

12. Richard C. Cabot, "The American Type of Psychotherapy," *Psychotherapy* 1, 1 (1909): 6.

13. *Psychological Bulletin* 4 (1907): 352–354.

14. Richard C. Cabot, "Creative Assertions," *Psychotherapy* 1, 2 (1909): 15.

15. Richard C. Cabot, "Work Cure," in *Psychotherapy* 3, 1 (1969): 24–29.

16. Richard C. Cabot, "The Literature of Psychotherapy," *Psychotherapy* 3, 4 (1909): 21.

17. Janet was, no doubt, well aware of his relatively greater popularity with American psychologists, as would appear evident in his self-serving comparison of his work with Freud's in an article entitled "Psychoanalysis" in the *Journal of Abnormal Psychology* 9 (1914): 1–35, 153–187.

18. Sidis's relocation of the "seat" of neurosis in the interpersonal realm prefigured Fromm's and Horney's important contributions to psychoanalytic theory. As early as 1918 William McDougall noted this development by observing that "Dr. Boris Sidis has, by applying the Freudian method, sought to show that fear is the source of all the psychoneuroses, all those troubles of thought and conduct which Freud attributes to the sex-impulse, and Adler to the self-assertive tendency and its opposite" ("The Present Position in Clinical Psychology," *Proceedings of the Royal Society of Medicine* 12 [1918]: 7).

19. Boris Sidis, "The Psychotherapeutic Value of the Hypnoidal State," in Morton Prince, ed., *Psychotherapeutics* (Boston: Richard G. Badger, 1909), p. 132.

20. Morton Prince, *The Unconscious* (New York: MacMillan, 1921), p. 149.

21. An unsigned review of Prince's book praised Prince for "rejecting [Freud's] far-fetched erotic interpretations" and demonstrating how Freud's work could be restated in a more acceptable fashion. *The Nation* 98 (April, 1914): 369–370.

22. Morton Prince, *The Unconscious,* p. 183.

23. Ibid., p. 196.

24. H. Addington Bruce, "Some Books on Mental Healing," *Forum* 43 (1910): 316–323; "The New Mind Cure Based on Science," *The American Magazine* 70 (1910): 773–778; and "Masters of the Mind," *The American Magazine* 71 (1910): 71–81.

25. H. Addington Bruce, "Some Books on Mental Healing," p. 318.

26. H. Addington Bruce, "The New Mind Cure Based on Science," p. 774.

27. H. Addington Bruce, "Some Books on Mental Healing," p. 317.

28. H. Addington Bruce, "Masters of the Mind," p. 81.

29. Maurice Green and R. W. Rieber, "The Assimilation of Psychoanalysis in America," p. 266.

30. By 1920, Brill and Jones were still the only two North American exponents of psychoanalysis who had met any measure of success in authoring book-length discussions of Freud's views. See A. A.

Brill, *Psychoanalysis: Its Theories and Practical Application* (Philadelphia: Saunders, 1912) and Ernest Jones, *Papers on Psycho-Analysis* (Condon: Bailliere, 1913).

31. Sigmund Freud, "Five Lectures on Psychoanalysis," *American Journal of Psychology* 21 (1910): 181–218; H. Addington Bruce, "Some Books on Mental Healing" and "Masters of the Mind;" and Ernest Jones, "Freud's Psychology." *Psychological Bulletin* 7 (1910): 109–128.

32. Sigmund Freud, *A General Introduction To Psychoanalysis* (New York: Simon and Schuster, 1963), p. 260.

33. Ibid., p. 188.

34. An excellent appraisal of Freud's views concerning the unconscious can be found in M. M. Gill, *Topography and Systems in Psychoanalytic Theory* (New York: International Universities Press, 1963).

35. See Paul Ricoeur, *Freud and Philosophy* (New Haven: Yale University Press, 1970).

36. Sigmund Freud, *An Outline of Psychoanalysis* (New York: W. W. Norton, 1949), p. 19.

37. Philip Rieff, *Freud: The Mind of the Moralist* (New York: Harper and Row, 1961), and *The Triumph of the Therapeutic* (New York: Harper and Row, 1966).

38. Hale, pp. 430–431.

39. Ibid., p. 431.

40. William A. White, *Mental Mechanisms* (Washington, D.C.: The Journal of Nervous and Mental Disease Publishing Company, 1911), p. 96.

41. In *Outlines of Psychiatry* (Washington, D.C.: Nervous and Mental Disease Publishing Company, 1923), White summarized the aim of psychoanalytic treatment by explaining:

    These patients come with no adequate philosophy of life . . . [and therefore] must be slowly changed by a process of reeducation in which the personality of the physician and his attitude toward the whole situation play a prominent part. (p. 58)

42. The almost utopian character of White's interpretation of psychoanalysis is revealed in his enumeration of "preventative principles

in the field of mental medicine":

> The full possibilities of the influence of the environment are only beginning to be appreciated. If a change in environment will actually change the shape of the skull in one generation, as has been recently shown by Professor Boas, what may we not expect from hygienic surroundings and proper educational methods? (*Mental Mechanisms,* p. 142).

43. Henri Bergson, cited in White, *Outlines of Psychiatry,* p. 19.

44. Carl Rahn, review published in *The Psychological Bulletin* 14 (1917): 327.

45. Edwin B. Holt, *The Freudian Wish and Its Place in Ethics* (New York: Henry Holt, 1915), p. 203.

46. Ibid., p. 100.

47. Ibid., p. 132.

48. Among the many excellent studies which have examined the covert religiosity and moralism in the professionalization of American social science are Mary O. Furner, *Advocacy and Objectivity: A Crisis in the Professionalization of American Social Science, 1865–1905* (Lexington, Ky.: University of Kentucky Press, 1975); Roy Lubove, *The Professional Altruist: The Emergence of Social Work as a Career, 1880–1930* (Cambridge, Mass.: Harvard University Press, 1965); David W. Noble, *The Paradox of Progressive Thought* (Minneapolis: University of Minnesota Press, 1958); and John C. Burnham, "Psychiatry, Psychology and the Progressive Movement," *American Quarterly* 12 (1960): 457–465.

49. Burnham, "Psychiatry, Psychology and the Progressive Movement," p. 463.

50. See, for example, Cabot's article entitled "Work Cure" in *Psychotherapy,* (Volume 1, No. 1, 24–29, and Volume 1, No. 2., 20–27); James Jackson Putnam, when describing psychoanalysis to readers of *Scientific American,* advocated its acceptance on the grounds that it leads to the "cultivation of social ideals" (*Scientific American Supplement* 78 [1914]: 391–392); and in *The Child's Unconscious Mind* (New York: Dodd, Mead, 1919), Winifrid Lay argued that psychoanalysis would make a more exact science of education by teaching us how to make use of the laws which govern our unconscious dispositions toward learning and educational authorities.

51. Burnham, "Psychiatry, Psychology and the Progressive Movement," p. 462.

52. The aesthetic vision of Emerson and Bergson made it possible for Putnam to turn his discussion of instincts and their relationship to human motivation into a discourse on the presence of "ideal possibilities" imparted to human life at a preconscious level. Metaphysically considered, "the most real' thing about a man may be defined, then, as the creative spirit which is immanent in him" (*Human Motives* [Boston: Little, Brown, 1915], p. 135).

53. Sigmund Freud in the preface to James Jackson Putnam, *Addresses on Psycho-Analysis* (London: Hogarth Press, 1951), p. iii.

54. Sigmund Freud, cited in Hale, p. 374.

55. Putnam, *Human Motives,* p. 72.

56. James Jackson Putnam, "A Plea for the Study of Philosophic Method In Preparation for Psychoanalytic Work," *Journal of Abnormal Psychology* 6 (1911): 252.

57. James Jackson Putnam, "Dream Interpretation and the Theory of Psychoanalysis, *Journal of Abnormal Psychology* 9 (1914): 58.

58. Ibid., p. 59. Nathan Hale has commented:

    It was as if the age of Transcendentalism were being reborn and its claims endorsed by natural science. America's "greatest modern discovery" was that the mind was not drably bound to inevitable laws of nature. Rather, mind was itself "creative," and education could now take a spiritual direction. (p. 247)

59. Putnam, "A Plea for the Study of Philosophic Method In Preparation for Psychoanalytic Work," p. 253.

60. James Jackson Putnam, "The Psychology of Health," *Psychotherapy* 1, 4 (1909): 40.

61. It is interesting to note the striking resemblance between Putnam's motivational hierarchy and that developed approximately forty years later by Abraham Maslow. See the chapter "Instincts and Ideas" in *Human Motives.* Also, and perhaps even more striking, is Putnam's discussion of independent ego energies in a paper still unfinished at the time of his death in 1918. Prefiguring the work of Heinz Hartmann and Robert White, Putnam argued that the higher mental processes are not simply a by-product of sublimation but

rather derive from independent mental energies. See his "Elements of Strength and Elements of Weakness in Psychoanalytic Doctrine" in *Addresses of Psycho-Analysis,* pp. 448–456.

62. Putnam, *Human Motives,* p. 141.
63. Ibid., p. vii.
64. L. Pierce Clark's review of *Human Motives,* in *Journal of Abnormal Psychology* 10 (1915): 366.
65. Putnam, "A Plea for the Study of Philosophic Method," p. 263.
66. Sigmund Freud, in a personal communication to I. C. P. Oberndorf and included in Oberndorf's *A History of Psychoanalysis in America* (New York: Grune and Stratton, 1953), p. 246.
67. G. Stanley Hall, in a letter to Martin L. Reymert on July 21, 1919. Cited in Dorothy Ross, *G. Stanley Hall: The Psychologist as Prophet,* (Chicago: University of Chicago Press, 1972), p. 408.
68. William James, in a letter to Theodore Flourney on September 28, 1909, and included in Henry James, ed., *The Letters of William James,* 2 vols. (Boston: Atlantic Monthly Press, 1920), 2: 328.
69. William McDougall, *Outline of Psychology* (New York: Charles Scribner's Sons, 1923), p. 131.
70. Robert S. Woodworth, "Some Criticisms of the Freudian Psychology," *Journal of Abnormal Psychology* 12 (1917): 174–194.
71. Bernard Hart, "The Concept of the Subconscious," *Journal of Abnormal Psychology"* (1910): 351–371.
72. E. E. Southard, "Sigmund Freud, Pessimist," *Journal of Abnormal Psychology* 14 (1914): 197–216.
73. Jastrow, *The House That Freud Built,* p. 174.
74. Ibid.
75. Walter D. Scott, "An Interpretation of the Psychoanalytic Method in Psychotherapy," *Journal of Abnormal Psychology* 3 (1909): 376.
76. Harry Woodburn Chase, "Psychoanalysis and the Unconscious," *The Pedagogical Seminary* 17 (1910): 314.
77. Frederick Lyman Wells, "Critique of Impure Reason," *Journal of Abnormal Psychology* 6 (1912): 89–93, and Knight Dunlap, *Mysticism, Freudianism and Scientific Psychology* (St. Louis: C. V. Mosby, 1920).

78. *The Nation* 96 (1913): 505.

79. Edna Heidebreder, "Freud and Psychology," *Psychological Review* 47 (1940): 195.

80. *Journal of Abnormal Psychology* 18 (1924): 129.

81. Adelson, "Freud in America," p. 467.

82. J. Victor Haberman noted in 1914 that Freud had received a more favorable reception in America than in Europe ("A Criticism of Psychoanalysis," *Journal of Abnormal Psychology* 9 (1914): 265–280). Frederick J. Hoffman, *Freudianism and the Literary Mind* (Baton Rouge, La.: Louisiana State University Press, 1945), explores the penetration of Freud's ideas into American intellectual thought. See also Stow Persons, *American Minds* (New York: Holt, 1958), and Phillip Rieff, *Freud: The Mind of the Moralist.*

83. Foremost among those volumes which have employed language vaguely suggestive of psychoanalytic theory for the ongoing "cult of the unconscious" are Emile Coue, *Self Mastery through Conscious Autosuggestion* (New York: American Library Service, 1922); Norman Vincent Peale, *The Power of Positive Thinking* (New York: Prentice-Hall, 1952); and Maxwell Maltz, *Psycho-Cybernetics* (Englewood Cliffs, N.J.: Prentice-Hall, 1960).

84. Mathews, "The Americanization of Sigmund Freud," p. 61.

85. See Heinz Hartmann, *Ego Psychology and the Problem of Adaptation* (New York: International Universities Press, 1958), and Robert White, *Ego and Reality in Psychoanalytic Theory: A Proposal Regarding Independent Ego Energies* (New York: International Universities Press, 1967).

86. Karen Horney, *Neurotic Personality of Our Times* (New York: Norton, 1937); *New Ways in Psychoanalysis* (New York: W. W. Norton, 1939); *Neurosis and Human Growth* (New York: Norton, 1945).

87. Thomas Harris, *I'm OK—You're OK* (New York: Avon, 1973), p. 22.

88. Ibid., pp. 22, 23.

89. Ibid., p. 49.

90. Ibid., p. 257.

Chapter Six

1. Joseph Jastrow, *Fact and Fable in Psychology* (Boston: Houghton Mifflin, 1900), p. 12.

2. Joseph Jastrow, *The Subconscious* (Boston: Houghton Mifflin, 1905), p. vii. Emphasis mine.

3. See, for example, Thomas Camfield, "The Professionalization of American Psychology, 1870–1917," *Journal of the History of the Behavioral Sciences* 9 (1973): 66–75.

4. John B. Watson commented that "behaviorism is a direct outgrowth of studies in animal behavior during the first decade of the twentieth century." Cited in Duane Schultz, *A History of Modern Psychology* (New York: Academic Press, 1975), p. 178.

5. James's often-overlooked essays entitled "Remarks on Spencer's Definition of Mind as Correspondence," "Great Men and Their Environment," and "The Importance of Individuals" are, in this context, important early installments in the humanistic attack upon behaviorism's reductionistic tendencies. For a discussion of the differences between James's and Skinner's use of evolutionary-adaptive models in the explanation of human behavior, see Don Browning, *Pluralism and Personality* (Lewisburg, Pa.: Bucknell University Press, 1980).

6. John B. Watson, "Psychology as the Behaviorist Views It," *Psychological Review* 20 (1913): 158–177.

7. John B. Watson, *Behavior: An Introduction to Comparative Psychology* (New York: Holt, Rinehart and Winston, 1967), p. 7.

8. H. W. Chase, "Consciousness and the Unconscious," *Psychological Bulletin* 9 (1912): 22. Chase's original article, "Psychoanalysis and the Unconscious," appeared in *The Pedagogical Seminary* 17 (1910): 281–327.

9. H. W. Chase, "Consciousness and the Unconscious," p. 23. The article, written by B. Hart, appeared in the *Journal of Abnormal Psychology* 4 (1917): 351–371.

10. A. P. Weiss, "Relation Between Functional and Behavior Psychology," *Psychological Review* 24 (1917): 354.

11. A. P. Weiss, "Consciousness and the Unconscious," *Psychological Bulletin* 15 (1918): 10.

12. K. S. Lashley, "The Behavioristic Interpretation of Consciousness," *Psychological Review* 30 (1923): 333. Emphasis mine.

13. William McDougall, *An Introduction to Social Psychology* (London: Methuen, 1908), p. 26.

14. An illuminating discussion of the role of "instinct" in American psychological thought can be found in R. J. Herrnstein, "Nature vs. Nurture: Behaviorism and the Instinct Doctrine," *Behaviorism* 7 (1972): 23–52.

15. The quoted material comes from Watson, *Behavior,* p. 106.

16. Watson, "Psychology as The Behaviorist Views It," p. 158.

17. Ibid.

18. John B. Watson, *Behaviorism* (New York: W. W. Norton, 1925), p. 3.

19. Ibid.

20. Ibid., p. 180.

21. Ibid., p. 192.

22. Ibid., p. 210. Watson's views concerning the unconscious and repression have remained the more or less standard behaviorist position on this subject. See, for example, John Dollard and Neal Miller's chapter entitled "The Unconscious: How Repression is Learned," in their *Personality and Psychotherapy* (New York: McGraw-Hill, 1950), pp. 198–221.

23. Ibid.

24. Ibid., p. 82.

25. The principal explanatory model employed by Watson was that of conditioned and unconditioned reflexes and implied that almost all behavior is stimulated by the external environment. Skinner, on the other hand, suggests that the "reflex" constitutes only a small portion of an individual's behavior. In Skinner's view, most behavior is randomly initiated and then, subsequently, shaped and controlled by environmental reinforcements. In Skinner's words, "behavior is shaped and maintained by its consequences."

26. B. F. Skinner, *About Behaviorism* (New York: Alfred A. Knopf, 1974), p. 20.

27. B. F. Skinner, *Science and Human Behavior* (New York: Macmillan, 1953), p. 252.

28. In *About Behavior,* Skinner writes:
    > The best-known division of mind is between consciousness and unconsciousness. . . . It is often said, particularly by psychoanalysts, that behaviorism cannot deal with the unconscious. The fact is that, to begin with, it deals with nothing else. (p. 157)

29. B. F. Skinner, *Beyond Freedom and Dignity* (New York: Vintage Books, 1972), p. 183.

30. Skinner, *About Behaviorism,* p. 158.

31. Skinner, *Beyond Freedom and Dignity,* p. 191.

32. John C. Burnham, "Psychiatry, Psychology and the Progressive Movement," *American Quarterly* 12 (1960): 457–465.

33. Weiss, "Relation Between Functional and Behavioral Psychology," p. 367.

34. David Bakan, "Behaviorism and American Urbanization," *Journal of the History of the Behavioral Sciences* 2 (1966): 5–28.

35. John B. Watson, in Carl Muchison, ed., *A History of Psychology in Autobiography,* vol. 3 (New York: Russell and Russell, 1961), p. 271.

36. Ibid., p. 274.

37. Ibid., p. 276.

38. Watson, *Behaviorism,* p. 17.

39. Bakan, "Behaviorism and American Urbanization," p. 12.

40. John B. Watson, *Psychology from the Standpoint of a Behaviorist* (Philadelphia: J. B. Lippincott, 1924), pp. xi-xii.

41. Robert S. Woodworth, *Contemporary Schools of Psychology* (New York: Ronald Press, 1931), p. 92.

42. Ibid.

43. David Bakan offers some insightful comments concerning Watson's synthesis of Darwinian and Wesleyan thought in his "Politics and

American Psychology," in R. W. Rieber and Burt Salzinger, *Psychology: Theoretical-Historical Perspectives,* (New York: Academic Press, 1980), pp. 125–144. Paul Creelan has also assessed the formative role which Watson's religious heritage had in the development of behavioral psychology. See both his "Watsonian Behaviorism and the Calvinist Conscience," *Journal of the History of the Behavioral Sciences* 10 (1974): 95–118, and his "Religion, Language, and Sexuality in J. B. Watson," *Journal of Humanistic Psychology* 15 (1975): 55–78.

44. Watson, *Behaviorism,* from the preface.
45. Creelan, "Religion, Language, and Sexuality in J. B. Watson," p. 58.
46. Edna Heidebreder, *Seven Psychologies* (New York: Appleton-Century-Crofts, 1933), p. 256.
47. Watson, *Behaviorism,* p. 248.
48. Peter Homans, *Theology After Freud* (Indianapolis: Bobbs-Merrill, 1970), p. 103.
49. B. F. Skinner, in Edwin Boring and Gardner Lindzey, eds. *A History of Psychology in Autobiography,* vol. 5 (New York: Appleton-Century-Crofts, 1967), p. 409.
50. To Watson, religion was identical with the imitation of pious behavior. In *Behaviorism* (p. 219), he wrote:

> In talking about the personality of an individual we often hear the phrase, "He is a deeply religious man." What does that mean? It means that the individual goes to church on Sunday, that he reads the Bible daily, that he says grace at the table, that he sees to it that his wife and children go with him to church, that he tries to convert his neighbor into becoming a religious man and that he engages in many hundreds of other activities all of which are called parts of a modern Christian's religion. Let us put all of these separate activities together and call them the *religious habit system* of the individual.

Skinner, in his third autobiographical volume, *A Matter of Consequences* (New York: Alfred Knopf, 1983), confesses that his psychology is a direct intellectual heir to the ascetic wing of Puritan theology. Interestingly, Skinner repeatedly acknowledges the structural similarity between his views and those of Jonathan Edwards. He does not, however, offer any hint that he is aware of the aesthetic strain in Edwards's thought such as has been amply analyzed by such noted intellectual historians as Perry Miller and William Clebsch. Skinner, instead, sees in Edwards only a confirmation of his own views that nature is an orderly system utterly determined by mechanistic laws and forces.

51. In his autobiographical essay in Carl Murchison's *A History of Psychology in Autobiography*, vol. 3 (New York: Russell and Russell, 1961), Watson wrote (p. 274), "I never knew what he [Dewey] was talking about and, unfortunately for me, I still don't know." Watson consistantly lumped Angell's and James's position with that of "monk's lore" and "old wives' tales." In attempting to account for James's unwillingness to accept a radical behaviorism, Watson suggested that James's motive was "not difficult to find . . . its roots lie in mysticism and early religious trends" (*British Journal of Psychology* (1929): 99).

52. George Santayana, "Living Without Thinking," *Forum* 68 (1922): 735. For a more persuasive treatment of Santayana's somewhat off-handed observation, see Lewis Brandt, "Behaviorism—The Psychological Buttress of Late Capitalism," in Allan Buss, ed., *Psychology in Social Context* (New York: Irvington, 1978).

53. George Santayana, p. 735.

54. Daniel Shea, Jr., "B. F. Skinner: The Puritan Within," *The Virginia Quarterly Review,* 50 (1974): 416–437.

55. David Bakan gives an excellent discussion of American Protestantism and what he calls its "exaggeration of agency and repression of communion" in the chapter entitled "Protestantism, Science, and Agency," in his *The Duality of Human Existance* (New York: Rand McNally, 1966).

56. See A. O. Lovejoy, "The Paradox of the Thinking Behaviorist," *The Philosophical Review* 31 (1922): 135–147, and Noam Chomsky, *For Reasons of State* (New York: Pantheon, 1971).

57. Santayana, "Living Without Thinking," p. 734.

58. James R. Angell, "Behavior as a Category of Psychology," *Psychological Review* 20 (1913): 255.

59. Ibid., p. 260.

60. Ibid., p. 268.

61. Ibid., p. 267.

62. Karl Mannheim, *Ideology and Utopia* (New York: Harcourt, Brace and World, 1968), p. 22.

63. Ibid., p. 17.

64. Ibid., p. 21.

65. My discussion here borrows from Don Browning's excellent critique of the ideological character of contemporary psychology in his *Pluralism and Personality* (Lewisburg, Pa.: Bucknell University Press, 1980).

66. Jon Krapfl and Ernest Vargas have edited an excellent volume of essays that offer a sympathetic treatment of behaviorism's positive contributions to ethical philosophy. See their *Behaviorism and Ethics* (Kalamazoo, Mich.: Behaviordelia, 1977).

67. B. F. Skinner, *Cumulative Record* (New York: Meredith Corporation, 1959), p. 36.

68. William Barrett, *The Illusion of Technique* (Garden City, NY: Doubleday, 1978), p.314.

69. Shea, Jr., "B. F. Skinner: The Puritan Within," p. 434.

Chapter Seven

1. Abraham Maslow, *Toward a Psychology of Being* (Princeton, N.J.: D. Van Nostrand Co., 1962), p. ix.

2. Anthony Sutich, cited in Abraham Maslow, *Religions, Values and Peak Experiences* (New York: Viking, 1970), pp. 70–71.

3. Commentary in *The Psychological Bulletin* 14 (1917), cited previously in Chapter 3, would appear worth repeating in this connection as it helps to explain why Jung's work received so little attention by American psychologists in the first part of this century:

   It seems a pity that a part of the immense labor which Jung must have undergone in writing his *Psychology of the Unconscious* could not have been expended in learning something of modern psychology, of which he shows an amazing ignorance (p. 10).

4. See, for example, Robert E. Valelt, "Carl Gustav Jung (1875–1961): Some Contributions to Modern Psychology," *Journal of Humanis-*

tic Psychology 2 (1962): 23–34, and John Levy, "Transpersonal Psychology and Jungian Psychology," *Journal of Humanistic Psychology* 23 (1983): 42–51.

5. Two helpful accounts of the relationship between phenomenology, existentialism, and humanistic psychology are Henry K. Misiak and Virginia Staudt Sexton, *Phenomenological, Existential, and Humanistic Psychologies* (New York: Grune and Stratton, 1973), and Rollo May's opening chapter in his *Existence* (New York: Simon and Schuster, 1958).

6. Carl Rogers, "Toward a Science of the Person," *Journal of Humanistic Psychology* 3 (1963): 72.

7. See Misiak and Sexton, *Phenomenological, Existential, and Humanistic Psychologies,* p. 108, and May, *Existence,* pp. 10 and 15. See also Joseph Gibert, "William James in Retrospect: 1962," *Journal of Humanistic Psychology* 2 (1962): 90–95, and Donald Meyer, "The Scientific Humanism of G. Stanley Hall," *Journal of Humanistic Psychology* 11 (1971): 201–213.

8. May, *Existence,* pp. 36, 10. May added (perhaps unaware of James's direct influence upon Whitehead and Husserl):

> There is an obvious similarity between existentialism, in its emphasis on truth as produced in action, and the process philosophies, such as truth as produced in action, and the process philosophies, such as Whitehead's, and American pragmatism, particularly as in William James. (p. 13)

9. Kurt Goldstein, *The Organism: A Holistic Approach to Biology Derived from Pathological Data in Man,* paperback edition (Boston: Beacon Press, 1963), p. 197. Goldstein later amplified these insights in his *Human Nature in the Light of Psychopathology* (Cambridge, Mass.: Harvard University Press, 1949).

10. *Journal of Humanistic Psychology* 1 (1961): vii.

11. See Joseph Rychlak's discussion of this issue in his *The Psychology of Rigorous Humanism* (New York: Wiley, 1977).

12. Examples of humanistic psychology's concern with returning psychology to the study of mental processes which in some way "transcend" the subject-object sphere are Andras Angyal's distinction between autonomy and homonomy in *Foundations For a Science of Personality* (New York: Commonwealth Fund, 1941), David Bak-

an's distinction between agency and communion in *The Duality of Human Existence* (Chicago: Rand McNally, 1966), and Ernest Schachtel's distinction between autocentricity and allocentricity in *Metamorphosis* (New York: Basic Books, 1959).

13. May, *Existence*, p. 91. Emphasis mine.

14. Rollo May, *Freedom and Destiny* (New York: W. W. Norton, 1981), p. 84.

15. Ibid., p. 176. May continued by explaining that after letting go, "the help of which he was not aware comes from the client's preconscious, and in Jungianism, it would probably be interpreted as a voice from the unconscious" (p. 178).

16. Walter A. Weisskopf, "Existential Crisis and the Unconscious," *Journal of Humanistic Psychology* 7 (1967): 58–65.

17. Ibid., pp. 60, 59.

18. Ibid., p. 60.

19. Ibid., p. 61.

20. Ibid., p. 64.

21. Ibid., p. 65.

22. Ibid., p. 65.

23. Maslow, *Toward a Psychology of Being*, pp. 191, 25. A more complete discussion of Maslow's work can be found in Salvatore R. Maddi and Paula T. Costa, *Humanism in Perspective* (Chicago: Aldine, 1972); Richard J. Lowry, *A. H. Maslow* (Monterey, Calif.: Brooks/Cole, 1973); and Frank G. Goble, *The Third Force* (New York: Grossman, 1976).

24. Maslow, *Toward a Psychology of Being*, p. 192.

25. Ibid., p. 25.

26. Maslow, *Religions, Values, and Peak Experiences*, p. xvi.

27. Abraham H. Maslow, *The Farther Reaches of Human Nature*, (New York: Viking, 1972), p. 333. Emphasis mine.

28. Ibid., p. 277.

29. Ibid., p. 112.

30. Ibid., p. 115.

31. Maslow, *Religions, Values, and Peak Experiences*, p. 45.

32. Ibid., p. 55.

33. Viktor Frankl, *Man's Search For Meaning* (New York: Pocket Books, 1963), p. 164.

34. Ibid., p. 157.

35. Ibid., p. 187.

36. Vicktor Frankl, *The Unconscious God* (New York: Simon and Schuster, 1975), p. 15.

37. Ibid., p. 25.

38. Ibid., p. 61.

39. Ira Progoff, *Depth Psychology and Modern Man* (New York: Julian Press, 1959), p. 7. See also his "Toward a Depth Humanistic Psychology," *Journal of Humanistic Psychology* 10 (1970): 121–130.

40. Ira Progoff, *The Symbolic and the Real* (New York: Julian Press, 1963), pp. 68, 73.

41. Gardner Murphy, quoted in Williard B. Frick, *Humanistic Psychology: Interviews with Maslow, Murphy, and Rogers* (Columbus, Ohio: Charles E. Merrill, 1971), p. 58.

42. Gardner Murphy, autobiographical essay, included in Edwin G. Boring and Gardner Lindzey, eds., *A History of Psychology in Autobiography,* 5: 253–282.

43. See, for example, Willard Frick, "The Symbolic Growth Experience," *Journal of Humanistic Psychology* 23 (1983): 108–125; Stephen Wilson, "In Pursuit of Energy: Spiritual Growth in a Yoga Ashram," *Journal of Humanistic Psychology* 22 (1982): 105–116; Roger Walsh, "The Consciousness Disciplines," *Journal of Humanistic Psychology* 23 (1983): 28–39; Larry Baron, "Slipping Inside the Crack Between the Worlds: Carlos Castenada, Alfred Schutz, and the Theory of Multiple Realities," *Journal of Humanistic Psychology* 23 (1983): 52–69.

44. Martin Gross, *The Psychological Society,* (New York: Basic Books, 1978), p. 8.

45. Ibid., p. 4.

46. Christopher Lasch, *The Culture of Narcissism* (New York: Warner, 1979), p. 33.

47. I would like to draw attention to the fact that the final section of this

chapter closely follows two articles which I have previously written about the wider cultural significance of Carl Rogers's psychology: "Carl Rogers, Religion, and the Role of Psychology in American Culture," Journal of Humanistic Psychology 22 (1982): 21–32, and "Rogers' Impact on Pastoral Counseling and Contemporary Religious Reflection," in Ronald Levant and John Shlien, eds., *Client-Centered Therapy and the Person-Centered Approach: New Directions in Theory, Research and Practice* (New York: Praeger, 1984).

48. Carl Rogers, "This is Me," in *On Becoming a Person* (Boston: Houghton Mifflin, 1961); autobiographical essay in E. G. Boring and G. Lindzey, *A History of Psychology in Autobiography,* vol. 5; and *A Way of Being* (Boston: Houghton Mifflin, 1980).

49. Rogers, autobiographical essay in Boring and Lindzey, p. 351.

50. Ibid.

51. Ibid., p. 354.

52. Ibid., p. 355.

53. Carl Rogers, *Client-Centered Therapy,* (Boston: Houghton Mifflin, 1965), p. 522.

54. In a personal communication dated March 21, 1981, Dr. Rogers responded to this point by informing me:

> You have rather shrewdly picked out Emerson. I did a great deal of personal reading during my adolescence (that is, reading not required by school or college), and Emerson was one of my favorites. . . . The notion that a divine force might be a struggling force, struggling to express itself through my life and yours, as well as through the physical universe, has always appealed to me.

55. Rogers, *A Way of Being,* p. 106.

56. Ibid., p. 122.

57. Carl Rogers, "The Formative Tendency," *Journal of Humanistic Psychology* 18 (1978): 25. Emphasis mine.

58. Rogers, *A Way of Being,* p. 88.

59. Ibid., p. 8.

60. Ibid.

61. Ibid., p. 124.

62. Ibid., p. 137.

63. Carl Rogers, taped dialogue with Paul Tillich, San Diego State College, 1966.

64. Rogers, *A Way of Being,* p. 83.

65. Ibid., p. 88.

66. Ibid., p. 228.

67. William McLoughlin, *Revivals, Awakenings, and Reforms,* (Chicago: University of Chicago Press, 1978), p. 2.

68. Ibid., p. 214.

69. William Clebsch, *American Religious Thought* (Chicago: University of Chicago Press, 1973), p. 94.

Chapter Eight

1. Peter Berger, "Toward a Sociological Understanding of Psychoanalysis," *Social Research* 32 (1965): 39.

2. Martin Gross, *The Psychological Society* (New York: Random House, 1978), p. 9. See also Richard Weiss, *The American Myth of Success* (New York: Basic Books,1969).

3. Clifford Geertz, *The Interpretation of Culture* (New York: Basic Books, 1973), p. 312.

4. Peter Berger and Thomas Luckmann, *The Social Construction of Reality,* (New York: Anchor Books, 1967).

5. Geertz, pp. 122, 125.

6. Thomas Jay Hudson, *The Law of Psychic Phenomena; A working hypothesis for the systematic study of hypnotism, spiritualism, mental therapeutics, etc.* (Chicago: A. C. McClurg, 1897), p. 14.

7. Thomas Jay Hudson, *The Evolution of the Soul* (Chicago: A. C. McClurg, 1904), p. 5.

8. Thomas Jay Hudson, *The Divine Pedigree of Man; or, the Testimony of Evolution and Psychology to the Fatherhood of God* (Chicago: A. C. McClurg, 1899), p. 37.

9. Ibid.

10. Ibid.

11. Ibid., p. 41.

12. Henry Addington Bruce, *The Riddle of Personality* (New York: Moffat, Yard, 1908); *Scientific Mental Healing* (Boston: Little, Brown, 1911); "Some Books on Mental Healing," *Forum* 43 (1910): 316–323; "The New Mind Cure Based on Science," *The American Magazine* 70 (1910): 773–778.

13. Henry Addington Bruce, "Religion and the Larger Self," *Good Housekeeping* 62 (1916): 55–61.

14. Henry Addington Bruce, "The Soul's Winning Fight with Science," *The American Magazine* 77 (1917): 21–26.

15. M. Scott Peck, *The Road Less Traveled* (New York: Simon and Schuster, 1978), p. 243.

16. Ibid., p. 281.

17. Ibid., p. 283.

18. The influence of psychological thought upon modern pastoral activities is assessed in both William Clebsch and Charles Jaekle, *Pastoral Care in Historical Perspective* (New York: Jason Aronson, 1964) and E. Brooks Holifield, *A History of Pastoral Care in America* (Nashville: Abingdon Press, 1983).

19. Morton Kelsey, *Transcend* (New York: Crossroad, 1981).

20. Accounts of Evans's life and works can be found in Charles Braden, *Spirits in Rebellion* (Dallas: Southern Methodist University Press, 1963), and John F. Teahan, "Warren Felt Evans and Mental Healing: Romantic Idealism and Practical Mysticism in Nineteenth-century America," *Church History,* 48 (March 1979): 63–80.

21. Warren Felt Evans, *Mental Medicine: A Treatise on Medical Psychology* (Boston: H. H. Carter, 1886) p. 46.

22. Ibid., p. 266.

23. Warren Felt Evans, *Esoteric Christianity and Mental Therapeutics* (Boston: H. H. Carter, 1886), p. 1.

24. Evans, *Mental Medicine,* p. 53.

25. Warren Felt Evans, *The Primitive Mind Cure: The Nature and Power of Faith, or Elementary Lessons in Christian Philosophy and Transcendental Medicine* (Boston: H. H. Carter, 1885), p. 87.

26. Evans, *Mental Medicine,* p. 104.

27. Ralph Waldo Trine, *In Tune with the Infinite* (New York: Crowell, 1897), p. 16.

28. Ibid., from the preface.

29. Evans, *Primitive Mind Cure,* p. 125.

30. A fascinating discussion of New Thought's "psychologization" of the Protestant ethic can be found in Alfred Griswold, "New Thought: A Cult of Success," *The American Journal of Sociology* (November 1934): 309–318.

31. Henry Wood, *Ideal Suggestions through Mental Photography* (Boston: Lee and Shepard, 1893), p. 41.

32. Ibid., p. 97.

33. The best discussions of Christian Science's relationship to Quimby's teachings are to be found in Julius Dresser, *The True History of Mental Science* (Boston: Alfred Budge and Sons, 1887), Charles Braden, *Spirits in Rebellion,* Frank Podmore, *From Mesmer to Christian Science* (New York: University Books, 1963), and Robert Peel's three-volume biography, *Mary Baker Eddy* (New York: Holt, Rinehart, and Winston, 1966, 1971, 1977).

34. Norman Vincent Peale, *The Power of Positive Thinking* (New York: Prentice-Hall, 1952), pp. viii, vii.

35. Norman Vincent Peale, *A Guide to Confident Living* (New York: Prentice-Hall, 1948), p. 154.

36. Norman Vincent Peale, *Faith is the Answer* (New York: Prentice-Hall, 1950), p. 52.

37. Peale, *Faith is the Answer,* p. 48.

38. Donald Meyer, *The Positive Thinkers* (Garden City, N.Y.: Doubleday, 1965), p. 268.

39. Meyer's insistence upon reading Peale as a spokesman for simple autosuggestion is unfortunate. His tendency to project his own animus upon historical materials makes his often-quoted analysis of popular psychology unreliable. To claim that Peale's notion of the unconscious was that of a static receptacle for suggestions fed it by our conscious minds hardly does justice to the following quotations: "he thereby *opens* himself to the recreative power that *flows* constantly through the universe" (*A Guide to Confident Living,* p. 11);

"All around you at this moment is divine healing energy . . . [which is] available to you if you will believe" (ibid., p. 161); "There is a Higher Power, and that . . . power is constantly available. If you *open to it, it will rush in* like a mighty tide" (*Power of Positive Thinking,* p. 267); "Every great personality I have ever known . . . seem in harmony with nature and *in contact with* the Divine energy" (ibid., p. 39).

40. Peale, *The Power of Positive Thinking,* p. 39.

41. In his *Alternative Altars; Unconventional and Eastern Spirituality in America* (Chicago: University of Chicago Press, 1979), Robert Ellwood draws attention to the fact that "Zen, Swedenborgianism, Theosophy, or Vedanta, for example, are in American life far from what they are or were in Japan, eighteenth-century England, or nineteenth-century India . . . [They] better approached through the American emergent and excursus heritage from Emerson, Thoreau, Whitman, the Shakers and Spiritualists" (p. 168).

42. Maharishi Mahesh Yogi, *Transcendental Meditation* (New York: Signet Books, 1968), from the cover.

43. Maharishi Mahesh Yogi, *On the Bhagavad Gita* (New York: Penguin Books, 1968), p. 250.

44. Maharishi Mahesh Yogi, *Transcendental Meditation,* pp. 80, 81.

45. Ibid., p. 250.

46. Whitney R. Cross, *The Burned-Over District* (Ithaca: Cornell University Press, 1950), p. 342.

47. R. Laurence Moore, *In Search of White Crows* (New York: Oxford University Press, 1977), p. 9.

48. Thomas Lake Harris, "Modern Spiritualism. Its Truths and Its Errors," cited in Moore, p. 18.

49. Ibid., p. 12.

50. Andrew Jackson Davis, *The Great Harmonia* (Boston: Mussey, 1852), p. 47.

51. Andrew Jackson Davis, *The Harmonial Philosophy* (London: William Rider, 1957), p. 76.

52. Ibid.

53. As Davis explained:

    > Spiritualism is the first religion that takes facts for its foundation,
    > rears its temples of thought on immutable principles of
    > philosophy, recognizes a Mother as well as a Father in God . . .
    > [and] liberates mankind from slavery to creeds and gives the
    > individual wholly to himself. (Ibid., p. 412)

54. In addition to R. Laurence Moore's *In Search of White Crows,*
    which examines "spiritualism, parapsychology, and American culture," I would refer the interested reader to Seymour H. Mauskopf
    and Michael R. McVaugh, *The Elusive Science: Origins of Experimental Psychical Research* (Baltimore: Johns Hopkins University
    Press, 1980).

55. William James, "Presidential Address of William James to the Society for Psychical Research," in Robert Maclehouse's ed., *Presidential Addresses to the Society for Psychical Research* (Glascow, 1912),
    p. 81.

56. F. W. H. Myers, "Presidential Address to the Society for Psychical
    Research," *Proceeding of the Society for Psychical Research* XV
    (1900): 110–127.

57. F. W. H. Myers, *Human Personality and Its Survival of Bodily
    Death* (London: Longmans, Green, 1936), p. 8.

58. Myers, "Presidential Address," p. 117.

59. I. Woodbridge Riley, review of *Human Personality,* in *Psychological Bulletin* 10 (1903): 556–565. Woodbridge's ten-page review of
    Myers's work made the symbolic importance of belief in the unconscious mind clear to his fellow psychologists. Of interest is the fact
    that he noted "The epilogue to these volumes reads like the *Philosophy of Spiritual Intercourse* of Andrew Jackson Davis, the 'Poughkeepsie' seer. In the one psychic research is urged as a duty much as
    in the other spiritualism was urged as a religion." Woodbridge, after
    reviewing Myers's theories, gently chided him for his failure to
    reduce the alleged phenomena to extant psychological theory.

60. Many more undoubtedly shied away from overt identification with
    the SPR so as to protect their scientific persona. Angell, for example,
    always felt that he could not professionally identify with the SPR's
    activities even though he privately confessed that "I have often

myself been tempted to undertake some of the lines which you have followed" (Mauskopf and McVaugh, p. 49).

61. G. S. Hall, quoted in Amy M. Tanner's *Studies in Spiritism* (New York: D. Appleton, 1980), p. xviii.

62. Richard M. Bucke, *Cosmic Consciousness* (New York: E. P. Dutton, 1969), p. 3. The *Psychological Bulletin* also reviewed Bucke's work, although with considerable disdain (20 [1923]: 706–707). The reviewer, obviously referring to James's laudatory remarks about the book, noted, "By some, though not by the reviewer, this book is regarded as a contribution to psychology."

63. Bucke, p. 17.

64. Ibid., p. 379.

65. Roberto Assagioli, *Psychosynthesis* (New York: Viking, 1971), p. 6.

66. Ibid.

67. "Statement of Purpose," in *The Journal of Transpersonal Psychology* 11 (1979).

68. In his *States of Consciousness* (New York: Dutton, 1975), Tart notes the importance of distinguishing between "lower," "ordinary," and "higher" states of consciousness. The first of these is exemplified in psychotic states and dreaming, which could be explained within a Freudian-like theoretical framework. Ordinary consciousness corresponds to the highly rational waking state of mind found in modern Western nations. The "higher states of consciousness," Tart explains, consist of mystical experiences, marijuana intoxication, meditative states, and psychedelic drug-induced states.

69. See Stanislav Grof, *Realms of the Human Unconscious* (New York: Viking, 1975).

70. Robert Monroe, *Journey Out of the Body* (Garden City, N.Y.: Anchor Books, 1977) p. 38.

Epilogue

1. If by symbols we mean concepts that disclose the relationship between the empirical and nonempirical realms of human experience, they are by definition indispensable to the larger cultural tasks

performed by modern psychology. It should be noted, however, that symbols have cognitive significance only to the degree that they are anchored in empirical fact. For regardless of the nature of the transcendent reality which a symbol attempts to signify, it must be drawn from the realm of public experience and public knowledge.

It follows that the validity of the unconscious as a symbol of our harmony with a transpersonal spiritual order is ultimately linked with both the cultural and scientific plausibility of a very particular set of psychological facts. The American psychological tradition has for this reason displayed an enduring tendency to distinguish between those sets of data which imply the existence of a "lower" unconscious and those which testify to a "higher" unconscious. From Emerson and Quimby to Maslow and Rogers, Americans have argued that a properly empirical psychology must include the data of telepathy, clairvoyance, mystical experience, cosmic consciousness, metaphysical healings, and peak experiences. For example, William James's psychological investigations of just such phenomena convinced him that "the fact that the conscious person is continuous with a wider self through which saving experiences come . . . is literally and objectively true." And it is, James contended, precisely on the authority of this "objective" fact that we are justified in holding our various overbeliefs or religious convictions. Moreover, James was aware that the psychological symbol upon which he grounded his religious faith was potentially testable and subject to confirmation, revision, or abandonment. Concern with earning the scientific community's endorsement of "facts" which support belief in our connection with a transpersonal spiritual reality led James and a good many of his fellow functionalists to become highly supportive of the efforts of the Society of Psychical Research. So, too, has it prompted humanistic psychologists to become actively involved with the field of transpersonal psychology.

2. Paul Tillich, *Systematic Theology,* 3 vols. (Chicago: University of Chicago Press, 1967), 1: 4,5.

3. Ibid., 3: 122. Emphasis mine.

4. Any number of modern writers have presented thoughtful arguments for the "superiority" of theological models which rest squarely upon empirically derived considerations of "the farther reaches of human nature." Peter Berger, for example, favorably compares the inductive

approach to religious thought with both the deductive style of biblically minded theologians and the reductionistic tendencies of religion's secularist opponents. His *The Heretical Imperative* (Garden City, N.Y.: Anchor Press, 1979) argues that the only intellectually defensible approach to theology in the modern world is that epitomized by Schleiermacher and his concern with anchoring religion in the individual's experience of the sacred. Theologian David Tracy likewise maintains that the pluralistic character of the modern intellectual climate demands that responsible religious reflections begin with descriptions of the psychological structure of what he calls "limit experiences." Insofar as qualitatively distinct experiences disclose a point or limit at which our individual existence gives way to a religious MORE, they constitute the fundamental data of religious discourse; see his *The Blessed Rage for Order* (New York: Seabury Press, 1975).

5. It is not inconsequential that whereas European psychologists traditionally seem to be concerned with what the unconscious "is," Americans have been almost exclusively interested in what it does. By symbolizing the point of harmony between the individual and a transpersonal spiritual power, the unconscious has bestowed renewed poignancy to the covenantal structure of the nation's religious heritage. The concept of the covenant, promising as it does that God has established lawful means whereby humanity might be saved, has encouraged Americans to interpret psychology in utilitarian and even soteriological ways. As early as 1835, Charles Finney voiced the characteristically American hope that the procuring of salvation could be reduced to a lawful science. To Finney's way of thinking, the concept of the covenant implied that being saved "is not a miracle or dependent upon a miracle in any sense . . . it consists entirely in the right exercise of the powers of nature." The practical implication of such a view was clear: "He who deals with souls should study well the laws of the mind." A more or less similar covenantal world view has, it would seem, furnished the presuppositions upon which Americans have set about describing the nature and utility of the unconscious. For although there has never been a consensus concerning the existence of a distinct psychological entity as an unconscious mind, there has been an enduring belief that the mind's unconscious reaches can potentially attune the individual to what Emerson called that "force always at work to make the best better and the worst good."

6. In his highly respected *Soul Friend: The Practice of Christian Spirituality* (San Francisco: Harper and Row, 1980), Kenneth Leech observes how the recent renewal of interest in meditational and contemplative forms of spirituality can be attributed to the conceptions of consciousness emanating from such disparate sources as Timothy Leary, Thomas Merton, Hermann Hesse, Yoga, Zen, and Transcendental Meditation. Further illustration of the important role which the unconscious plays in modern religious thought are the many books by Morton T. Kelsey, such as *Transcend: A Guide to the Spiritual Quest* (New York: Crossroad, 1981), *Dreams: A Way to Listen to God* (Ramsey, N.J.: Paulist Press, 1979), and *The Other Side of Silence: A Guide to Christian Meditation* (Ramsey, N.J.: Paulist Press, 1976), in which he continuously reiterates his conviction "that there is a depth in humankind called the unconscious through which one experiences the spiritual world" (*Transcend,* p. 17).

Index

Index

Society for Psychical Research, 87, 190–92
Southard, E. E., 121
Spiritualism, 188–90
  James's (William) interest in, 102
  relationship to mesmerism, 187, 189
  relationship to Swedenborgianism, 187–88
  religious character of, 189–90
Starbuck, Edwin, 66–67, 89
Structural psychology, 55–56, 98, 208n
Sunderland, LaRoy, 37–38
Sutich, Anthony, 151
Suzuki, D. T., 186
Swedenborg, Emanuel, 81, 188
Swedenborgianism, 45, 88, 178, 188
Symbolic dimensions of psychology, 5, 199–200, 240n. *See also* Unconscious, as a religious symbol; symbolic aspects of

Tart, Charles, 194–95
Teilhard de Chardin, 127, 163
Thurstone, L. L., 99
Tillich, Paul, 6, 126, 127, 160, 194, 198
Tocqueville, Alexis de, 13
Townshend, Rev. Chauncy, 34–35
Transactional Analysis, 127
Transcendental Meditation, 186–87
Transpersonal psychology, 194
Trine, Ralph Waldo, 181–82

Unconscious
  alleged parapsychological attributes of, 31–33, 59, 100, 171, 176, 191, 195
  the "American" unconscious, 5, 126, 165, 242n
  antisocial properties of, 110–12
  behaviorists' objections to, 132–37
  cultural dimensions of doctrines about, 11, 61–65, 100, 165, 174–75, 242n
  in early developmental psychology, 67–72
  functions of, 4–5, 73–74
  "levels" of, 34–36, 72, 102, 119, 156, 162, 190, 192, 195

as point of contact with a higher reality, 15–16, 26, 36, 45, 88, 103, 119, 126, 128, 159–60, 162
in the psychology of religion, 65–67, 91–93
psychopathological aspects of, 87, 105–12
reeducable nature of, 106, 107, 114
relationship to belief in the power of positive thinking, 47–48, 181–85
relevance to moral philosophy, 93–94, 116, 146–49
as religious symbol, 44–45, 128, 163–65, 175–78, 195, 198–200
as reservoir of untapped potentials, 87–91, 105, 106, 115, 118, 124, 157, 160, 169, 181, 193
sexual nature of, 110–11, 113
as source of self-actualization, 154–55, 160, 162, 171
symbolic aspects of, 5, 6, 92–95, 128, 165, 172, 174–75, 198–99, 240n
as vehicle of divine influence, 15, 43–44, 88–92, 119, 162, 176, 179, 185, 199–200
Urbanization, 61, 76, 138–40, 174

Waldstein, Louis, 74
Watson, J. B.
  behaviorist views of, 134–35
  early life of, 137–38
  religious background and views of, 137–41, 228n
  repudiation of subjectivist language, 131, 134–35
Watts, Alan, 186
Weiss, A. P., 132, 138
Weisskopf, Walter, 157–58
Wells, Frederick L., 123
White, Robert, 125
White, William A., 113–14
Whitehead, Alfred, 163
Wiebe, Robert, 62, 76, 116
Worcester, Rev. Elwood, 102–3